MAKING SENSE
OF THE NEW
ADOPTION LAW

A Guide for Social and Welfare Services

Nick Allen

Russell House Publishing

First published in 2003 by:
Russell House Publishing Ltd.
4 St. George's House
Uplyme Road
Lyme Regis
Dorset DT7 3LS

Tel: 01297–443948
Fax: 01297–442722
e-mail: help@russellhouse.co.uk
www.russellhouse.co.uk
© Nick Allen

British Library Cataloguing-in-publication Data:

A catalogue record for this book is available from the British Library.

ISBN: 1-903855-31-4

Typeset by Saxon Graphics Ltd, Derby
Printed by Cromwell Press, Trowbridge

About Russell House Publishing

RHP is a group of social work, probation, education and youth and community work practitioners and academics working in collaboration with a professional publishing team.

Our aim is to work closely with the field to produce innovative and valuable materials to help managers, trainers, practitioners and students.

We are keen to receive feedback on publications and new ideas for future projects.

For details of our other publications please visit our website or ask us for a catalogue. Contact details are on this page.

Contents

Preface		*iv*
1.	Origins and Themes	1
2.	The Legal Effects of Adoption	13
3.	Openness in Adoption	21
4.	Providing an Adoption Service	23
5.	Adoption Agencies and Adoption Support Agencies	30
6.	Domestic Baby Adoption	34
7.	The Adoption of Looked After Children	52
8.	Non-agency Domestic Adoption	99
9.	Eligibility to Adopt	105
10.	Assessment of Adopters	109
11.	Adoptions with a Foreign Element	114
12.	Access to Information After Adoption	122
Appendix: Special Guardianship Orders		132
Index		136

Preface

'Despite the gathering momentum in research activities during recent years, the whole subject of adoption is still surrounded by emotion and prejudice; it is also subject to the vested interests of different pressure groups.' These words may have been written more than 30 years ago (Mia Kellmer Pringle and others, *Growing Up Adopted* (National Foundation for Educational Research in England and Wales, 1972), page 30) but having followed the twists and turns of the ten-year-long debate in this country leading up to the Adoption and Children Act 2002, I feel bound to ask: what's changed? Adoption remains a subject easily capable of generating much tension and disagreement – disagreement about, for example, parent/child relationships, or the role of child welfare agencies and their staff, or the role of the law. This book is concerned with the law. Its primary purpose is to explain how the adoption process in England and Wales will operate under the new rules introduced by the 2002 Act. However, because of the particular way that adoption is viewed in these countries, the Act cannot be properly understood without taking account of the prevailing social and political contexts. For this reason, I have endeavoured to include contextual material where appropriate. There is a great deal of such material, much of it fascinating, and what appears here is only a selection.

Although people will hold different opinions about different aspects of the 2002 Act, some points attract wide agreement. The Government described it as representing 'probably the most radical overhaul of adoption law for 25 years' (John Hutton MP, speaking in the House of Commons on 26 March 2001). This description is accurate because most of the Adoption Act 1976 – the principal statute in the existing law – has been replaced. There will be new supplementary rules and regulations too. It is also true that the idea of a new adoption law was universally welcomed. In fact it was demanded for several years by leading adoption organisations, especially BAAF. A further point will be endorsed by many (though not, I imagine, the Department of Health). The Act is overly complex. Indeed, in terms of accessibility and intelligibility to the average member of the public, it can only be described as a severe disappointment. Although adoption cases can never be simple, I do not believe that their features come anywhere close to justifying the tortuous structure and language employed in this new law. The contrast with the original text of the Children Act 1989 is considerable in this respect.

I referred earlier to the significance of the political context. The change in the political climate surrounding adoption – especially adoption from local authority care – has been particularly noticeable over the past few years. As is explained in the opening chapter of this book, the 2002 Act is based largely on the excellent work undertaken by the Adoption

Law Review in 1991 and 1992. But how many people would have predicted then that this part of our family law would come to be reformed against a background of National Standards, Performance Assessment Framework Indicators, Ranked Bar Charts, Taskforces and Beacon Councils? No matter how incongruous these trappings of New Labour governance may appear when placed in the discretionary and sensitive arenas of child care planning and adoption, the fact is that they exist and so they have to be taken on board when examining the legal framework.

Readers should note that while I have aimed to explain fully the effect of the main provisions of the 2002 Act, on numerous points my explanation cannot be complete because of the absence of supplementary government regulations. These regulations will have to be issued during 2004 if the Act is to be implemented on time. For the record, secondary legislation is expected on the following topics:

- The form of entries in the Adopted Children Register.
- The meaning of 'adoption support services'.
- The local authority's duty to provide adoption support services.
- Organisations approved to assist local authorities in the provision of the statutory adoption service.
- Local authority plans for adoption services.
- The exercise of functions by adoption agencies (including the assessment of adopters).
- The registration of voluntary adoption agencies.
- The form of giving consent to placement for adoption.
- Modification of the local authority's Children Act duties following placement for adoption.
- Legal procedures for obtaining an adoption order or placement order.
- The operation of the Adoption and Children Act Register.
- The independent review mechanism.
- The preparation of privately commissioned home study reports.

- Requirements to be complied with by intercountry adopters.
- The probationary period for intercountry adopters.
- Local authority obligations in intercountry cases.
- The recognition of foreign adoption orders.
- Fees charged by local authorities to prospective adopters in intercountry cases.
- Information to be kept by adoption agencies in relation to individual cases.
- The transmission of birth record information from the Registrar General to adoption agencies.
- The type of adoption information to be released to adopted persons by courts.
- The disclosure by agencies of protected information (including counselling for persons seeking information).
- The disclosure to birth relatives of information about a past adoption.
- The Adoption Contact Register.
- Special guardianship orders.

The implementation timetable was announced by the Department of Health in May 2002. It was expected that the Act would be fully in force by the end of 2004. Some changes in the law, however, would be introduced early, during 2003. These changes would relate to adoption support services, the independent review mechanism (for people who are turned down as prospective adopters) and intercountry adoption. The legal technique used to achieve all this consisted of amending the existing Adoption Act 1976 so that it would enable appropriate Department of Health regulations to be made on these three topics. (Readers who are seeking these so-called transitory provisions can find them in paragraphs 3, 5 and 12 of Schedule 4 to the 2002 Act.) These regulations – some of which are noted below – will have only temporary effect because they will be superseded by new regulations made upon full implementation of the 2002 Act (presumably in 2004). To avoid unnecessary complication, the main text of this book does not refer to early implementation of particular provisions. It has been written on the basis that the whole of the

2002 Act is in force (and therefore as if the Adoption Act 1976 and its supplementary regulations were old law).

The following developments in adoption law, policy and practice have occurred since the text of this book was written:

◼ In February 2003 secondary legislation was made by the Department of Health with a view to bringing the adoption work of local authorities and voluntary adoption agencies within the scope of the Care Standards Act 2000 – and therefore within the remit of the National Care Standards Commission – on 30 April 2003. This matter is considered in Chapter 5 of this book. The four principal pieces of legislation were: the Care Standards Act 2000 (Commencement No.17 (England) and Transitional and Savings Provisions) Order 2003; the Voluntary Adoption Agencies and the Adoption Agencies (Miscellaneous Amendments) Regulations 2003; the National Care Standards Commission (Fees and Frequency of Inspections) (Adoption Agencies) Regulations 2003; and the Local Authority Adoption Service (England) Regulations 2003. The last instrument contains some interesting provisions. Regulation 3 requires each local authority in England to produce a 'children's guide' to its adoption service. This guide is to be provided to all prospective adopters with whom the authority has placed a child and to every child (subject to his age and understanding) who may be, or has been, placed for adoption by the authority. Regulation 10 provides that each local authority shall ensure that there is, having regard to the size of the authority and the need to safeguard and promote the welfare of relevant children, 'a sufficient number of suitably qualified, competent and experienced persons working for the purposes of the adoption service'. Accompanying all this legislation were the national minimum standards for local authority adoption services in England and voluntary adoption agencies in England and Wales.

◼ In March 2003 the Health and Social Care (Community Health and Standards) Bill was presented to the House of Commons. Part 2 of this Bill, when passed and implemented, will have the effect of changing significantly the arrangements in England concerning the regulation and inspection of adoption agencies and adoption support agencies. Significant change has, of course, already been effected in this field through the Care Standards Act referred to in the previous paragraph, but the Labour government has evidently come to the conclusion that the institutional aspects of that recent reform are capable of improvement. Under the 2003 Bill, the National Care Standards Commission will be replaced by the Commission for Social Care Inspection (CSCI). The CSCI will assume – from April 2004 – the regulatory and inspection functions of both the NCSC and the Social Services Inspectorate. References in this book to the NCSC and the SSI should be read accordingly.

◼ In January 2003 the Sexual Offences Bill was presented to Parliament. One of the many effects of this Bill will be to abolish the criminal offence of incest and put in its place two new offences: sex with an adult relative (penetration) and sex with an adult relative (consenting to penetration). The significance of all this for adopted persons is revealed in the Explanatory Notes on the Bill prepared by the Home Office: 'Adoptive relatives are excluded from [these offences]. Paragraph 30 of Schedule 4 makes a consequential amendment to the Adoption and Children Act 2002, to the effect that the provision in the 2002 Act that makes an adoptive child a child of the adoptive parents, does not apply in relation to these offences. Therefore, for example, it will not be an offence under these clauses for an adoptive brother and sister aged over 18 to have sexual intercourse.' This is essentially a repeat performance of the existing law as described in Chapter 2 below.

◼ In December 2002 the Department of Health published a consultation document entitled *The Draft Adoption Support Services (Local Authorities) (Transitory and Transitional Provisions) (England) Regulations and Draft Accompanying Guidance*. This represented the beginning of the early implementation of the provisions of the 2002 Act concerning adoption support services, noted earlier in this preface. According to the Department of Health, the contents of the consultation document reflected submissions made by agencies in response to the earlier publication *Providing Effective Adoption Support* (on which see page 94 of this book). The intention was to make the necessary regulations in March 2003 with a view to their introduction at the end of April. In the event, agencies were not ready for all this and the timetable was put back. The definitive Adoption Support Services (Local Authorities) (England) Regulations 2003 were made on 21 May with a commencement date of 31 October. The regulations were accompanied by *Adoption Support Services Guidance* and Local Authority Circular LAC (2003) 12. According to the circular, this initial phase of the new framework for adoption support provisions 'acts as a stepping stone for those local authorities starting from a low base in adoption support provision ensuring that they make significant progress prior to the implementation of the full framework'. As was indicated earlier, these regulations were made under a provision in Schedule 4 to the 2002 Act that had the effect of modifying the Adoption Act 1976 until such time as the Department of Health felt able to introduce the main adoption support provisions of the 2002 Act, contained in sections 2, 3 and 4. The regulations to be made in pursuance of sections 2, 3 and 4 are likely to be more ambitious than the 2003 legislation. As it is, that legislation imposes a variety of significant obligations on local authorities in England. The *Guidance* points out that it is particularly targeted on meeting the needs of adoptive families created when children are adopted from care. It covers both new adoptions and existing adoptions where the adopted person is under 18. No attempt will be made here to analyse the detail of the legislation. Suffice it to say that adoption practitioners will need to study the *Guidance* very carefully in order to absorb the important distinctions drawn in the regulations between, for example, agency and non-agency placements, adoptive parents and birth relatives, financial support and non-financial support, assessment of needs and the actual delivery of support services, and placing authorities and so-called recovering authorities. Any allowance payable by an authority under the Adoption Allowance Regulations 1991 immediately before 31 October 2003 is to be treated after that date as financial support payable under the 2003 regulations.

In January 2003 the Government issued the Intercountry Adoption (Hague Convention) Regulations and the Adoption (Amendment) Rules. These instruments were made under the Adoption (Intercountry Aspects) Act 1999 and the Adoption Act 1976 and provided for the introduction of the 1993 Hague Convention into our domestic law from 1 June 2003. The Hague Convention provisions of the 1999 Act were brought into force on that day by means of a separate order. The effects of the Hague Convention and the 1999 Act are explained in Chapter 11 of this book. The new rules and regulations prescribe the procedure to be followed in England and Wales where the UK is the so-called receiving State, as well as the procedure where the UK is the State of origin. Appropriate modifications are made to the 1976 Act, the Adoption Agencies Regulations 1983 and the Adoption Rules 1984. In May 2003, as Convention implementation was approaching, the Department of Health published a revised version of its *Intercountry Adoption Guide*. Its stated aim was to provide an overview of the law relating to intercountry adoption. It contained some useful – though complicated – flowcharts. It should be noted that although the UK's ratification of the Hague Convention has been an extremely lengthy process, the rules and regulations noted here will have only temporary effect. They will have to be revised (during 2004 presumably) so that they fit into the new general adoption law framework to be introduced under the Adoption and Children Act.

■ In April 2003 the Department of Health issued the Adoption (Bringing Children into the United Kingdom) Regulations. These regulations, which came into force on 1 June 2003, formed another part of the Government's strategy of early implementation of selected aspects of the Adoption and Children Act. Together with a new section (section 56A) of the Adoption Act 1976, they have the effect of strengthening – and superseding – the Adoption of Children from Overseas Regulations 2001 which are described on page 119 of this book. They apply where a person who is habitually resident in the British Islands (a) brings a child who is habitually resident outside the British Islands into the UK for the purpose of adoption by them or (b) brings into the UK a child already adopted by them under a foreign adoption effected within the previous six months. Adoptions arranged under the Hague Convention are excluded from these provisions, however. The Department of Health's revised *Intercountry Adoption Guide*, noted above in relation to the Hague Convention, also covered these non-Convention adoptions. When the Adoption and Children Act is fully implemented, section 56A and the 2003 regulations will be replaced by section 83 of the 2002 Act and a further set of regulations. Section 83 is described on page 120 of this book.

■ In March 2003 the Department of Health released statistical information revealing that 3400 looked after children had been adopted in England during the year ending 31 March 2002. This confirmed the steady upward trend evident in recent years – a trend which, of course, has been sought by both main political parties.

■ In May 2003 there was published the first Annual Report of the Adoption Register for England and Wales (described in Chapter 7 of this book under the title of the National Adoption Register). Covering the Register's first twelve months of full operation from April 2002 to March 2003, the report revealed that the Register had generated 1800 potential links for children, 600 of which had been designated viable. 30 children had had matches approved at adoption panel. Statistical information on registered children and approved adopters was provided in the report and this served to demonstrate yet again how difficult the matching process can be. According to the report's statistical commentary: 'The majority of children under analysis by the register have multiple special needs. The evidence after discussion with agencies is that adopters are generally unable/unwilling to meet these needs, although approved for them.'

There are two acknowledgements to be recorded here. First, the title of Chapter 1 of this book has been taken from the Finer Report on One-Parent Families, which was published to widespread acclaim in 1974. That report, whose recommendations were unfortunately far too bold for the government of the day, had a considerable influence on my own approach to family law studies. Second, I owe a huge debt to my wife Anne. This relates not only to her assistance on various aspects of adoption and fostering work, derived from her great professional experience and expertise, but also to her support for me personally during the writing of this book.

Nick Allen
June 2003

CHAPTER 1

Origins and Themes

Introduction

When the Adoption and Children Act completed its passage through Parliament on 7 November 2002, it brought to a close what is arguably one of the most remarkable episodes of law reform ever seen in this country. This may be a strong claim to make but it is justified not so much because of the size of the Act or the scale of public interest and controversy surrounding the adoption process – formidable though these are – but more because of the tortuous, roller coaster-like history of the legislation. For this is a law whose development can be traced back thirteen years, across three governments and four Parliaments. Over this period, inevitably, the content and the intensity of the debate fluctuated, as individual cases and other events served to highlight – if not always in a proportionate way – particular aspects of the law and practice. The impact of legal and political developments in areas linked to adoption (and there are many of them) was also felt. As a result, there came about greater understanding of some things but more confusion about others.

How do we explain the strange history of the 2002 Act? After all, it is not as if we were unused to legislating on adoption. Some experienced practitioners will recall only too clearly the passage and implementation of the Children Act 1975, following the report of the Houghton Committee of 1972[1]. Many of the provisions of that Act were truly ground-breaking and yet they were enacted with relatively little public debate and controversy. Provocative newspaper headlines and 'hard-hitting' television documentaries on adoption – now almost commonplace – were then conspicuous by their absence. What has changed? To understand the 2002 Act and its troubled background, it is necessary to acknowledge a number of social, political and legal truths of our time, some well-known, others less obvious. The first of these concerns adoption itself. It ceased to be a narrow, secret sanctum of family law a long time ago. Its deployment in recent decades has revealed a move away from the relatively calm (albeit poignant) waters of the voluntary relinquishment of British-born babies by unmarried mothers to the very different and multi-faceted territory of children in care (and therefore child maltreatment) and inter-country arrangements. The second truth concerns family law as a whole. Whereas reform in this field could once be conducted on a predominantly technical level, with debate confined largely to 'experts', it has now been politicised. The role of 'the family', its contribution to society, and even its meaning, have become, for a complex set of reasons, political and therefore electoral issues. Family law has gone the same way, so that any proposals for legislative reform, even apparently modest ones, are liable to generate controversy across a wide area very rapidly.

This phenomenon can be seen at work in areas as diverse as divorce, cohabitation, assisted reproduction, child support, transsexualism and the recognition of same-sex relationships. The media both reflects and fuels this wider interest in family law and the curious result is a debate that takes place on two levels: the professional and the public. In the adoption field, for example, the publication of detailed academic research in *Adoption Now*[2] and the holding of follow-up seminars nationally and regionally took place more or less at the same time as media stories concerning the treatment of children and prospective adopters by agencies. The extent to which the two levels of debate coalesce remains unclear.

This leads on to the third truth. A heightened public interest in 'the family' and family law, including adoption, presents both opportunities and pitfalls for politicians in government. On the one hand a government can look forward to an enhancement of its credibility and popularity through its willingness to address major concerns (for example, about vulnerable children living away from home). The clearest demonstration of this political, and party political, dimension lies in the announcement by the Prime Minister's office – not the Department of Health – of the review of adoption law that led directly to the 2002 Act. On the other hand, on matters as sensitive as family composition, family breakdown and child rearing, misunderstood remarks or unsure reactions to intervening events – perhaps involving one individual or one family – can result in a government being wrong-footed to the accompaniment of media and Parliamentary derision. This inevitably injects additional risks into the law reform process. A quite separate danger attached to the political process lies in the temptation to portray what is in fact a complex situation in overly simplistic terms.

All these factors have been in play during the protracted gestation period of the 2002 Act. When and how they have impacted becomes clear when the chronology is examined.

The Three Stages of the Reform Process

1. 1989–1993: Gaining momentum

In June 1989, during a debate on the Children Bill (later to become the Children Act 1989) the then Minister of Health informed the House of Commons that the government intended to 'embark on a full review of adoption law'. This exercise, it was said, would provide an opportunity for detailed consideration of all matters relating to adoption in the light of the changes that had taken place since the last major review (in 1972). While the Children Act did effect amendments to adoption law, the amendments were largely technical. Adoption law has traditionally been both reviewed and revised separately from other areas of child law and there was never any intention to use the 1989 Act as a vehicle for comprehensive adoption law reform. The government's announcement was therefore consistent with previous practice.

Although the Adoption Law Review, as it came to be known, was organised and driven by the Department of Health, it was conducted by a multi-disciplinary group of lawyers and civil servants drawn from a variety of government departments and the Law Commission (the standing law reform agency in England and Wales). And although adoption agencies and other interested groups were not directly represented on the Review (an arrangement which drew criticism from British Agencies for Adoption and Fostering) there were ample opportunities for these bodies – and, indeed, interested individuals – to have their say by way of comment on discussion papers that the Review group produced between September 1990 and January 1992. Four discussion papers emerged: *The Nature and Effect of Adoption, Agreement and Freeing, The Adoption Process* and *Intercountry Adoption*. Accompanying these were three background papers: *International Perspectives, Review of Research relating to Adoption* and *Intercountry Adoption*. The large number and the variety of organisations and individuals who submitted comments on the ideas floated in these documents reflected very clearly the wide practical effects and implications of the adoption process. Apart from the expected responses from local authority social services departments, voluntary agencies, health authorities and the legal profession, there were submissions from – among others – the Grandparents' Federation, Rights of Women, the Society of Genealogists, the Joint Council for the Welfare of Immigrants, the National Fertility Association, the Ecumenical Coalition against Child Exploitation and the Committee of London and Scottish Bankers.

The report of the Adoption Law Review, containing 45 main recommendations, was published in October 1992. According to a foreword to the report written by the then (Conservative) junior Health Minister, its basic message was that 'although numbers have decreased, adoption as the basis of permanent transfer of a child from one family to another continues to provide an important service for children'. Ministers, it was said, were not committed to proceeding with any of the recommendations for change; they would take decisions in the light of public responses and the availability of resources. To that end, comments on the report were sought by the end of the year. A debate on the report was held in the House of Commons in November 1992 and it is here that we can discern indications of some of the points of tension arising between government and adoption agencies that were set to recur in later years. The junior Health Minister suggested that there was no room for dogma when dealing with an issue as complex and important as adoption: 'what is needed is common sense, compassion and a sound legal framework.'[3] Having noted the increasing interest in both official and unofficial inter-country adoption, he said that he recognised that 'one of the main reasons why some would-be adoptive parents attempt inter-country adoption outside the existing legal framework is their anger and frustration at what they see as the obstructive attitude of

some local authorities'. He went on: 'I do not condone such attempts by prospective parents to short-circuit the system, but local authorities must understand that public confidence in the fairness of their policies is destroyed if adherence to fashionable or politically correct notions appears to influence their decisions more than consideration of the interests of the individual child.' Three aspects of agency practice were called into question: age ('rigid and inflexible age limits have no place in modern adoption practice and should not be imposed by any local authorities'), race ('there are appalling instances of children being removed from foster parents merely on the ground that they are of a different race from the child') and the placement of children with single people ('I expect that in every case of a child seeking adoptive parents the authorities should make the most strenuous possible efforts to place that child with a married couple').

A year was to elapse before the Department of Health felt able to commit itself to reasonably firm proposals (a delay of several months was said to have been caused by arguments over whether to extend agencies' powers to charge prospective adopters for their services). These were contained in a white paper presented by the then Secretary of State, Virginia Bottomley, and entitled *Adoption: The Future*.[4] Not surprisingly, the proposals were numerous and varied. Some required an Act of Parliament, others could be implemented by government regulations or guidance addressed to agencies. Many of them were based directly on the recommendations of the Adoption Law Review. On two particular matters, the government announced further consultation exercises: placement orders (designed to supersede orders freeing a child for adoption) and the role of adoption agency panels. But generally, the way seemed clear for an early statute and the Department of Health stated in the white paper that primary legislation to amend the Adoption Act 1976 would be brought forward 'as soon after the 1993–94 Parliamentary session as the legislative programme allows'.

2. 1994–2000: Loss of nerve

Consultation documents on placement orders and adoption panels were duly published by the Department of Health in April and June 1994 but contrary to general expectation, no Adoption Bill appeared in the autumn of that year. Nor did one appear in 1995. It was suggested in some quarters that the anticipated financial costs of reform were holding ministers back but it seems clear that, even if this was the case, other factors were at work.

At the beginning of 1995, another piece of family law reform was brought before Parliament: the Family Homes and Domestic Violence Bill. This Bill, which was not regarded as in any way contentious, was designed to rationalise court procedures relating to the occupation of the matrimonial home. It had been drawn up by the Law Commission's family law team following an extensive consultation exercise. (It is a point of interest that some members of this team had played a leading role in the Adoption Law Review.) However, the Bill ran into a furious, and wholly unexpected, storm of opposition in the final stages of the Parliamentary process and the government, giving the appearance of panic, withdrew it. Critics of the Bill – supported by the *Daily Mail* – had seized upon provisions which were said to provide excessively generous treatment to the unmarried partners of home-owners, and, as one senior peer subsequently put it, 'their fear was that the Bill would virtually conflate the status of marriage with the status of concubinage'. The government sought to make amends for this extraordinary surrender by reintroducing the family home provisions, cosmetically altered so as to placate the critics, in the next Parliamentary session, but it committed a tactical error by incorporating them in the wider Family Law Bill, a measure primarily designed to revolutionise the law of divorce. Although this Bill did eventually become law in 1996, the government (and, it should be said, the Law Commission, whose report formed the basis of the Bill) met another barrage of criticism from the family values lobby. By this stage the end of the 1992 Parliament, and therefore a general election, were rapidly approaching. Given such political difficulties, it would have been entirely understandable had the Conservative government concluded that introducing a Bill on adoption – opening up lengthy debate on, among other things, adoption by unmarried couples, stepparent adoption, gay and lesbian parenting, transracial placements and intercountry arrangements – would be electorally unproductive. There remained a problem, however. The Department of Health had set in motion the Adoption Law Review and had thereby generated both public and professional expectations. The solution evidently chosen involved, first, the publication in February 1996 of adoption guidance addressed to local authority social services departments, and second, the publication in March 1996 of a *draft* Adoption Bill.

The guidance, though delivered under the hand of the Chief Inspector of the Social Services Inspectorate[5], was clearly designed for consumption by the general public, especially prospective adopters, and the media. It urged adoption agencies to pursue 'a more positive approach to adoption'; it contained a warning against concentrating too heavily on the age of applicants; it referred to 'unfair and distressing experiences of some prospective adopters who have felt that they have been dealt with in an insensitive and discourteous manner'; it stated that it was 'unacceptable for prospective adopters to be ruled out because the adoption agency considers them to have received too high a level of education, have time-consuming jobs or an income above a certain level'; it also contained statements about single applicants, race and culture, intercountry adoption and post-adoption contact with birth relatives. Finally, it explicitly reminded social workers of the importance of adopting a sensitive approach to the assessment of applicants: 'prospective adopters should not be made to feel that they are being interrogated and they should never be subjected to the personal views of social workers.' Viewed from a social work perspective, the tone of this tirade was no doubt provocative but it seemed to reflect a growing consensus across the main political parties. In welcoming the government's 1993 white paper, David Blunkett – then the Labour Party's spokesman on health – had said that 'we all have an interest in putting behind us any nonsense about political correctness and any prejudice…What matters is not age, status, weight, height or anything else but solely the needs of the child'.

The draft Adoption Bill, running to 104 clauses, appeared a month later. In a foreword to the 'Consultative Document' that contained the Bill, the then Secretaries of State for Health and for Wales stated that 'publication of the Bill in advance of its introduction into Parliament provides a further opportunity for those involved in the adoption service – practitioners, parents, adopters and adopted persons as well as the general public – to consider these provisions and comment'. Publication of the Bill was said to be 'the final phase' of the consultation process, which would terminate on 28 June 1996. In normal circumstances statements such as these, taken together with the massive detail in the Bill, would be regarded as indications of imminent legislation. But the government had by this time established a clear track-record of caution in matters relating to adoption law and it cannot have come as any great surprise to informed observers that the draft Adoption Bill failed to make an appearance in John Major's last Parliamentary session as Prime Minister. Instead, the government's parting shot in this field consisted of new regulations, made in February 1997, altering the duties of adoption agencies[6]. Even this relatively modest initiative led to controversy, after the Secretary of State for Health (now Stephen Dorrell) told the press that 'the changes will help to remove political correctness from adoption and introduce more independence and transparency'. An official of the British Association of Social Workers responded by describing the changes as little more than election posturing, an observation that was probably justified. In a leading article, the *Daily Telegraph* suggested that the government's announcement 'should play well with voters who are appalled by stories about parents considered too fat, too white or too middle-class to adopt and are indignant that priority is occasionally given to homosexual couples'[7]. On this rather sour note, the Conservative Party's protracted – and, it has to be said, botched – attempt to reform adoption law came to an end.

The advent of a Labour government led by Tony Blair inevitably changed the situation. Labour's overwhelming majority in the House of Commons meant that it could be confident of pushing through its legislative programme without much difficulty, and its support for the 1993 white paper, reaffirmed in 1996 after the draft Bill was produced, led many to expect an early initiative. It was a Labour government, after all, which had sponsored the 1975 reforms. But, to the consternation of interested groups, nothing happened. When asked about an Adoption Bill, the Department of Health merely gave holding answers. In March 1998, for example, it told Parliament that it was 'unable to find legislative time in the immediate future for the comprehensive reform of adoption'[8], while in its social services white paper of November 1998 it stated that it would keep the working of the adoption service under careful review and would 'consider whether fresh legislation would help to overcome some of the delays without denying the rights of birth families to take part in the process'[9]. This is not to say that the Labour government was inactive on the adoption front. As we shall see, significant developments did take place. For reasons which are still unclear, however, primary legislation did not form part of its early strategy. In the words of one agency director, 'government has chosen to go down the path of managerialism rather than legislation to achieve its policy objectives'[10].

In July 1998 the House of Commons Select Committee on Health produced a report on children being looked after by local authorities. Since a significant number of such children are, or could be, the subject of adoption plans, this aspect of child care was clearly within the Committee's remit. After taking evidence from various groups, the Committee concluded that 'local authorities too often do fail to take adoption sufficiently seriously as an option, unnecessary delays occur, and insufficient support is offered to adoptive parents'. It recommended that the Department of Health should issue further guidance to authorities. Whether primarily because of this report or not, guidance did emerge a month later, in a circular entitled *Adoption – Achieving the Right Balance*[11]. Unveiling the guidance – described in a government press release as 'tough new guidelines' – the junior Health Minister, Paul Boateng, said that for too long adoption had been regarded as the last and least acceptable option for looked after children. He went on: 'These new guidelines aim to end misguided practices and reinforce the point to local authorities and social workers that children who need stable and secure families may well be best served by the adoption process. This fresh approach to adoption policy and practice forms an important part of the government's commitment to see a radical improvement in children's services.' The circular itself was fairly detailed and contained sections entitled Race, Culture, Religion and Language, Avoiding Delay, Responsibility of Senior Managers, Training, Prospective Adopters, Assessment Criteria, Intercountry Adoption, Post-adoption Support and Contact Arrangements. Some of the provisions reflected the earlier guidance of 1996. None of them, however, changed the law, and in that respect they lacked bite. They also contained generalities and so the wide discretion held by adoption agencies remained intact. It was, perhaps, significant that representatives of the agencies were reported as suggesting that the new guidance would make little difference to practice in most parts of the country.

During this period, the priorities of the Department of Health lay elsewhere. September 1998 saw the launch of the *Quality Protects* programme, a large-scale three-year exercise covering a wide range of children's social services. This involved the fixing of national objectives and targets, the production by local authorities of Management Action Plans, the delivery by government of a new special grant and the creation of an attendant bureaucracy to monitor, advise, exhort and report[12]. Because, however, the programme covered children being looked after by local authorities, adoption inevitably featured in the exercise. The first stipulated objective in the *Quality Protects* programme was 'to ensure that children are securely attached to carers capable of providing safe and effective care for the duration of childhood'. Two sub-objectives referred to adoption. The first of these required local authorities 'to maximise the contribution adoption can make to providing permanent families for children in appropriate cases'. According to the Department of Health, the intention was to ensure that adoption was considered as soon as it became clear that there was no realistic prospect of the birth family providing the basis for safe and adequately effective parenting, and to avoid children staying unnecessarily long in the care system. The second sub-objective required local authorities 'to reduce the period children remain looked after before they are placed for adoption, or placed in long-term foster care'[13]. Although these objectives were, necessarily, cast in vague terms, and although the placement of looked after children forms only one aspect of the adoption process, the fact that adoption played a part in the *Quality Protects* programme enabled the government to maintain that it was not standing still on the issue. This strategy was confirmed very clearly in a Parliamentary debate on adoption and fostering that took place in the summer of 1999. Asked directly about the prospect of legislation, a Department of Health spokeswoman said this: 'Legislation is not essential to achieve important improvements in adoption practice ... Measures to improve the standard and quality of adoption and foster care are making good progress, and many of those measures are being introduced through the *Quality Protects* programme which was introduced last September ... It is likely that the *Quality Protects* programme will be allowed to run its course before a more radical view is taken to deal with some of the weaknesses in the adoption services.'[14]

In one area of adoption law, however, the Labour government did feel able to move forward. An international agreement on intercountry adoption had been concluded at the Hague in 1993. This was an important development, heralding uniform international procedures governing the placement of children with foreign nationals, but it could be implemented in the UK only by Act of Parliament. In 1999 the Government was able to find a way of moving ahead with this without opening up to debate the much larger question of domestic adoption law. A Liberal Democrat Member of Parliament who had been given – through the annual MPs' ballot – the opportunity of presenting a Bill on a topic of his choice, decided, no doubt after obtaining government support, to sponsor a Bill to implement the Hague Convention. This secured an easy passage through Parliament and emerged as the Adoption (Intercountry Aspects) Act 1999. It was a step forward, albeit of limited proportions in the overall adoption context. As far as domestic adoptions were concerned, there seemed little chance of an early Bill. As late as 3 February 2000, the junior Health Minister, John Hutton, told the House of Commons that he was 'not convinced' of the need for a change in the law[15]. Within two weeks, however, the situation had been transformed.

3. 2000–2001: Waterhouse and beyond

It was entirely in line with the twists and turns in the path to adoption law reform that what proved to be the critical turning point, in February 2000, had its origins in a development that occurred nearly four years earlier on an apparently unrelated matter. On 13 June 1996 John Major told the House of Commons that a discussion of child abuse in residential care had taken place in Cabinet that morning; that he had been 'personally horrified' by what he had learned; and that wide-ranging reviews would be set up in the near future. So it was that there came to be

established, first, the Utting Review of the safeguards against the abuse of children living away from home and second, a Tribunal of Inquiry chaired by a former High Court judge, Sir Ronald Waterhouse. While the immediate cause of Major's statement, and the exercises he set in motion, was the failure by various authorities to deal properly with the long-running scandal of abuse in children's homes in north Wales, both the Utting Review and the Waterhouse Inquiry had far wider implications. The evidence submitted and the ensuing reports[16] took their place in a long line of published material exposing deficiencies in the regulation of child care arrangements, both public and private, across the country. The Utting Review was published towards the end of 1997 and its recommendations were taken up through a variety of mechanisms, including the *Quality Protects* programme. The report of the Waterhouse Inquiry necessarily took far longer to emerge. By the time it did arrive, steps were already being taken to strengthen selected areas of child care law, notably through the Care Standards Bill and the Children (Leaving Care) Bill, but, as has been noted, adoption was not part of this agenda. This was not in the least surprising in the context of Waterhouse because adoption had not been within the Inquiry team's terms of reference. For this reason, no doubt, it did not feature in any of the 72 recommendations.

The first indication that the Government had decided to make adoption, and specifically the reform of adoption law, part of its post-Waterhouse strategy came on 17 February 2000, two days after the publication of the report. In a briefing to political journalists, the Prime Minister's Official Spokesman, Alastair Campbell, said that the Prime Minister had viewed Waterhouse as a dreadful report and felt that the Government needed to know whether adoption had a role in some of the long-term solutions to some of the problems identified in it. The report of the briefing went on:

> There were problems in the field of adoption. There were long, unacceptable delays in adoption amongst children in care. For example, the

average wait for children in care over the age of five between going for adoption and actually being adopted was five years. There was also huge variability between different areas on adoption rates, ranging from 2 per cent in some shire counties to 31 per cent in others. There were also disincentives for local authorities, for example when one local authority placed a child with a couple recruited by another agency they had to pay the second authority a sizeable fee for the process – around £12,000. Real hurdles had been put in the way of couples who wanted to adopt. Work was currently being done by the Health Department and Home Office. But the Prime Minister wanted to see whether new adoption laws were required.[17]

How precisely adoption came to be linked in the Prime Ministerial mind with the horrors laid bare in the Waterhouse report – a link not made by the Inquiry team itself – remains unclear. In his briefing the Official Spokesman said simply that the issue of adoption 'was one that people had pressed upon the Prime Minister in the past through letters and visits to his [constituency] surgery, although not in the context of anything as ghastly as this'. Whatever the true reasons, the announcement marked the end of the strategy of procrastination pursued by the Department of Health and signalled what was in effect a resuscitation of the reform plans of the early 1990s.

There was, of course, a draft Adoption Bill ready and waiting in Whitehall but this had been published by a Conservative government and so perhaps for presentational and party political reasons it was decided not to pick this up directly. Instead, the Performance and Innovation Unit of the Cabinet Office was instructed to carry out a speedy review. *The Prime Minister's Review*, as it was called, was completed in eight weeks and published in July 2000. It was followed by a white paper entitled *Adoption: a new approach* (accompanied by draft National Adoption Standards) in December of that year. This stated that legislation would be brought forward during 2001 'to overhaul and modernise the legal framework for adoption'[18]. Although the PIU review and the

white paper contained much detail, one striking feature of both documents is worth noting at this stage: they were overwhelmingly directed towards the needs of children being looked after by local authorities. Such an emphasis was not particularly surprising given the circumstances in which the PIU was given its task, and of course it could be said to demonstrate a clear appreciation of the changing nature of the adoption process in the period since the Houghton Report. At the same time, however, it ran the risk of distorting the true position by confining to the margins what the white paper described in a throwaway paragraph as 'step-parent and other adoptions'[19]. It could also be said to have played into the hands of those politicians and commentators who wished to heap opprobrium onto local authority social services departments. In this respect, the two documents were markedly different from the more rounded blueprint emanating from the Adoption Law Review in 1992.

Following the publication of the white paper it simply remained for the Department of Health to introduce its new Adoption Bill into Parliament but even this stage in the process was mishandled. With a general election almost certain to be held in mid-2001, it was thought that a Bill on the subject was unlikely to appear until later that year, in the new Parliament. Only then would there be sufficient time for proper scrutiny and debate. But only a few weeks after the white paper appeared, Tony Blair, evidently under pressure in the House of Commons, inexplicably committed his government to legislation in the current Parliamentary session. Either he failed to understand that the size of a suitable Bill would make it impossible to deal with in the limited time then available, or he decided to go ahead anyway for public relations reasons. The cause of the pressure was the case of the so-called internet twins which for a variety of reasons (explained later in this book) gave rise to a veritable media frenzy. Such was the level of public excitement that the case became the subject of a Parliamentary exchange between the Prime Minister and the Leader of the Opposition and it was here that the commitment to legislate was given[20]. The effect of this was to require the Department of Health to bring forward a Bill far earlier than it had anticipated. In the event, it managed to do this on 15 March 2001, when the Adoption and Children Bill was published. Although a general election was still expected to bring an end to the Parliamentary session in the summer this had not been officially announced, which meant that the Bill had to be treated – in a sort of pretence – according to normal Parliamentary procedures. This is the reason why the Bill was subjected to a full-scale House of Commons debate on 26 March and then sent for detailed consideration by a committee of MPs who knew perfectly well that it stood no chance of becoming law. As one of them observed, there was an air of unreality about the whole exercise. The cost to the public purse must have been substantial. To the surprise of nobody, the Bill fell in May, leaving the Government to reintroduce it after its victory at the polls on 7 June.

In introducing the initial Bill to the House of Commons on 26 March, junior Health Minister John Hutton – who, it will be recalled, had played down the need for adoption legislation only a year earlier – said that it was long overdue. He went on:

> By common consent, the current legislation is considered to be outmoded, out of date and unsuitable for the kind of adoption service that we need today. As a result, it is failing to meet the needs of children and families and, therefore, the needs of society as a whole. The need to recast both the law and the practice of adoption so that they better serve the interests of children is clear and obvious. The Adoption Act 1976 is based on legislation dating back to 1958 and it is not consistent with the Children Act 1989. There is an overwhelming case for bringing the framework of legislation up to date. That is precisely what the Bill seeks to achieve.[21]

The Bill received all-party support and so its passage through Parliament, though interrupted by the election, was never in doubt. It duly received Royal Assent on 7 November 2002.

Themes

What is one to make of the extraordinary saga described above? A number of themes do emerge fairly clearly when the developments are examined in the round. First of all, adoption has been well and truly captured by the political and media worlds. Whereas the practices and policies of agencies were once the exclusive property of a relatively small group of professionals, they are now caught in a very public spotlight and as a result are far more susceptible to questioning and adverse comment. It was no exaggeration for the Social Services Inspectorate to say in November 2000 that 'public, political, media and professional interest in adoption has never been higher'[22]. Governments have therefore become cautious about adoption legislation, the timing of which has assumed electoral significance. This leads on to the second point, which concerns the level and quality of debate. The adoption of children is a very serious matter. It is also a fascinating one, involving a range of emotions. Consequently, it is both understandable and right that it attracts high public interest. But the 'discovery' of the subject by politicians and newspapers – both tabloid and broadsheet – has led to a gross over-simplification of what is often an extremely complex process. This applies particularly to the approval of prospective adopters by agencies (an issue to which the media has returned time and again) and to decisions to place for adoption children being looked after by local authorities. Stark newspaper headlines such as 'Adoption is the answer'[23] and 'Is it politically correct to harm a child for life?'[24] are not particularly helpful when it comes to generating a rounded and informed discussion of these matters.

Third, the period preceding the publication of the Adoption and Children Bill saw an almost total preoccupation on the part of the Government with adoption outcomes for looked after children, at any rate, until the internet twins episode. Debate on adoption reform and discussion of the treatment and life chances of children in care became fused, so that a skewed vision of the adoption process was presented to the public. This intertwining of what are actually quite separate issues reached its climax in the Prime Minister's unexpected reaction to the Waterhouse Report.

The last point to be made here concerns the winners and the losers in the reform process. Leaving aside the interests of children themselves – who, needless to say, were said to be uppermost in everybody's minds – there can be no doubt that the group which gained the most during this period were prospective adopters. Although they had no organising body through which their wishes and feelings could be articulated, members of the public wishing to adopt succeeded in attracting almost universal sympathy from the media and from the political class (the case of the internet twins threw up a rare exception to this trend) and this led directly to changes both in Department of Health guidance to agencies and in the law itself. Publicity was given to cases involving individuals and couples from different parts of the country who had for one reason or another met with difficulties when trying to adopt. The fact that some of them had previously experienced problems, including protracted and expensive IVF treatment, in conceiving a child of their own only served to heighten the poignancy of their situation. A significant number of MPs appear to have been heavily influenced by individual cases originating in their constituencies.

By way of contrast, there is no doubt that adoption agencies, and in particular local authority social services departments and their social workers, were losers during the period under consideration. These were the bodies, of course, which frequently had the pivotal role of approving adopters, preparing children for adoption and actually selecting future parents for children. Far from receiving support for this demanding set of tasks, they were vilified, both in Parliament and in the press. Anecdotal evidence, concerning cases in which mistakes may well have been made, was often used as a base on which to construct unlikely and unprovable generalisations, such as the preposterous suggestion that

the adoption system is 'run by people who are inefficient at doing something they are largely opposed to anyway'[25]. These were invariably compounded by a defective understanding of the existing law and Department of Health guidance. As has already been seen, the view that decision-making within agencies was governed by so-called political correctness gained substantial ground during the 1990s. Evidence to support this proposition was usually based on a small selection of individual cases. More specifically, it was suggested that decisions were being taken by 'ideologues who have ruled it is better for a child to languish in a care home than to be adopted by "pushy, over-achieving" middle-class parents'[26]; that smokers were 'persecuted'[27]; and that there was a preference within agencies for 'irregular lifestyles'[28]. One MP said that in talking to people in the social services profession (sic) he had sensed 'a certain sniffiness and suspicion of the people who opt for overseas adoption'[29]; another referred to 'social workers' obsession with birth families' and said that the youngest and the least-trained social workers were involved in adoption cases[30]; yet another stated that he heard stories suggesting that 'social workers sometimes come to the task with little idea of what bringing up children is about and carry out tests as though from a book'[31]. These examples could be multiplied.

Nor were ministers in the Department of Health reluctant to lend their weight to the criticisms. John Hutton, announcing the publication of the first Adoption and Children Bill, said that 'we have already begun the process of encouraging social services departments to see adoption as a positive, responsible choice', the implication being that this idea had not previously occurred to agency workers[32]. In a Parliamentary debate on the Bill, he said that he was aware of 'cases in which potential adopters have been told that they cannot adopt because they are too old, or in one case, because they were too middle class'. Such 'blanket bans', he said, failed to put the needs of children first[33]. Identical comments had been made by Alan Milburn, the Secretary of State, three months earlier when the Government's white paper was published[34].

This relentless barrage of vituperation, and the course of the adoption debate generally, reinforced what has long been learned from the child protection field: social services departments and their employees, in seeking to discharge their statutory functions and tackle the consequences of family breakdown, are easy targets for critics and are unable to field criticisms effectively. Their vulnerability was demonstrated particularly clearly during the case of the Bramleys, in which prospective adopters decided to abduct the two children placed with them rather than comply with an agency request to return them. Although the true facts of the case were not – and could not be – immediately revealed, still less properly understood, widespread sympathy for the couple's use of self-help was matched by unbridled hostility on the part of the media towards the local authority concerned and the social work profession in general. As one national newspaper put it: 'It has come to something when the reputation of one of the agencies of the state that touches so directly and intimately on people's lives has fallen so low that it is regarded with universal suspicion.'[35] Given this unfavourable climate, it was only to be expected that some people would call for a radical change in the organisational aspects of adoption, even extending to the removal of functions from local authorities, and sure enough one commentator did jump to this conclusion, with considerable attendant publicity. 'There are no good reasons', she wrote, 'for social services departments to hang on to adoption, when so many are uninterested or even antagonistic, as well as unequipped for the task.'[36] Local authorities will probably have viewed with chagrin the way in which this particular commentator was able to base her provocative conclusions partly on reports published by the Department of Health's Social Services Inspectorate. Although these reports in fact contained many references to high quality adoption work being carried out by local authority practitioners, there were enough

uncomplimentary remarks – often of the 'could do better' variety – in both the reports themselves and the accompanying letters from the Chief Inspector of the SSI to provide suitable ammunition for those not well disposed towards public sector services[37]. Even though many of the harshest criticisms may have been applicable to only a small minority of authorities, the sector as a whole was inevitably tainted. Damage was also sustained as a result of the Department of Health's decision in October 2000 to apply the notion of league tables to local authority adoption services. While newspapers predictably talked of authorities being 'named and shamed' and being visited by 'hit squads' of experts, agency representatives voiced concern about the knock-on effects of this exercise on the recruitment of adopters and social workers[38].

A further group of people, however, may be identified as losers in the protracted adoption debate. The position of birth parents – who in socio-economic terms are unlikely to share the same background as those who apply to adopt – received remarkably little attention. Those who sought to restore some balance to the debate were liable to receive short shrift. One MP stated that 'there is a difficulty when social workers put the possibility of reconciliation with the birth family above every other priority'[39]. Another – the co-chairman of the all-party Parliamentary committee on adoption – went so far as to say that he was 'fed up with people putting the case for the rights of birth parents'[40]. Such an approach reveals a striking contrast with the thinking behind the Children Act 1989, which sought to emphasise partnership with parents, the support of families of children in need, the encouragement of parental contact where a child is living away from home, as well as the notion of parental responsibility. While the Government certainly did not abandon these principles, its frustration with the continuing poor profiles of children leaving care, coupled with evidence (from Waterhouse and other reports) of large-scale abuse of children in local authority establishments, appears to have led to a new imperative, one which is not favourable to birth relatives. The Government's decision to go in for adoption targets and timescales for local authorities – targets which would, if achieved, eliminate legal relationships between many more parents and their children – only served to highlight the size of the change that was underway.

Notes

1. *Report of the Departmental Committee on the Adoption of Children,* Cmnd 5107.
2. *Adoption Now: Messages from Research* (1999).
3. Tim Yeo MP, *Hansard* (House of Commons) 12 November 1992, col 1046.
4. Cmnd 2288 (1993).
5. CI (96) 4 of 1 February 1996.
6. The Adoption Agencies and Children (Arrangements for Placement and Review) (Miscellaneous Amendments) Regulations 1997.
7. *Daily Telegraph* 18 February 1997.
8. Baroness Jay, *Hansard* (House of Lords) 26 March 1998, col 1336.
9. *Modernising Social Services,* Cmnd 4169, para 3.28.
10. Jim Richards, Catholic Children's Society (Westminster) *A Denial of the Right to Family Life* in *Adoption: The Continuing Debate* (Institute of Economic Affairs, 1999), page 45.
11. LAC (98) 20.
12. DH Circular LAC (98) 28 of 11 November 1998: *The Quality Protects Programme: Transforming Children's Services.*
13. The objectives were refined by the Department of Health in September 1999 in *The Government's Objectives for Children's Social Services.*
14. Baroness Hayman, *Hansard* (House of Lords) 14 June 1999, cols 86–90.
15. Westminster Hall debate, *Hansard* (House of Commons) 3 February 2000, col 251.
16. Sir William Utting, *People Like Us: The Report of the Review of the Safeguards for Children Living Away From Home.* (November 1997); Sir Ronald Waterhouse, *Lost in Care.* HC (1999–2000) 201 (February 2000).
17. Lobby Briefing 11.30 a.m. Thursday 17 February 2000, 10 Downing Street Newsroom.
18. Cmnd 5017, para 9.1.
19. Para 8.3.
20. *Hansard* (House of Commons) 17 January 2001, col 336.
21. *Hansard* (House of Commons) 26 March 2001, col 698.
22. *Adopting Changes: Survey and Inspection of Local Councils' Adoption Services* (Department of Health, November 2000), para 1.1.
23. *Sunday Telegraph,* 20 February 2000.
24. *Mail on Sunday,* 22 March 1998.
25. 'This Adoption Scandal', *Daily Mail,* 24 April 1999.
26. *Sunday Telegraph,* 20 February 2000.
27. *Daily Telegraph,* 18 February 1997.
28. Melanie Phillips, 'Adoption is a cruel mess we must reform', *Sunday Times,* 17 January 1999.
29. Vincent Cable MP, *Hansard* (House of Commons) 30 January 2001, col 284.
30. David Davis MP, *Hansard* (House of Commons) 26 March 2001, cols 740–1.
31. Andrew Stunell MP, *Hansard* (House of Commons) 30 March 2001, col 1238.
32. Department of Health Press Release, 15 March 2001.
33. *Hansard* (House of Commons) 26 March 2001, col 699.
34. *Hansard* (House of Commons) 21 December 2000, col 580.
35. *Independent,* 15 January 1999 (leading article).
36. Patricia Morgan, *Adoption and the Care of Children* (Institute of Economic Affairs Health and Welfare Unit, 1998), page 154.
37. *For Children's Sake: An SSI Inspection of Local Authority Adoption Services* (DH, 1996); *For Children's Sake Part 2: An Inspection of Local Authority Post-Placement and Post-Adoption Services* (DH, 1997); SSI letter CI (96) 39; SSI letter CI (97) 16.
38. 'Eight councils put on adoption "shame" list', *Guardian,* 11 October 2000; 'Hit squads sent to tackle councils' adoption failure', *Independent,* 11 October 2000; 'Task force to tackle adoption headache', *Western Morning News* (Plymouth), 11 October 2000.
39. Desmond Swayne MP, *Hansard* (House of Commons) 30 March 2001, col 1242.
40. Julian Brazier MP, *Hansard* (House of Commons) 26 March 2001, col 744.

CHAPTER 2

The Legal Effects of Adoption

Introduction

According to section 46(1) of the 2002 Act, an adoption order 'is an order made by the court on an application under section 50 or 51 giving parental responsibility for a child to the adopters or adopter'. So begins the Act's description of the consequences in law of adoption in England and Wales. This description, set out in the form of sections and subsections of the legislation, is clearly drafted and coherently structured, and it is analysed in detail below. What it does not do, however – and what it cannot do – is convey the reality of the adoption process. For those involved, especially the child and the adopters, it means far more than simply the granting of 'parental responsibility'. The reality is perhaps better conveyed by comments said to have been made by two children who in 1980 were the subject of an application made by their step-father. One of the children, aged 13, told a social worker that adoption would 'make the family united'. The other, aged 10, was reported as saying that adoption would make her step-father her 'proper Dad'[1]. This is just one of many reported adoption cases – arising in an astonishing variety of factual contexts – where the special features of adoption have been highlighted. For example:

- In *Re H*[2] Lord Justice Ormrod posed the question: 'What do the adoptive parents gain by an adoption order over and above what they have already got on a long-term fostering basis?' He said: 'To that the answer is always the same – and it is always a good one – adoption gives us total security and makes the child part of our family and places us in parental control of the child; long-term fostering leaves us exposed to changes of view of the local authority, it leaves us exposed to applications, and so on, by the natural parent. That is a perfectly sensible and reasonable approach; it is far from being only an emotive one.'

- In *Re A*[3] (another foster carers' application) a member of the court said this: 'In the present case it seems to me that it cries out from the facts that this child needs the security of the [adopters'] family and that that security should not be susceptible of disruption by any possible threat to the [adopters] of harassment or intervention by the natural parents. That the adoption order should be made is the natural solution.'

- In *Re S*[4] (a grandparents' application) a member of the court stated: 'The feature of the case which impresses me as of major importance is that this child of four and a half has, throughout his sentient life, been brought up bonded to the applicants as mother and father. It seems to me that the paramount factor affecting his future welfare is to make an order that will secure him in his de facto relationships in such a way as to minimise the risk of [the mother], or anyone else, seeking to disrupt them. This an adoption order can achieve… The legal relationships will then coincide with the actual relationships on which [the child] is, by now, totally reliant.'

■ In *Re O*[5] (a case in which a baby had been voluntarily given up by his birth mother) the court said: 'Although in recent years views in relation to adoption have, to an extent, altered, there can be no doubt that adoption gives the adoptive parents and the child greater security and confidence in the relationship. After all, if an adoption order is made, the adopters become the child's parents. If there is not an adoption order in place, the people with whom the child is living *may* always fear that there will be a change of status. There is a risk, unquantified in this case, that the mother might have a change of mind and reappear on the scene.'

The message conveyed by these statements is very clear: adoption offers a child and his carers a particularly strong chance of security, stability, finality, permanence and freedom from interference. In the words of British Agencies for Adoption and Fostering, adoption provides 'a method of achieving an unrivalled level of permanent security for children separated from their original families'[6]. All this is brought about in large measure by the statutory provisions concerning the legal consequences of adoption which will now be described.

Allocation of Parental Responsibility to Adoptive Parents

Adoptive parents acquire parental responsibility in respect of the adopted child from the date of the adoption order. This they will keep until the child attains the age of 18, unless the child is re-adopted – an eventuality expressly catered for by section 46(5). According to Schedule 6, the expression

'parental responsibility' has the meaning given by section 3 of the Children Act 1989. This was the position under the Adoption Act 1976 following its amendment by the 1989 Act, so there has been no change in this basic legal position.

The term 'parental responsibility' means 'all the rights, duties, powers, responsibilities and authority which by law a parent of a child has in relation to the child and his property'. This definition has been part of English family law since 1991, when the Children Act 1989 came into force, so it is now very well established and very well known to child care professionals. Just as the courts before 1989 were reluctant to explain the old statutory term 'the parental rights and duties', so they have held back from listing the various components of parental responsibility. This lack of absolute certainty appears not to have caused major problems in practice. Certainly in the adoption context, problems of interpretation are unlikely to arise because of the extinguishment of the parental responsibility and parental status of the relevant birth parent(s). The so-called total legal transplant means that the adopters take over from the birth parents both in law and in fact, and therefore disputes over the scope of parental responsibility or the exercise of it are no more likely to arise than when a child is brought up by their birth parents.

Extinguishment of Parental Responsibility

An adoption order is not the only court order to result in the granting of parental responsibility. The same thing happens when a residence order, a special guardianship order or a care order is made under the Children Act. However, the special feature of adoption is its effect of extinguishing 'the parental responsibility which any person other than the adopters or adopter has for the adopted child immediately before the making of the order'[7]. This rule will serve, therefore, to remove all the relevant rights and powers from birth parents, other individuals having parental responsibility (for example, under a residence order) and any local authority having parental responsibility. These others will lose an important legal link with the child.

Extinguishment of Orders

Section 46(2)(b) makes it clear that an adoption order will have the effect of extinguishing any order previously made under the Children Act.

Extinguishment of Maintenance Liability

Since adoption is intended to make the adopters full and sole parents in the eyes of the law, the Act provides for the automatic extinguishment – from the date of the adoption – of any agreement or court order relating to maintenance payments for the child[8]. There is an exception to this covering payments under trusts and similar arrangements[9].

Transfer of Legal Parenthood

In order to make complete the creation of a new legal family, the Act provides that the adopters shall not only have parental responsibility for the child but also be treated as parents for legal purposes. Although this arrangement reflects the effect of the previous legislation, the drafting of the 2002 Act is significantly different. The reason for the new wording lies in the decision of the House of Commons – ultimately accepted by the House of Lords as well – to permit joint adoption applications made by unmarried couples, including gay and lesbian couples. The previous legislation permitted joint applications only by married couples and the provisions concerning the child's post-adoption status in such cases were geared to the applicants' marriage. Clearly, this arrangement cannot be employed for applicants who are not married.

According to section 67(1), an adopted person is to be treated in law as if born as the child of the adopters or adopter. Section 67(5) makes this rule effective from the date of the adoption. Legal parenthood is conferred on the adopter or adopters in this way. The law's assumption that the child was *born* to the adopters does, of course, involve a fiction and a similar assumption reflected in the initial draft of the Adoption and Children Bill attracted criticism from (among others) the Family Rights Group on the grounds that it was offensive to birth parents[10]. Section 67(2) provides that an adopted person is the legitimate child of the adopters or adopter and, if adopted by a couple, is to be treated as the child of the relationship of the couple. The perceived need to secure legitimate status for the adopted child is a hangover from earlier times when the stigma of illegitimacy was more intensely felt. Today, when well over 30 per cent of births occur outside marriage and cohabitation is commonplace, such a policy will seem outdated to some. Indeed, the very labels 'legitimate' and 'illegitimate' have been so comprehensively expunged from everyday discourse that many people probably regard them as having been consigned to legal history. Section 67(2) shows that this is not the case.

It follows from the above that the adopted person is to be treated in law as not being the child of any person other than the adopters, and section 67(3)(b) expressly provides for this result. The birth parents consequently lose their legal parenthood: it is transferred to the adopters on the date of the order, along with parental responsibility. This transfer of parenthood will have life-long effect.

The Extended Family

The transfer of legal parenthood effected by section 67 (above) has a knock-on effect on the child's wider family: since the adopted child is to be treated in law as if born as the child of the adopters, it must follow that the adopters' own parents become the child's new legal grandparents, and that the adopters' own children become the child's new legal siblings. This change is followed through in respect of all other relatives. All the child's birth relatives become strangers as a matter of law. Section 68 states that the child's new legal relatives may be referred to as 'adoptive' relatives.

Losing Legal Ties Without Losing Contact

The comprehensive severance of legal ties between the child and his birth relatives (graphically described in one case as 'the statutory guillotine') has always been the hallmark of adoption and in cases of closed adoption – stereotypically involving the voluntary relinquishment of a new-born infant by a young single mother to strangers – the legal position may well sit comfortably alongside the reality. Such cases are far fewer today, however, and in situations where continuing contact of some sort is going to take place between the child and one or more members of his birth family, it may seem strange for the law to insist on putting the same distance between them. This is the case, however. No matter how much contact takes place with a birth relative, there will be no legal relationship with them after adoption. Conversely, there will be a full legal relationship between the child and all of his adoptive relatives, no matter how meagre the contact.

The superior courts have acknowledged the existence of these theoretical problems in open adoptions but are generally relaxed about them. In *Re C*[11], for example, a married couple were applying to adopt a girl of 10 who had experienced a disruptive and insecure childhood, which included nearly seven years spent in residential care with her two older brothers. The girl was particularly attached to her elder brother, then aged 18 – indeed, the judge stated that their relationship 'ought to be preserved at all costs' – and it was this factor that led the judge to refuse an adoption order, even though the applicants were known to be willing to support the relationship. He said: 'If I made an adoption order S and M would cease to be C's brothers although they are children of the same family. That may seem a little bit high-flown and

theoretical; but it is a wholly undesirable and unnecessary result to bring about if the security of C can be brought about in a way that does not create that nonsense…It worries me from the point of view of C's own feelings. If anybody was to tell her that technically M was no longer her brother, she would I think be bitterly and desperately hurt.'

On appeal, the House of Lords made an adoption order subject to a condition as to continuing contact between C and her brother. Adoption was needed to provide security and the judge's evaluation of C's reaction to learning that technically M was no longer her legal brother was 'quite unreal'. When interviewed, C had made it clear that she wanted to be adopted. It would mean, she said, that she would then know that 'no one could ever take her away from her mum and dad'. As for the impact on her brother, she said that she could not see how adoption would affect her relationship with him nor how she felt for him and he for her.

In the earlier case of *Re D*[12], the Court of Appeal made similar observations. A stepfather was seeking to adopt his wife's two children and their birth father was agreeable to this. The social worker who had compiled a welfare report expressed misgivings about an adoption, one reason being that the effect of an order would be to cut off the children entirely from the birth father's family. The response of the Court of Appeal was to point out that an order would not necessarily have that effect: 'There is no magic in an adoption order. The fact that the child becomes a child of the new family does not, in itself, automatically cut off the children from the natural family. Of course it may do…It may have in law that effect, but there is no reason why, if everyone is agreeable, children like these should not see their paternal grandparents should it be desirable.'

Of course, the argument that continued contact with the birth family does not preclude the appropriateness of severing legal ties can be pushed too far. In many cases there will come a point at which adoption, with all its consequences, becomes simply untenable. A recently reported example is *Re B*[13], where the child was firmly established in a local authority foster home but was seeing his birth father and his paternal grandmother very frequently indeed, she being employed at the boy's school, and all the parties living within a very short distance of each other. As the Court of Appeal pointed out, to make an adoption order in such circumstances – as the local authority in fact wished – was inconsistent with the reality that the child was both a member of his foster carer's family and a member of his father's family.

Nationality and Property Rights

It is not surprising that the effect of an English adoption order is to make the child a British citizen if he was not such a citizen beforehand, provided one of the adopters is a British citizen. This rule is contained in section 1(5) of the British Nationality Act 1981, not the 2002 Act. It will, of course, be especially relevant in intercountry adoption cases. British citizenship will give the child the right of abode in the UK for the purposes of the immigration laws, thereby removing any possibility of expulsion in the future.

As for property rights, these will as a rule flow from the transfer of legal parenthood under section 67. Inheritance rights will consequently attach to the adoptive family in place of the birth family. Sections 69–73 contain complex provisions concerning the impact of adoption on wills and similar legal instruments. These are outside the scope of this book and professional legal advice will invariably be needed if questions arising out of such documents occur.

Prohibited Degrees and Incest

According to section 74(1), section 67 does not apply for the purposes of (a) the table of kindred and affinity in Schedule 1 to the Marriage Act 1949 or (b) sections 10 and 11 of the Sexual Offences Act 1956. This repeats the existing law and has the effect of preserving legal ties with the birth family for the purposes of the law relating to eligibility to

marry and the law relating to incest. Adopted children aged 16 or 17 who intend to marry and who wish to be certain that the marriage will not fall foul of the prohibitions prescribed by the Marriage Act 1949, for example, by their unwittingly marrying a sibling, are in a position to obtain information via the Registrar General that should confirm the position[14].

The Adopted Children Register

The Adopted Children Register is retained by section 77(1). This is the formal record of all adoptions taking place in the courts of England and Wales. According to section 77(4), a certified copy of an entry in this Register is to be received as evidence of the adoption without further or other proof; and under section 77(5), where the entry refers to the date or place of birth of the adopted person, as it usually will, such a copy is also to be received as evidence of that date or place 'in all respects as if the copy were a certified copy of an entry in the registers of live-births'. This further demonstration of the special nature of the adoption process is a logical by-product of the construction of a new legal family for the child and although the provisions were originally drawn up when most adoptions were baby adoptions, they apply irrespective of the circumstances. Schedule 1 to the Act requires the court making the adoption order to communicate the order to the Registrar General, in order that a new entry can be made in the Register and an appropriate annotation can be made in the register of live-births. The form of the new entry is a matter for government regulations and changes may be needed here in order to make workable the new provisions in the Act concerning joint adoptions by same-sex couples.

Irrevocable Nature of Adoption

Most court orders made in children's cases are expressly stated to be capable of variation or discharge at a later date. This is a sensible arrangement, given the changing nature of family relationships. Provisions for the variation and revocation of adoption orders, however, are conspicuous by their absence. Such provisions would be inconsistent with the permanence, finality and change in status that adoption is intended to signify. The only exception to this position relates to the very rare case in which a child born to unmarried parents is adopted by one of those parents who subsequently marries the other parent[15]. It is a fact, of course, that in some cases the undoubted psychological benefits that are supposed to flow from an unbreakable legal bond between adopter and child prove elusive. Indeed, in some cases, the legal tie proves to be utterly intolerable. Significant emotional turmoil must be generated in what, one hopes, is the small number of cases in which a party to an adoption desperately desires to reverse the process. But this is seen by the law as a price that has to be accepted if the majority of adopters and their children are to get the best possible chance of building a full relationship free from intrusion. One thing is obvious: the irrevocability of an adoption decision makes it all the more important to undertake appropriate pre-placement enquiries, planning and preparation. The remarkable case described in the next paragraph vividly illustrates what may happen when these things do not occur.

The most well-known modern case on the irrevocable nature of adoption is *Re B*[16], in which a man of 35 asked the High Court to set aside his adoption order which had been made by the Liverpool county court when he was four months old. His was a typical 1950s baby adoption, his placement having been arranged by the matron of a nursing home. The adopters were described as a middle-class couple who had been trying to adopt a baby for years. Serious factual mistakes were made during this process, however, the most important of which was that the matron – and therefore the adopters – acted in the belief that the child was 'of Syrian Jewish stock', whereas in fact he was the son of a Kuwaiti Muslim. When the Jewish adopters began to discover the truth nine years later,

they said that their world had been 'pulled down over our heads'. They did not, however, take steps to challenge the adoption order. This move was made much later on by their son, in adulthood, in order to resolve what the High Court described as an 'appalling dilemma', but the court rejected the argument that it could set aside the order even though a fundamental mistake of fact had been made. On appeal, Lord Justice Swinton Thomas said that 'to allow considerations such as those put forward in this case to invalidate an otherwise properly made adoption order would, in my view, undermine the whole basis on which adoption orders are made, namely that they are final and for life as regards the adopters, the natural parents, and the child'. He went on to express the view that it would gravely damage the life-long commitment of adopters to their adoptive children if there was a possibility of the child or the parents subsequently challenging the validity of the order. This Court of Appeal ruling has not been affected by the 2002 Act.

Adoption with Conditions

Section 12(6) of the Adoption Act 1976 allowed the court to attach conditions to adoption orders and this power was occasionally used to give formal effect to a post-adoption contact arrangement, as in the case of *Re C*, described previously. In 1992, however, the Adoption Law Review recommended the repeal of this provision, arguing that 'it is unrealistic to make an adoption order conditional upon the fulfilment of certain conditions'[17]. This recommendation has been accepted and there is therefore no equivalent of section 12(6) in the 2002 Act. If the court wishes to make a formal provision for contact, it can do so by means of a contact order under the Children Act 1989 (this facility having been available since 1991).

Adoption by Step-Parents

The old law's insistence on removing legal parenthood from birth parents in all cases presented problems in cases where step-parents wanted to adopt. If a step-father adopted alone, it would have the absurd effect of cutting off his wife's legal tie with the child and making him the child's sole legal parent. A joint application by step-father and birth mother was therefore necessary; but this was unsatisfactory too, because it involved the mother going through a sort of legal panto-mime only to end up as an adoptive parent for the purposes of the law. A legal framework designed for adoption by strangers was never going to accommodate in-family arrange-ments appropriately, and it is not surprising that its rigidity was heavily criticised.

The 2002 Act now makes special provision for step-parent adoptions. Section 51(2) has extended the range of permissible single appli-cants so as to include a person who is 'the partner of a parent of the person to be adopted'. According to section 144(7), a person is the partner of a child's parent if the person and the parent are a couple but the person is not the child's parent; and according to section 144(4), 'a couple' means (a) a married couple or (b) two people, whether of different sexes or the same sex, living as part-ners in an enduring family relationship. These convoluted provisions are a by-product of the new rules relating to the eligibility of unmar-ried couples to adopt jointly. A step-parent may therefore apply on their own. If an adop-tion order is made in their favour, the order will not extinguish the legal parenthood, or the parental responsibility, of their partner: under section 67(2), the child is to be treated in law as the child of the relationship. The legal parenthood, and the parental responsibility, of the absent birth parent is, of course, extin-guished[18]. The result of all this is that the step-parent becomes an adoptive parent, as under the previous law, while their partner remains a birth parent. A similar division applies to extended family members. As with all adop-tions, the making of the order will be recorded in the Adopted Children Register and the relevant entry in the register of live-births will be annotated. The form of an adoption certifi-cate in a step-parent case will be prescribed in due course by government regulations.

Adoption by Grandparents

Adoption by grandparents continues to be available under the 2002 Act. No special provision is made for these cases in the Act which means that the legal re-ordering of family relationships is followed through in the usual way. The grandparent consequently becomes the child's adoptive parent and the grandparent's own children (including, in many cases, one of the child's birth parents) become the child's adoptive siblings.

Adoption by Birth Parents

Adoption by a single birth parent also contin-ues to be available. The effect here is to sever the legal ties between the child and the other birth parent and that birth parent's family. Section 67(2) applies, so that the child is to be treated in law as the legitimate child of the adopter.

Adoption of 18-Year-Olds

Sections 47(9) and 49(4) introduce a new rule under which 18-year-olds can be adopted, provided the application for their adoption is lodged with the court prior to their eighteenth birthday. This novelty was recommended by the Adoption Law Review, which reported 'concern that some older children are prevented from being adopted by delays which occur between the application and the court's decision'[19]. In these cases, the provisions of the Act concerning the effect of adoption need to be read with some latitude. While the order will certainly make the 'child' a permanent member of the adopters' legal family, it cannot possibly have the effect of conferring parental responsibility on the adopters because parental responsibility as a legal concept is defined by reference to the under-18s and therefore only has meaning in relation to them[20]. By the time an 18-year-old is adopted, nobody will have parental responsibility for him.

Notes

1. *Re D* (1981) 2 FLR 102.
2. (1982) 3 FLR 386.
3. [1987] 2 All ER 81.
4. [1987] 2 All ER 99.
5. [1999] 2 FCR 262.
6. *The BAAF Response to the Review of Adoption Law* (1993) page 13.
7. Section 46(2)(a), repeating section 12(3) of the Adoption Act 1976.
8. Section 46(2)(d).
9. Section 46(4).
10. Memorandum submitted to the House of Commons Select Committee on the Adoption and Children Bill (April 2001).
11. [1988] 1 All ER 705.
12. Note 1 above.
13. [2001] 2 FCR 89.
14. Section 79(7).
15. Section 55, repeating the existing law.
16. [1995] 3 FCR 671. The full story of this case is told in Clare Dyer, 'Pitching a tent in no-man's land', *Guardian*, 15 March 1993.
17. Para 5.8.
18. Section 67(3).
19. Para 25.1.
20. Section 3(1) of the Children Act 1989.

CHAPTER 3

Openness in Adoption

Open adoption is not a concept known to English law. The 2002 Act does not refer to it, nor did any of the earlier adoption legislation. And yet it has become firmly established as a central feature of agency policy and practice[1]. Why is this? The main reason resides in the fact that widely differing meanings are given to the term. In 1990, the Adoption Law Review stated that 'open adoption is generally used in this country to refer to adoptions where some links are maintained between the birth and adoptive families, in contrast to the classic position where contact ceases'[2]. However, the Review went on to point out that elements of 'openness' could be identified in other stages of the adoption process. Openness included:

■ Inviting birth parents and relatives to make known their views about the sort of adoptive family which they would like the child to have.
■ Encouraging birth parents to share information about their family history and background with the adoptive family and to put on record the reasons for the adoption, together with gifts or mementoes for the child.
■ Arranging for birth parents and prospective adopters to meet.
■ Disclosing the parties' identities and welfare reports during the legal proceedings.

■ Arranging for the adoptive parents to keep the birth family informed of the child's development.
■ Telling the child about their adopted status and its effects.
■ Preserving some form of contact between the child and their birth family both after placement and after the court hearing.
■ Enabling adopted adults and their birth families to renew contact with each other.

If open adoption is understood in this wide sense, it quickly becomes apparent that it is in fact reflected in the legislation. Indeed, several of the elements of openness referred to above are tightly regulated by it. The words 'open' and 'openness' do not, however, actually feature. One example of this approach may be seen in section 46(6) of the Act. This states that before making an adoption order the court 'must consider whether there should be arrangements for allowing any person contact with the child'. Openness may therefore be regarded as a complex of ideas or practices which the legislation validates but does not necessarily demand. This has meant that agencies have been able to develop policies and approaches largely at their own speed, unrestrained by a legal straitjacket. Such a highly discretionary framework was explicitly endorsed by the Adoption Law Review: 'The extent to which a particular form of openness is likely to be appropriate will vary greatly according to the needs of the child and the circumstances surrounding the adoption. It will very often be a matter for the discretion of the agency or the court to decide exactly what the best approach is likely to be.'[3]

The various provisions of the 2002 Act that may be said to be linked to ideas of openness are analysed in subsequent chapters of this book.

Notes

1. John Triseliotis and others, *Adoption: Theory, Policy and Practice* (1997), Chapter 4; DH, *Adoption Now: Messages from Research* (1999), Chapter 5; DH, *Intermediary Services for Birth Relatives: Practice Guidelines* (2000).
2. Inter-departmental Review of Adoption Law, *Discussion Paper Number 1*, para 67.
3. *Review of Adoption Law* (1992), para 4.2.

CHAPTER 4

Providing an Adoption Service

Introduction

According to British Agencies for Adoption and Fostering, adoption is first and foremost a service for children needing families[1]. This view is widely shared within Parliament, the Government, local authorities, the voluntary sector and the general body of child care practitioners in this country, and it is therefore not surprising to see it reflected in the provisions of the law. But acceptance of the notion of a service in this context raises key questions. Who should have the responsibility for providing this service? To what extent should the nature of the service be prescribed? How much discretion should be allowed to those responsible? What checks should there be? These questions are considered in the present chapter. The first question can be disposed of quickly. Since 1988 local authorities have had statutory responsibility for the provision of an adoption service and the 2002 Act maintains this position. The removal of adoption work from the local authority sector was considered by the Government's Performance and Innovation Unit as part of its review of adoption in 2000 but the idea was rejected[2]. The answers to the remaining questions are far more complex and contentious.

Historical Background

Provision for a local authority-led national adoption service was first made by the Children Act 1975, following recommendations contained in the Houghton Report[3]. At that time, not every local authority acted as an adoption agency, some authorities having chosen to leave service provision to the voluntary sector. Section 1 of the 1975 Act changed everything. It imposed on every local authority a duty to 'establish and maintain within their area a service designed to meet the needs, in relation to adoption, of (a) children who have been or may be adopted, (b) parents and guardians of such children, and (c) persons who have adopted or may adopt a child'. For this purpose, local authorities were required to provide 'the requisite facilities' or secure that they were provided by approved adoption societies (the voluntary sector). Because some local authorities had previously been inactive in this field, it was obvious that the implementation of section 1 would have to be held over until the necessary administrative arrangements had been made. There were also, of course, significant resource implications. For this reason, the Department of Health and Social Security, as it then was, accepted that at least one year's notice would be required for the introduction of the new service. However, in order to pave the way for implementation, the Department in 1976 set out in a circular its own view of what section 1 would eventually require:

> Local authorities should establish an adoption service as an integral part of their social services

provision in partnership with adoption societies operating in their area. The Act does not lay down the form that this partnership should take; it will vary according to the needs of the area – of children, prospective adopters and natural parents – and according to the adoption societies operating in the area, the particular category of clients they serve (e.g. whether they have to be of a particular religious faith) and the extent to which they are likely to meet the new criteria for approval. Each authority will have to consider and assess which groups are not covered by voluntary agencies; ideally, where authorities are not already acting as adoption agencies, the local authority service and the voluntary service should be complementary, with the minimum of duplication or parallel working…It will be necessary for each authority to ensure oversight of the service available in the area. This will involve at least one senior, experienced officer with a recognised executive responsibility for adoption who should have access to the Director's management team to ensure that an adequate adoption service is provided in conjunction with their other social services for families and children and in liaison with voluntary agencies. The officer involved will need to have direct links with the area teams to ensure that: (a) the social workers are knowledgeable about the adoption service; (b) they receive advice and guidance; and (c) the service is available to local families and children, including children in care.[4]

In the event, implementation of section 1 was delayed for 12 years, until January 1988[5]. This was an eternity in terms of adoption and child care policy and practice. The annual number of adoption orders in England and Wales had declined from 21299 in 1975 to 7201 in 1987; the proportion of children adopted at the age of 10 or over had grown from 19 per cent in 1975 to 27 per cent in 1987; the proportion of looked after children adopted had grown from one and a half per cent in 1975 to three per cent in 1987; and the number of voluntary adoption societies had markedly declined[6]. The delay in implementation – extraordinary even by English family law standards – meant that when the Adoption Law Review was set in motion in July 1989, the national statutory adoption service had been in existence for only 18 months. In these circumstances, it is

hardly surprising that when the report of the Review was delivered in 1992, no proposals for significant change in this part of the law were made. For the same reason, no proposals for change were made in the Conservative government's white paper of 1993[7].

Formal signs of central government dissatisfaction with the adoption service framework began to emerge in 1996. In its draft Adoption Bill published in March of that year, the Department of Health proposed to expand the provisions of section 1 in two ways: firstly, by inserting an explicit reference to intercountry adoption, an issue over which some local authorities and social workers were felt to be obstructive, and secondly by requiring authorities to prepare, publish and review plans for their adoption services. The second, more critical, development took place in December 1996 with the publication by the Social Services Inspectorate of *For Children's Sake*. This was a report of an exercise described as the largest evaluation of local authority adoption services ever undertaken. Six social services departments were inspected, in the course of which data was collected on 111 staff, 375 children, 122 stepparent applicant households and 373 households of other prospective adopters. It is clear that despite the relatively small sample size, alarm bells had sounded among the inspection team. In a covering letter written to all SSDs, the Chief Inspector of the SSI highlighted the principal areas of concern[8]:

- Significant numbers of children and applicants were waiting for unacceptably long periods for placements.
- Adoption work had a low profile and was often seen as peripheral to mainstream child care concerns.
- Adoption expertise was located with very few staff. Many child care workers were not familiar with adoption processes and had limited access to training. Step-parent applicants were often dealt with by staff with little relevant expertise.
- Most authorities had not reviewed their services to ensure that they met current needs. They were concerned almost

entirely with their in-house provision and in some cases were not fulfilling the planning responsibilities imposed by the legislation. Public information was usually poor.

■ Delays were not monitored systematically enough and more pro-active recruitment was required to ensure that appropriate placements were available to meet each child's needs.

If these findings are compared with the expectations set out in the original 1976 DHSS circular (above), it is easy to see why the SSI expressed the view that its report represented 'a very challenging management agenda'. It seems that too few SSDs managed to convince central government that this challenge was being met because when the Performance and Innovation Unit presented the *Prime Minister's Adoption Review* in July 2000, its report – confined, admittedly, to the adoption of looked after children – contained observations that closely resembled those made by the SSI three and a half years earlier. One of the principal conclusions drawn by the PIU was that 'a step change in local authority performance on adoption and permanence' was required[9]. This conclusion was accepted by the Government in the white paper that preceded the 2002 Act and so paved the way for a strengthened statutory and administrative framework[10].

The Statutory Provisions

Maintenance of the adoption service

The relevant provisions here are modelled on those contained in the Adoption Act 1976. Section 3(1) of the Act requires every local authority to continue to maintain within their area a service designed to meet the needs, in relation to adoption, of (a) children who may be adopted, their parents and guardians, (b) persons wishing to adopt a child, and (c) adopted persons, their parents, natural parents and former guardians. For this purpose, every local authority must provide 'the requisite facilities'. Those facilities must

include making, and participating in, arrangements (a) for the adoption of children, and (b) for the provision of adoption support services. 'Adoption support services' means (a) counselling, advice and information in relation to adoption, and (b) such other services as are specified in government regulations e.g. financial support[11]. References in these various provisions to 'adoption' are to the adoption of persons, wherever they may be habitually resident, effected under the law of any country or territory, whether within or outside the British Islands[12]. This makes it clear that adoptions with a foreign element fall within the scope of the local authority's service obligations.

Section 3(4) enables a local authority to provide any of the requisite facilities by securing their provision by registered adoption societies or other organisations approved for the purpose by government regulations. However, the facilities must be provided in conjunction with the local authority's other social services and with local adoption societies 'so that help may be given in a co-ordinated manner without duplication, omission or avoidable delay'[13]. The Department of Health expects most local authorities to become members of consortia over time[14].

Assessments for adoption support services

Section 4 contains new provisions on assessment. A local authority must, at the request of any person covered by section 3(1) (above), carry out an assessment of that person's needs for adoption support services (as defined by section 2(6) (above)). Such an assessment will be followed, where the authority considers it appropriate, by a decision to provide services and by the preparation of a plan. It may also involve requests for help directed at other local authorities and adoption societies, and notification of relevant needs to health and education agencies.

This new statutory duty will be filled out in due course by government regulations and guidance and this explains why the provisions of section 4 lack detail. It is clear, however, that like other provisions of the Act and the

National Standards (mentioned below) they are a reflection of the Government's desire (a) to see more people come forward to adopt looked after children and (b) to see more such adoptions succeed. This desire was very clearly expressed in its white paper of December 2000, where it was stated that adopters regarded post-adoption support as 'the least satisfactory part of the adoption process' and where it was noted that 18 per cent of adoptive placements broke down during 1999–2000 before an adoption order was made[15]. It was also expressed by ministers during the Parliamentary debates on the Act[16]. Despite the emphasis on looked after children, the terms of section 4 extend to all types of adoption, though whether distinctions are introduced by regulations and guidance remains to be seen. Chapter 7 of this book contains further discussion of this important provision.

Local authority plans for adoption services

Drawing on a provision in the Conservative government's 1996 Bill, section 5 requires every local authority to prepare and publish a plan for the provision of its adoption service. Supplementary regulations will govern the content of these plans and will make provision for review and consultation. Special directions can be given by the Department of Health to a particular local authority, such as an authority singled out for attention by the Adoption and Permanence Taskforce[17]. The Department is fully aware of the fact that, as it put it, 'the organisation of adoption work and its place within the competing priorities of other social services work is not standardised'[18]. How far this variation survives the implementation of section 5 remains to be seen.

Default power of central government

Section 14 enables the Department of Health to make an order declaring a particular local authority to be in default in respect of a duty, or collection of duties, imposed on the authority by the Act. This can occur only if the minister is satisfied that the authority has failed, without reasonable excuse, to comply with the duty in question. Directions can be attached to the order for the purpose of ensuring that the duty is complied with.

This type of power is commonplace in local government law (there is one in the Children Act 1989 and section 14 is modelled on it) and is aimed at large-scale breakdowns in services. Although it is rarely used, a threat to invoke the power – however veiled – can be an influential tool.

The National Standards

Development of the National Standards

The idea of introducing National Standards into the framework for the provision of an adoption service was first mentioned in the Performance and Innovation Unit's report on adoption, published in July 2000[19]. The PIU recommended the development of Standards in relation to the recruitment and assessment of adopters, adoption allowances, contact with birth relatives and what it called 'the key stages of the process of planning for and delivering permanence and adoption'[20]. All of these recommendations were made with looked after children in mind.

Because National Standards are not in themselves legal instruments (although they can be incorporated into such instruments) being mere administrative tools, they are relatively easy to process. They also, of course, sound impressive. They are issued by central government but their delivery is in the hands of non-governmental agencies (in this case, local authorities). All of these factors render Standards an attractive proposition for a government keen to be seen as responding vigorously to a known problem, and they no doubt played a part in Tony Blair's decision to pursue the PIU recommendations at once, in advance of a white paper. In his foreword to the PIU report he wrote: 'I am determined to make early progress. It is clear from the PIU report that there are some things we can get on with quickly. Over the next few months we will therefore…draw up new National Standards, which local authorities will need to follow, setting out timescales for making decisions about children and clear criteria for assessing adopters, so that children do not drift in care and those wanting to adopt know what to expect and can be confident they will be treated fairly.' Draft Standards were subsequently developed by a working group, 'organised' by British Agencies for Adoption and Fostering, and published for consultation in December 2000. 187 organisations and individuals submitted comments on the draft, which was said to have been 'broadly welcomed'. The finalised Standards were issued in August 2001.

Content of the National Standards

The Standards finalised in 2001 apply only to looked after children, reflecting the thrust of the PIU report and the Government's white paper. Intercountry and step-parent adoptions were to be the subject of separate documents, as was the subject of adopted adults and their birth siblings. The Standards are divided into six sections, A to F, covering the following: Children, Prospective Adopters, Adoptive Parents, Birth Parents and Birth Families, Councils and Adoption Agencies and Services. Each section contains individual numbered standards. These will not be described here. They are considered in later chapters of this book under appropriate headings. It may be noted at this stage, however, that they range from the general to the very specific. Examples of the former include Standard A6 (children will be given clear explanations and information about adoption, covering what happens at each stage) including at court (and how long each stage is likely to take in their individual case) and Standard C7 (where there are difficulties with the placement or the adoption breaks down the agencies involved will co-operate to provide support and information to the adoptive parents and the child without delay). Examples of the latter include Standard A3(a) (a match with suitable adoptive parents will be identified and approved by panel within six months of the agency agreeing that adoption is in the child's

best interest) and Standard D3 (birth parents will have access to a support worker independent of the child's social worker from the time adoption is identified as the plan for the child).

Although the finalised Standards resemble the draft ones sent out for consultation, some intriguing changes of substance were made, presumably on the grounds that the original text was either too ambitious, too cautious or open to misinterpretation. For example, draft Standard A7 stated that: 'The family of choice for the looked after child is one that reflects his or her birth heritage, if this can be found without unnecessary delay.' There were obviously second thoughts about this proposition because it was transformed into the following finalised Standard A9(a): 'Every effort will be made to recruit sufficient adopters from diverse backgrounds, so that each child can be found an adoptive family within the [prescribed] timescales, which best meets their needs, and in particular which reflects their ethnic origin, cultural background, religion and language.' Is the finalised standard stronger or weaker than the draft? Opinions may differ on this question.

Enforcement of the National Standards

The important issue of Standards enforcement – especially as regards the more specific Standards, such as those laying down timescales – was approached with a measure of uncertainty. The PIU recommended that the Department of Health should make regulations (i.e. law) supplemented by guidance requiring local authorities to implement *key elements* of the National Standards[21]. These key elements were not specified. When the Government published its adoption white paper, it said that it would put in place 'a number of mechanisms' to monitor Standards implementation. Some of them would be included in the initial set of minimum standards against which the new National Care Standards Commission would inspect councils and voluntary adoption agencies. The Standards would also be used to inform SSI inspections[22]. Clearer information emerged through two Department of Health circulars, the first issued in August 2001 alongside the finalised Standards, the second issued in December 2001[23]. The first circular pointed out that some of the rules contained in the Standards were already enshrined in legislation or official guidance. It went on to say, however, that meeting *all* the Standards would 'ultimately become a statutory duty for local councils and voluntary adoption agencies'. In the meantime, they were to be regarded as good practice guidance. The second circular contained the Government's decision that all Standards not already enshrined in legislation or guidance were to have the status of statutory guidance under section 7 of the Local Authority Social Services Act 1970 with effect from 1 April 2003. This date was also the planned commencement date for inspection of adoption services by the National Care Standards Commission but it preceded, by a considerable margin, the planned commencement date of the 2002 Act itself. The Standards would therefore enter into force against a background of the existing adoption law.

The precise effect in law of section 7 guidance has remained remarkably obscure over the years but the Department of Health's understanding of the position was as follows: 'A council should follow guidance issued under section 7 unless there is a good reason for them not to do so, but any deviation from the guidance should not be significant and must be capable of justification.'[24] To a lawyer, this description would mean that the Standards fell some way short of a full statutory duty, which is of course how they were classified in the Government's first circular. It seems clear, therefore, that the expression 'statutory duty' was being used rather loosely in this particular context.

Practice Guidance to Support the National Standards

Draft practice guidance to support the National Standards was published in August 2001[25]. Following the layout of the Standards themselves, its stated aim was to 'clarify what needs to be done, when and how it can be achieved in order to put each of the Standards into practice'. The final document will be updated to reflect changes in the law. Unlike the Standards, the practice guidance is aimed only at a professional audience.

The Adoption and Permanence Taskforce

Like the National Standards, the Adoption and Permanence Taskforce owes its existence to the report of the Performance and Innovation Unit. It is not referred to in the 2002 Act and it has no status in law: it is a purely administrative device, unlike the National Standards which, as explained above, will have a quasi-legal status. The PIU envisaged the Taskforce as having two principal functions[26]. It would:

■ Conduct an intensive visit programme focusing on poor performing areas to look at the reasons for poor performance and agree plans for improvement.
■ Provide a source of whole systems expertise to feed into drawing up best practice guidelines and National Standards.

This recommendation was accepted by the Government and the Taskforce was set up in October 2000. Announcing the change, the junior Health Minister said that the Taskforce was 'at the centre of our action to lever improvements in performance on adoption and permanence'[27]. Eight local authorities were immediately named (and, inevitably, 'shamed' via the attendant media publicity) as the first to be given the opportunity of working with the Taskforce. Although the second wave of selected authorities, announced in October 2001, was said to include councils whose adoption service was good, and although the Taskforce itself disclaimed any intention of inspecting adoption services or criticising council management[28], there is no escaping the fact that the Taskforce became – initially at any rate – part of the regulatory framework for adoption.

Notes

1. *The BAAF Response to the Review of Adoption Law* (1993), para 30.4.
2. *Prime Minister's Review: Adoption* (July 2000), para 6.5; John Hutton MP, *Hansard* (House of Commons), 26 March 2001, col 699.
3. *Report of the Departmental Committee on the Adoption of Children*, Cmnd 5107 (1972).
4. Circular LAC (76) 15, para 14.
5. See 'A statutory adoption service' (editorial), *Adoption and Fostering*, 11:1 (1987), page 1.
6. Inter-departmental Review of Adoption Law, *Discussion Paper Number 3* (1991), para 7; PIU Report (note 2 above), Chapter 2.
7. *Adoption: The Future*, Cmnd 2288.
8. CI (96) 39. Similar concerns were expressed in the later report on post-placement and post-adoption services *For Children's Sake Part 2* (August 1997).
9. Para 4.14.
10. *Adoption: a new approach*, Cmnd 5017 (December 2000).
11. Section 2(6).
12. Section 2(8). This provision is based on section 9 of the Adoption (Intercountry Aspects) Act 1999.
13. Section 3(5).
14. *Adoption: a new approach* (note 10 above), para 7.27.
15. Para 2.8, citing Chapter 7 of *Adoption Now: Messages from Research* (DH, 1999).
16. John Hutton MP, *Hansard* (House of Commons), 26 March 2001, col 706 and Alan Milburn MP *Hansard*, 29 October 2001, col 658.
17. DH Explanatory Notes on the Adoption and Children Bill (October 2001), para 39.
18. *Draft Practice Guidance to Support the National Adoption Standards for England* (2001), page 48.
19. Note 2 above.
20. Paras 5.4, 5.5, 5.22, 5.25, 5.42 and 6.18.
21. Para 6.19.
22. Note 10 above, paras 4.7 and 4.8.
23. LAC (2001) 22 and LAC (2001) 33.
24. Circular LAC (2001) 33, para 11.
25. LASSL (2001) 5.
26. Note 2 above, para 6.21.
27. John Hutton MP, speech at BAAF, 11 October 2000.
28. *Adoption and Permanence Taskforce First Annual Report* (DH, October 2001).

CHAPTER 5

Adoption Agencies and Adoption Support Agencies

Historical Background

Under the Adoption Act 1976 an 'adoption agency' meant either a local authority with social services functions or an approved adoption society[1]. These were the organisations which together were expected to provide the requisite facilities to make up a national adoption service, as described in the previous chapter. Although the two types of agency were very different in nature, each was tightly regulated under legislation – which included the 1976 Act itself – and official guidance. Accountability was secured in a number of ways. Since all adoption orders must be obtained from the courts, the actions of agency workers in an individual case stood to be scrutinised in the courtroom, by guardians ad litem, professional advocates and the judges themselves. Some criticisms could be severe. In the case of *Re C*[2], for example, the county court judge found that the agency had never explained to the prospective adopters that the child's birth father was 'still on the scene' and wanted contact. He accused the agency of having acted recklessly, or at any rate of having treated the adopters lamentably. When the case reached the Court of Appeal, it was noted that the agency had failed to carry out certain duties it owed to the father under the Adoption Agencies Regulations. The agency's general handling of the case was described by the court as 'inept and insensitive'. No doubt other agencies – or at least their legal advisers – took note. More systematic accountability was secured through agency inspections carried out by the Social Services Inspectorate. These inspections could be agency-specific or else geared to a sector as a whole. The reports of inspections would be published and might form the basis of further Department of Health guidance. Several major sector-wide SSI reports were in fact produced during the 1990s[3].

This regulatory framework was changed significantly by the Care Standards Act 2000. As is well known, this Act established the National Care Standards Commission and the General Social Care Council, and it introduced completely new arrangements for the registration and inspection of children's homes, care homes, independent hospitals and clinics, domiciliary care agencies and child minders and other day care providers. What is probably not so widely appreciated, however, is that the regulatory provisions of this large and complex statute also extended to voluntary adoption agencies and the adoption functions of local authorities. In summary, the adoption provisions of the Act had the following effect:

- The job of approving and inspecting voluntary adoption agencies was given to the National Care Standards Commission (for agencies in England) and the National Assembly for Wales (for agencies in Wales).
- Section 11(3) of the Adoption Act 1976 was amended to make it a criminal offence for a person to take part in the management or control of a body of persons which existed for the purpose of making adoption arrangements and which was not a local authority or a voluntary agency registered under the 2000 Act.
- Local authority adoption functions (viz. functions under the 1976 Act of making or participating in arrangements for the adoption of children) were brought within the inspection powers of the NCSC and the National Assembly for Wales.

Implementation of these changes was not expected to occur before 2003, by which time, of course, the Adoption and Children Act would have been passed. All this makes for a complicated picture. The enactment of the 2002 Act could not have been anticipated by the Department of Health when the Care Standards Bill was introduced in 1999 because it was only in December 2000 that adoption legislation was clearly signalled. However, the arrival of the 2002 Act on the statute book necessarily involved the making of amendments to the adoption provisions of the 2000 Act in order that the two statutes could contain appropriate cross-references. The effect of these amendments is described below.

The Significance of Being an Adoption Agency

According to section 2(1) of the 2002 Act, 'an adoption agency' means either a local authority or a registered adoption society. A 'registered adoption society' is defined by section 2(2) to mean a voluntary organisation which is an adoption society registered under Part 2 of the Care Standards Act 2000. An 'adoption society' means a body whose functions consist of or include making arrangements for the adoption of children[4]. The combined effect of these provisions is broadly similar to the effect of the former law, described at the beginning of this chapter.

The agencies are, as one would expect, affected in a large number of ways by the provisions of the Act. They will also be affected by rules and regulations to be made under the Act by the Department of Health. Some parts of this legislation confer powers and privileges on agencies, other parts seek to regulate them by the imposition of duties. A pivotal provision is section 92. This makes it a criminal offence, punishable by fine or imprisonment, for a person other than an agency to take any one of a number of specified steps concerning adoption, including offering a child for adoption to a person other than an agency. (Various exceptions are laid down, covering for example placements with relatives and step-parent adoptions.) This section is based on a similar provision in the Adoption Act 1976 which was derived from the recommendations of the Houghton Committee made in 1972. It reflects the long-standing policy of channelling as many 'stranger adoptions' as possible through agencies staffed by, and regulated by, child care professionals. It is designed therefore to make agencies the exclusive providers of adoption arrangement services in such cases. The other provisions in the Act that impinge on the work of adoption agencies are considered in later parts of this book under appropriate headings. It may be useful, however, to summarise the main ones here:

- Whenever an agency is coming to a decision relating to the adoption of a child, the paramount consideration of the agency must be the child's welfare throughout his life[5].
- The exercise of all the adoption functions of agencies is liable to be controlled by government regulations[6].
- Where an adoption order application relates to a child placed by an agency, that agency must submit a welfare report to the court[7].

- Information kept by an agency about an adoption can be disclosed only in restricted circumstances. In some circumstances, information has to be disclosed[8].
- All agencies are obliged to provide statistical and other general information on demand to the Department of Health, or, in Wales, the Assembly[9].
- Government inquiries can be held into any matter connected with the functions of an agency[10].

The importance of Department of Health regulations for adoption agency work cannot be exaggerated. Many sets of regulations will be made in the run-up to the Act's commencement, covering a variety of matters. The Adoption Agencies Regulations 1983 will have to be revoked because they were drafted so as to fit in with the Adoption Act 1976, but they are bound to be replaced by something similar. All of these new regulations, like the old ones, will have the force of law and agencies will ignore them at their peril.

Registration of Voluntary Adoption Agencies

Unlike the Adoption Act 1976, the 2002 Act makes no provision for the approval of voluntary adoption agencies. This is because, as was explained earlier, the procedure for approval was radically altered by the Care Standards Act 2000. Under that Act, voluntary agencies were to be registered, and inspected, by the National Care Standards Commission (in England) and the National Assembly for Wales (in Wales). This arrangement has not been altered by the 2002 Act, although references to the Adoption Act 1976 in the 2000 Act have been changed to references to the new legislation. Part 2 of the 2000 Act provides a framework for the registration procedure, decision-making by the registration authorities, cancellation of registration, and appeals. Government regulations will supplement these provisions. The Act also makes provision for the preparation and publication of 'national minimum standards' by the Department of Health and the Welsh Assembly. These standards, which are not the same as the National Adoption Standards referred to in Chapter 4 above, have to be taken into account by the registration authorities when they make decisions about agencies[11]. Draft regulations and standards for VAAs were published in September 2002, with a view to their introduction in April 2003[12].

Inspection of Adoption Agencies

Whereas the Care Standards Act 2000 provides for the *registration* of only voluntary adoption agencies, it provides for the *inspection* of all adoption agencies, including local authorities. Part 2 of the Act covers voluntary adoption agencies while Part 3 covers local authorities. The provision for national minimum standards (above) is extended by Part 3 to local authorities, and these will be taken into account by the National Care Standards Commission when deciding what action to take following an inspection[13].

Adoption Support Agencies

According to section 8(1) of the 2002 Act, an adoption support agency is an undertaking the purpose of which, or one of the purposes of which, is the provision of adoption support services. These 'support services' are themselves defined in section 2(6) and, as was explained in Chapter 4 above, they consist largely of counselling, advice and information in connection with adoption. Section 8(2) makes it clear, however, that the following will *not* be regarded as adoption support agencies:

- voluntary adoption societies registered under the Care Standards Act 2000
- local authorities
- local education authorities
- health authorities
- the Registrar General.

Having defined these agencies, section 8(3) goes on to amend the Care Standards Act 2000 in such a way as to bring them within the scope of the registration and inspection provisions of that Act. This is the real purpose of section 8, as was made clear in the Government's Explanatory Notes on the Adoption and Children Bill:

> The purpose of these new provisions is to allow agencies other than adoption agencies to provide support services in connection with adoption (for example, specialist birth records counselling, and other services to be set out in the new national framework for adoption support) while ensuring that organisations operating in this sector are properly regulated. An adoption support agency may be voluntary or profit-making, and both organisations and sole practitioners providing adoption support services will be required to apply for registration as an adoption support agency. Registration will ensure that adoption support services are provided to an appropriately high standard by staff with the necessary training and expertise.[14]

The statutory profile of registered adoption support agencies was significantly enhanced in the autumn of 2002 when the Government agreed to make special provision in the Act for the birth relatives of people adopted in the past. The details of this legislation, contained in section 98 of the Act, and the debate preceding it may be found in Chapter 12 of this book.

Notes

1. Section 1(4).
2. [1991] FCR 1052.
3. *For Children's Sake: An SSI Inspection of Local Authority Adoption Services* (1996 and 1997); *Meeting the Challenges of Changes in Adoption: Inspection of Voluntary Adoption Agencies* (1999); *Adopting Changes: Survey and Inspection of Local Councils' Adoption Services* (2000).
4. Section 2(5).
5. Section 1(1) and (2).
6. Section 9.
7. Section 43.
8. Sections 56–65.
9. Section 13.
10. Section 17.
11. Section 23 of the 2000 Act.
12. DH local authority social services letter LASSL (2002) 8.
13. Section 49. Draft standards were published in September 2002.
14. DH Explanatory Notes to Bill 34 (2001), para 42.

CHAPTER 6

Domestic Baby Adoption

Introduction

Although the subject of adoption provokes many disagreements, all commentators today proceed from one fact: domestic baby adoption, once the norm, is now rare. 'Domestic baby adoption' for present purposes means the adoption of a UK-born infant who has been voluntarily given up (or 'relinquished', to use a commonly employed term) by their mother. When the Houghton Committee produced its report on adoption law reform in 1972, this type of arrangement was still encountered on a significant scale. Indeed, many of that committee's most important recommendations (for example, those concerning freeing for adoption) were drawn up with it in mind. Even then, however, change was known to be underway. The Committee referred to the decline in the annual number of adoption orders since the peak year of 1968 and said:

> This fall is the result of a smaller number of babies being offered for adoption, for there is no shortage of suitable couples wishing to adopt. The increasing number of legal abortions, more use of contraception, and the changing attitude to illegitimacy, which has resulted in a higher proportion of unmarried mothers keeping their babies, are among the factors which may accentuate this trend. Unmarried mothers are gradually becoming less disadvantaged, and there is a significant increase in tolerance and understanding towards them and their children.[1]

The extent to which this trend was accentuated during the 1970s and 1980s has been well documented. An indication of the scale of transformation is provided by a study by the Social Services Inspectorate of voluntary adoption agencies published in 1999. The SSI inspection team found that 'most VAAs had experienced a significant decrease in the volume of work with birth parents considering adoption for their baby. Two agencies had had no such referrals, the remainder (with one exception) handled only one or two cases a year'[2]. Indeed, in a Department of Health review of research published in the same year it was suggested that this reduction in the number of relinquished babies was 'the most significant feature' of the dramatic change in the character of adoption witnessed over the previous 25 years[3].

In the light of the above, it is hardly surprising that domestic baby adoption received relatively little attention in the period leading up to the Adoption and Children Act. The focus lay elsewhere, especially with looked after children. It is significant that on the two occasions when government ministers did seek to raise the issue of relinquishment as a beneficial social measure, they were widely criticised for doing so. The first of these interventions occurred in March 1996, shortly before the publication by the Conservative government of its draft Adoption Bill[4]. The junior Health Minister, John Bowis, was quoted as saying: 'We are trying to promote adoption as an acceptable and valid alternative to abortion and the burden of bringing up an unwanted child. But we are most certainly not putting pressure on any mother to use this route if she doesn't want to.'[5] In the event, this statement (like the draft Bill) came to nothing. A much bigger ripple in the pond, however, was caused in January 1999 when the Labour Home Secretary, Jack Straw, delivered a speech to the Family Policy Studies Centre. He said this:

> We need to find ways of presenting adoption as a positive, responsible choice to natural mothers who are not able to care for their babies. This is a sensitive area, and we will have to be careful in getting the message right. But it is in no one's interest, not the mother's nor the child's, nor the prospective parents', to allow a situation to develop whereby a crisis point is reached in the baby's first year because the ability of the mother, often a teenage mother, to cope has been misjudged by those well-meaning but not very professional people who are making the judgment.[6]

These comments, which of course included a thinly-veiled attack on social workers (who were evidently thought to play a key role in the counselling of young pregnant women) were said to be designed to 'start a debate' on adoption and it is true that the issue of relinquishment did occupy the national and regional media for a few days[7]. As with the Bowis intervention three years earlier, however, the matter was not pursued. This was not really surprising. The fact is that by the 1990s relinquishment of a baby for adoption was widely seen as both an act of folly and an act of betrayal. It was liable to carry the same sort of stigma for a woman as an unwanted extra-marital pregnancy had done in earlier times. As the vice-president of the Association of Directors of Social Services so graphically put it, 'it is society itself that has decided it no longer wants to see babies farmed out to middle-class mothers'[8].

In spite of all this, baby relinquishments do still occur and the 2002 Act does apply to them. The purpose of the present chapter is to explain the way in which key issues in this dwindling band of cases will be handled under the new legislation.

The Need for Immediate Agency Involvement

The Houghton Committee felt that the decision to place a child with a particular couple was the most important stage in the adoption process[9]. Consequently, the law should demand appropriate safeguards at the placement stage. Although the evidence submitted to it was mixed, the Committee clearly took a dim view of placements arranged directly by relinquishing birth mothers and placements arranged by third parties and it recommended that, subject to limited exceptions, such independent placements be prohibited by the criminal law. The recommendation was implemented by section 28 of the Children Act 1975 (subsequently section 11 of the Adoption Act 1976) although the provision did not become operative until 1982. Section 92 of the 2002 Act maintains this general prohibition of independent adoption placements but the wording of the legislation has been completely revised, evidently in an attempt to make it more accessible. It is, after all, aimed at ordinary members of the public, not child care professionals. According to section 92(1) and (2), a person who is neither an adoption agency nor acting in pursuance of an order of the High Court must not take any of the following steps:

a) Asking a person other than an adoption agency to provide a child for adoption.
b) Asking a person other than an adoption agency to provide prospective adopters for a child.
c) Offering to find a child for adoption.
d) Offering a child for adoption to a person other than an adoption agency.
e) Handing over a child to any person other than an adoption agency with a view to the child's adoption by that or another person.
f) Receiving a child handed over to them in contravention of paragraph (e).

g) Entering into an agreement with any person for the adoption of a child, or for the purpose of facilitating the adoption of a child, where no adoption agency is acting on behalf of the child in the adoption.

h) Initiating or taking part in negotiations of which the purpose is the conclusion of an agreement within paragraph (g).

i) Causing another person to take any of the steps mentioned in paragraphs (a) to (h).

The reference to people acting in pursuance of a High Court order is of no great importance: it is generally understood to cover those rare cases where a child has been made a ward of court and the court has authorised his placement for adoption. A more significant provision is section 92(3), which exempts from prohibitions (d) to (i) above cases in which the prospective adopter is a parent, relative[10] or guardian of the child or the partner of a parent. These exemptions are based on the previous law and can be traced back to the recommendations of the Houghton Committee, which was concerned with the particular risks attaching to placements with strangers, as opposed to in-family arrangements. The legal effect of infringing any of the prohibitions prescribed by section 92 is that the person concerned commits a criminal offence, punishable by fine (of up to £10,000) or imprisonment[11]. Whether proceedings are actually brought against an offender lies within the discretion of the Crown Prosecution Service. Where the charge relates to the paragraph (f) prohibition – receiving a child – the prosecution must prove that the defendant knew or had reason to suspect that the child was handed over unlawfully; and where the charge relates to the paragraph (i) prohibition – causing a third party to take a prohibited step – the prosecution must prove that the defendant knew or had reason to suspect that the step taken would contravene the law.

It is clear from the language of section 92 that the objective is to regulate placements for *adoption*. Genuine fostering placements – which of course can eventually lead to adoption – are not caught by this part of the statute, just as they were not caught by section 28 of the Children Act 1975[12]. It is also clear from the language that the only definite legal consequence of infringement is criminal liability. The legislation does not therefore prevent an adoption going ahead where an illegal placement has been identified. This was the position under the previous law and the courts confirmed it on a number of occasions[13]. As a matter of policy this must be right. If it were otherwise, the court would be prevented from making the very order that would most benefit the child in question (whose interests, of course, come first). The illegal behaviour in these cases, while serious enough to make possible a criminal prosecution, is not deemed serious enough to act as a bar to adoption.

Adoption applications following illegal placement

If an application for adoption is made in a case where the terms of section 92 have been broken, that breach of the law will have to be weighed in the balance by the court along with all the other relevant factors. The child's welfare will of course be paramount. Under the previous legislation it was ruled that these tainted applications should be determined in the High Court and there is no reason to think that this rule no longer applies[14]. It may be noted at this stage that as a result of section 42(5) of the Act, prospective adopters who have not received the child through an agency (or after a High Court authorisation) are able to file an application only after they have accumulated three years' care and possession of the child, unless they obtain permission from the court prior to reaching that point. This is a departure from the previous law, which prescribed a minimum care period of twelve months for non-agency adoption by strangers[15]. As with all non-agency adoption applications, notice of intention to adopt has to be given to the local authority[16].

Dealings with the Birth Mother

It is clear (indeed, obvious) that the circumstances of birth mothers who decide to relinquish their baby for adoption will vary widely, despite their low numbers. Of the many reported cases arising out of relinquishment decisions, *Re P*, decided in 1976[17], illustrates the historical stereotype. This concerned a baby born to a girl of 15 who lived with her divorced mother and her brothers and sisters in what was described as a Victorian terraced council house in South London. The family was entirely dependent on welfare benefits. The baby's father was 17 and was no longer in a relationship with the mother. The mother initially gave her consent to adoption but subsequently retracted it. At a rather different point on the spectrum is the case of *Re B*, first heard in 2000[18]. Here, the baby was born to a 28-year-old woman who was described by the judge as intelligent and reflective. She had in fact already relinquished her first child for adoption and when she discovered that she was expecting a second, planned the same thing for her too. She had no doubts about this: she told a social worker that she had no maternal instinct and that she had known for many years that she did not want children. She stated that she was ashamed of her pregnancies ('once is forgivable – twice is incomprehensible'), having kept her second pregnancy secret from both the father and her own family. According to the report of the case, she did not look at the baby when she was born and she discharged herself from hospital the day after the birth. The baby was placed from hospital in foster care at four days old.

Given this sort of variation, it is no surprise that adoption legislation and guidance are framed in only very general terms when dealing with obligations to, and services for, relinquishing birth mothers. It has already been seen how the 2002 Act has maintained the obligation of local authorities to provide an adoption service. This service extends to children who may be adopted and their parents, so relinquishments plainly fall within its scope[19]. The 'requisite facilities' that must be provided include making arrangements for adoption and the provision of adoption support services (defined as meaning counselling, advice and information in connection with adoption) and section 4(1)(a) of the Act

entitles a birth mother to an assessment of her needs for such support services. This is really as far as the Act itself goes on this subject. It is certain, however, to be supplemented in important respects by regulations made under section 9. These are likely to follow the pattern of the Adoption Agencies Regulations 1983 which, among other things, required an agency that was considering adoption for a child to provide a counselling service for the mother and to explain to her the legal implications and procedures of adoption[20]. On top of these statutory obligations there will be applicable the National Adoption Standards and accompanying Practice Guidance. The first set of Standards published in August 2001 contained a discrete chapter (Chapter D) devoted to Birth Parents and Birth Families. According to the introductory statement: 'Birth parents and birth families are entitled to services that recognise the lifelong implications of adoption. They will be treated fairly, openly and with respect throughout the adoption process.' The nine Standards themselves read as follows:

1. Agencies will work with birth parents and significant birth family members to enable effective plans to be made and implemented for their child(ren).
2. Every effort will be made to ensure that birth parents and significant birth family members have a full understanding of the adoption process, the legal implications, and their rights.
3. Birth parents will have access to a support worker independent of the child's social worker from the time adoption is identified as the plan for the child.
4. Birth parents and birth families (including siblings) will have access to a range of support services both before and after adoption, including information about local and national support groups and services.
5. Birth parents will have the opportunity to give their account of events, and to see and comment on what is written about them in reports for the adoption panel, and in information passed to the adopters.

6. Birth parents and families will be supported to provide information that the adopted child needs. This will include information about the adopted child's birth and early life, the birth family's views about adoption and contact and up-to-date information about themselves and their situation.
7. Where it is in the child's best interest for there to be ongoing links, including contact, with birth parents and families (including siblings separated by adoption), birth families will be involved in discussions about how best to achieve this and helped to fulfil agreed plans, e.g. through practical or financial support.
8. Where adoptive parents have agreed to inform the agency of the death of the adopted child or the breakdown of the adoption, birth parents or the 'next of kin' at adoption will, if they wish, be informed by the adoption agency.
9. Birth parents and birth families will be informed of their right to make representations and complaints.

It is important to note that these Standards were formulated with all domestic agency adoptions in mind. Like the other Standards, they were put together not so much for baby relinquishment cases but for the numerically greater category of looked after children. Nor were any distinctions made between mothers and fathers.

Unlike the Standards document, the draft Practice Guidance, also published in August 2001, did refer specifically to relinquishment. It suggested that: 'As much preliminary work as possible should be undertaken with the birth parent/s before the child is actually born, to ensure that the decision to place for adoption is based on the fullest possible consideration of all the alternatives available. As the Adoption Act 1976 provides that agreement given to adoption within 6 weeks of the birth is ineffective, a birth mother must be allowed at least 6 weeks before confirming her decision to relinquish. Agencies should ensure birth parents have access to advice, counselling and support during this period.'

There were also references to unmarried fathers, described below. The Practice Guidance will have to be revised appropriately once the 2002 Act comes into force, so as to reflect the new legal framework.

Dealings with the Birth Father

Introduction

Just as the circumstances of birth mothers in relinquishment cases differ widely, so do the circumstances of fathers. In fact, there may well be more variation. For one thing, the identity of these men (or boys) is not always known. For another, they may have no desire to be involved in the decision-making process; or if they do have such a desire, it may be thwarted by maternal hostility or indifference. Very few, if any, of these fathers will be married to the mother and the fact that the mother has decided to relinquish the child at the earliest possible moment will almost certainly mean that the father will lack the legal status of having parental responsibility for the child within the meaning of the Children Act 1989. Parental responsibility will be vested exclusively in the mother. In view of these factors, it is hardly surprising that English adoption law, and therefore agencies and the courts, have tended to play down the position of the father in the relinquishment process. Change is underway, however, and this reflects complex attitudinal shifts in relation to illegitimacy, extra-marital relationships, parenting roles and openness. (The new parental responsibility provisions contained in the 2002 Act – allocating joint parental responsibility to an unmarried father who becomes registered as the child's father under the Births and Deaths Registration Act – are additional evidence of these.) By October 2000 a judge of the Court of Appeal could say this:

> The climate has undoubtedly shifted since the mid-1980s, and the shift is towards according greater involvement of natural fathers, even

though there has been no marriage and even though there has been no formal order of parental responsibility.[21]

Legislation and guidance

Although the previously-noted general provisions of the 2002 Act relating to the adoption service (including adoption support services) and the National Adoption Standards, do extend to birth fathers, it is likely that special provisions will be found in regulations and practice guidance. The Adoption Agencies Regulations 1983, made under the previous Adoption Act, certainly contained special provisions, for regulation 7(3) read as follows:

Where the father of a child does not have parental responsibility for the child and his identity is known to the adoption agency, it shall so far as it considers reasonably practicable and in the interests of the child – (a) carry out in respect of the father the requirements of paragraph (1)(a) as if they applied to him [*these were the requirements to provide a counselling service and to explain the adoption process*]; (b) obtain the particulars of him referred to in Parts III and IV of the Schedule [*these included personal details and health information*]; and (c) ascertain so far as possible whether he intends to apply for custody of the child. [*The reference to 'custody' became obsolete in 1991: the paragraph should have referred to a residence order under the Children Act 1989.*]

A number of issues arose out of this provision which will have to be addressed again under the 2002 Act. The first point to note is that it applied only to birth fathers lacking parental responsibility. Fathers with parental responsibility are entitled to play a full part in adoption proceedings. However, as has already been noted, in baby relinquishment cases it is unlikely that the father will have this status: if the mother is set on adoption – which will of course have the effect of transferring parental responsibility permanently to the adopters – what purpose would be served by sharing that responsibility with the father for a strictly limited period? A second point relates to the apparently unfettered discretion of the

agency. The obligations set out in the regulation were not absolute; they were stated to apply only so far as the agency considered reasonably practicable and in the interests of the child. Although this clearly provided an agency with a justification for not working actively with a known birth father, case law developments suggested that compelling reasons would have to be found for this to occur. This leads on to the third point, which concerns the identification of the father by the mother.

No statutory or guidance provisions relating to the father can be put into effect if the identity of the father is not known and the circumstances of a relinquishment case may well leave the mother as the sole provider of this information. What if she refuses to provide it, or provides it on condition that the father is not informed by the agency of her plans? For many years the assumption was that birth mothers could not be compelled to reveal identifying information[22] but the question was directly explored in November 2000 by the High Court in the cases of *Re H and G*[23]. The timing of these cases was advantageous in that it enabled the court to consider the impact of the family life and fair trial provisions of the European Convention on Human Rights (incorporated into English law by the Human Rights Act 1998). The overall effect of the judgment was to leave agencies with the discretion to proceed with a placement despite the absence of information about the father, but also to reaffirm the court's power to insist on disclosure – possibly at a very late stage in the process – if the circumstances warranted it. The stronger the father's claim to having family ties with the child and mother, e.g. through a period of cohabitation with the mother prior to the birth, the greater the likelihood of the court taking steps to have him notified of the adoption application. Where the father was shown to have had a 'substantial relationship' with the mother, the desire of the mother for secrecy could not prevail over notice to the father unless there were strong countervailing factors. Among such countervailing factors might be rape or other serious domestic violence that placed the mother at serious physical risk. In one of the two cases being considered, the court directed that steps should be taken to inform the father of the adoption proceedings. The mother was 'requested' to give the father's name and address to the agency and to the court. This action was taken despite the fact that the agency had from the start dealt with the mother on the basis of confidentiality and despite the fact that by the time of the court's direction the child had been living with the (unsuspecting) prospective adopters for nine months. In the other case, the court was content for the father not to be involved: although the birth parents had at one time been engaged to be married, the court was not satisfied that their relationship had 'sufficient constancy to create de facto family ties'. The judge went on to make the following general observations on the issue of confidentiality:

> I recognise the importance of supporting unmarried mothers who wish to place babies for adoption and do not wish their family and friends or the natural father to know of the birth of the child. It is highly desirable that babies not able to be brought up by the natural mother should be cared for by local authorities and placed for adoption within a framework of confidentiality so far as it can be maintained. The European Convention, however, underpins the evolving culture in our adoption legislation of greater involvement of natural families in post-adoption placements and knowledge of the natural father…A considerable degree of confidentiality is clearly important but it ought not, in the majority of cases, to deprive the father of his right to be informed and consulted about his child. In my view, social workers counselling mothers ought to warn them that, at some stage, the court will have to make a decision in adoption proceedings as to whether to add the father as a respondent [i.e. as a party] to the proceedings. The father should, therefore, be told as soon as possible in order to reduce delay, and certainly before the child is placed with prospective adopters. If the mother refuses to disclose the identity of the father, her reasons must be carefully considered and, unless those reasons are cogent, it would be wise for the local authority to seek legal advice at an early stage.

The tenor of this important judgment has made it more likely that birth fathers will be brought into relinquishment cases against the wishes of the mother. Whether agencies will be given heavier duties under the regulations towards fathers who lack parental responsibility, so as to reflect the European Convention and the English case law, remains to be seen.

Dealings with the Extended Birth Family

Although the 2002 Act does not refer expressly to an agency's dealings with a child's extended birth family, it is clear that agencies are expected to work with a range of relatives where appropriate. The National Adoption Standards, set out earlier in this chapter, contain explicit references to 'significant birth family members' and it is not difficult to see how in a relinquishment case (involving a very young mother, for example) grandparents and perhaps others could become heavily involved in the arrangements. The Standards provide that birth parents *and birth families* will have access to a range of support services both before and after adoption[24]. This assumes, however, that extended family members are actually aware of the child's existence and the mother's plans for him. Suppose they are not aware? Cases will arise, for example, where the relinquishing mother insists on the birth of her child being kept secret from her family. This can create dilemmas for an agency similar to those encountered in relation to birth fathers, of the sort discussed earlier. (Indeed, the cases of *Re H and G*, mentioned above in the context of birth fathers, did involve women who demanded confidentiality in relation to both the father and their own relatives.)

By coincidence, the question of disclosing to relatives the fact of the child's birth and the mother's intention to relinquish him was addressed by the High Court around the same time as that court was considering the position of fathers. In the case of *Re R*[25], the relinquishing mother revealed that she had some siblings but she was adamant that they should not be made aware of her child's existence. She told the agency that 'given her own family dynamics, she did not feel that she or her family could offer R all that R needed in terms of a secure future'. She was '110 per cent sure' that the relatives were not in a position to care for R and she expressed concern that any further enquiries could create extreme difficulties within the wider family unit. However, when the agency made a freeing application to the court, the guardian ad litem – commenting that the mother 'appeared to have an obsession of secrecy' – raised the issue of informing the relatives and argued that the European Convention on Human Rights might have an important role to play. As has been seen, this argument was also run in *Re H and G*. It is clear that the judge was against compulsory disclosure as a matter of policy. He said this:

> Although no statistics are available, many children must have been adopted over the years, outside their birth families, and with no knowledge by, or investigation of, other members of the birth family. Adoption exists to serve many social needs. But high among them has been, historically, the desire or need of some mothers to be able to conceal from their own family and friends the fact of the pregnancy and birth. So far as I know, it has not previously been suggested, nor judicially determined, that that confidentiality of the mother cannot be respected and maintained. If it is now to be eroded, there is, in my judgment, a real risk that more pregnant women would seek abortions or give birth secretly, to the risk of both themselves and their babies…There is, in my judgment, a strong social need, if it is lawful, to continue to enable some mothers, such as this mother, to make discreet, dignified and humane arrangements for the birth and subsequent adoption of their babies, without their families knowing anything about it, if the mother, for good reason, so wishes.

He found that there was nothing in the European Convention to make it obligatory for the relatives of R to be told of his relinquishment. The mother was an intelligent person and the judge saw no reason to doubt the sincerity of her reported views. He did stress that his conclusion was reached on the particular facts of the case: 'this judgment is not intended in any way to suggest that the extended family can simply be ignored on the say-so of a mother.' Normally, he said, there should be wide consultation with, and consideration of, the extended family, and that should be dispensed with only after due and careful consideration. The effect of this judgment was to leave agencies free to use their discretion and it seems clear that their discretion is less trammelled when it comes to informing relatives than it is in regard to fathers. In many cases it will not be that difficult for the agency to argue that going against the mother's wishes in this matter would have such an uncertain outcome as to jeopardise the arrangements for the future welfare of the baby. Perhaps the most that can be said is that if the mother does insist on secrecy, her reasons need to be explored and discussed thoroughly. A failure to address the issue properly at the outset could lead to delay at a later stage in the process when the court is seised of the adoption application itself.

Placement of the Child

It was noted earlier how the Houghton Committee of 1972 considered that the placement decision was the most important stage in the adoption process. It is a curious fact that this view has become fully reflected in the law only through the 2002 Act. Unlike the previous legislation, the new Act contains detailed provisions about placement. These have been introduced with looked after children particularly in mind, and they are considered in that context in Chapter 7 of this book, but they also apply to baby relinquishment cases so they need to be noted here too.

The 2002 Act draws a distinction between adoption placements that are agreed by the child's parents (viz. parents having parental responsibility for the child) and contested placements. Since baby relinquishment is by definition a consensual process (to begin with, at any rate) it is the agreed placement provisions that are relevant. These are contained in sections 18, 19 and 52 of the Act. Under section 19(1), where the adoption agency is satisfied that each parent with parental responsibility has consented to the child being placed for adoption with prospective adopters identified in the consent, or being placed for adoption with *any* prospective adopters who may be chosen by the agency, the agency is authorised to place the child for adoption. According to section 52(5), 'consent' means consent given unconditionally and with full understanding of what is involved, while section 52(7) provides that consent under section 19 must be given in the form to be prescribed in government rules. These important provisions reflect very clearly the serious nature of placement of a child for adoption, and they are reinforced by section 102, which enables rules to be made providing for CAFCASS staff to witness documents that signify consent to placement. Through these formalities, the genuineness of the birth mother's consent can be tested at the outset. It should be noted, however, that special provision has been made for babies who are placed for adoption in the first six weeks of life (i.e. the classic relinquishment cases). Under section 18(1), such children can be placed by an adoption agency without the usual formalities being complied with. This facility is necessary for a number of reasons, for example because of the sheer impracticality of getting the formalities completed in time in those fast-track cases where the plan is for the child to go to the adopters almost immediately upon discharge from hospital. The Act therefore permits an immediate placement, although as is explained below section 19 consent should be obtained from the mother at the six-week point if the adoption is to proceed smoothly.

Under section 18(3), a child who is placed by a local authority (as opposed to a voluntary adoption agency) is looked after by that authority for the purposes of the Children Act 1989. This means that the various local authority obligations set out in Part III of the 1989

Act kick in, although section 53(1) of the 2002 Act permits modification of these obligations by government regulation (so as to disapply, for example, the duty to promote parental contact). A similar overall result is achieved in relation to VAA placements by section 53(3), by reference to section 61 of the Children Act.

The Birth Mother's Consent to Adoption

Although some of the Act's provisions draw a clear distinction between consent to placement and consent to the making of an adoption order, in the case of voluntary relinquishment the former is all that is needed for an order to be made, provided the consent to placement was given by the mother more than six weeks after the birth of the child. This is the effect of section 47(4). If for any reason the birth mother's consent to an adoption *order* is required, such consent is, again, valid only if provided after the six-week point (section 52(3)). The time restriction is long-standing and is based on the need to give the relinquishing mother sufficient time to recover from the effects of the birth. The provision of consent by the mother does not necessarily signal the end of her involvement in the adoption process. Section 141 of the Act, innocuously entitled 'Rules of procedure', provides that the court rules relating to adoption applications must require the mother to be notified of the date and place where the application will be heard, and notified of the fact that she can attend court if she wishes, or be required by the court to attend. Mothers who prefer not to be further involved in this way are catered for by section 20. This enables a mother who has already given placement consent under section 19 to give an 'advance consent to adoption', which need not be linked to particular adopters. Under section 20(4), the mother may then give notice to the adoption agency that she does not wish to be informed of any adoption application. Once that is done, the notification duty under the section 141 rules disappears. It can be seen that section 20 is, in effect, the new legislation's equivalent of the discredited (and now abandoned) freeing for adoption provisions of the Adoption Act 1976.

Birth mothers under a disability

In the exceptional case where the relinquishing mother is under a disability to the extent that she is not in a position to provide a valid consent to adoption, the matter will have to proceed in the hands of the local authority via a placement order (on which see Chapter 7). This is because of section 18 of the Act, mentioned earlier. Agency placements can proceed only under section 19 – which requires a genuine consent – or a section 21 placement order. Section 52(1) – repeating the principle of the previous law – allows the mother's consent to a placement order to be dispensed with if the court is satisfied that she is incapable of giving it.

Birth Mothers who Change Their Mind

Background

In 1971 adoption law in England and Wales began to turn decisively against relinquishing birth mothers who changed their mind. It was in that year that the House of Lords delivered its decision in the landmark case of *Re W*[26]. The case had the most straightforward facts. The mother was an unmarried woman who at the age of 21 gave birth to her third child. It had been an unplanned pregnancy. Although she was looking after her two older children satisfactorily, she felt that life with three small children in cramped accommodation would be impossible. She therefore relinquished the baby, who went to the prospective adopters at nine days old. The mother signed the adoption consent form ten months into the placement but sought to revoke her consent seven weeks later, on the day before the adoption application was due to be heard by the court. She wrote:

I would like to withdraw my consent to the adoption of my child. Sir, when I had my child I just moved into a [council] flat and I had so much to do but now I would like to have my child back as I have enough accommodation for him. I have always wanted him back. I was so mixed up at the time, I have two children with me at the moment of my own and I can look after them very well and I would like to have [the child] back with me.

The county court judge decided to dispense with the mother's consent on the ground – then contained in the Adoption Act 1958 – that it was being withheld unreasonably. He was evidently influenced by the danger of upsetting settled arrangements and also by the mother's unhappy track record in personal relationships. 'It does seem', he said, 'she does make relationships with men who are very unsatisfactory as far as one can see. She may be unlucky. I can't put it out of my mind…I can't help feeling there is a grave risk of another association and another unwanted child arriving on the scene. A grave risk.' In the Court of Appeal, however, this decision was overturned. The judge was said to have delivered what was described as a 'welfare judgment', which was impermissible. He had failed to attach sufficient weight to the Draconian effect of an adoption order; and he had failed to recognise the quasi-penal nature of the dispensing provisions of the legislation. Before a mother could be said to be withholding consent unreasonably, it had to be shown that she had been guilty of culpable conduct. Vacillation on her part could satisfy this test but only if it was exceptionally prolonged and repeated, which was not the case here. According to Lord Justice Sachs, it was natural and to be expected that a mother might change her mind. As for the danger of psychological disturbance caused by moving the child, the same judge expressed his concern about 'a whole class of adoption cases being in effect decided by the psychiatric specialist profession' and he suggested (as did the two other members of the court), that any such danger needed to be weighed against 'a second and better known set of risks occurring when a child is told that the parent it has been taught to regard simply as 'mother' is not truly the child's mother'.

In upholding the mother's veto in this case, the three very experienced Court of Appeal judges expressed themselves in unusually strong language. ('The Adoption Act', said one, 'is not – as counsel for the applicants also rightly conceded – a piece of legislation intended to deprive even prostitutes of the right of parenthood if they are in fact good mothers.') And their judgments probably represent the high-water mark of the parental rights perspective in relinquishment cases. When the case went on further appeal to the House of Lords, a very different approach – also strongly expressed – was pursued, one that has held sway ever since. The Court of Appeal's insistence that blameworthiness on the mother's part had to be demonstrated was firmly rejected. 'Unreasonableness', said Lord Hailsham, 'is one thing. Culpability is another. It may be that all or most culpable conduct is unreasonable. But the converse is not necessarily true.' Furthermore – and crucially – in assessing the reasonableness of the mother's change of mind, the welfare of the child was highly relevant because a reasonable mother would always give great weight to what was better for the child. Welfare, according to Lord Hailsham, 'is relevant in all cases if and to the extent that a reasonable parent would take it into account. *It is decisive in those cases where a reasonable parent must so regard it*'[27]. Applying this test, the House of Lords went on to find that the county court judge had had adequate material to justify dispensing with the mother's consent. He had not exaggerated the risks attached to moving the child from a stable and secure home and was justified in thinking that there was – as he had put it – an enormous question mark in relation to the mother. Consequently, the adoption order was confirmed.

The judges who presided at the Court of Appeal stage of this case sought to point out the danger in elevating the welfare of the child as a factor in applications to dispense with a relinquishing mother's consent. Lord Justice Russell, for example, said: 'The question whether a parent's consent is unreason-ably withheld is not to be solved merely by a view formed by a court, or by a child welfare officer, or a man or woman in the street that life with the proposed adopters would be, if I may use the phrase, a better bet for the child. This truism must be clearly appreciated by any who may interest themselves in cases such as the present case. Were it otherwise the Act would have allowed consent to be dispensed with whenever the adoption order would in the view of the court be in the best interests of the child.' In the event, of course, these warnings were dismissed and it was no surprise to find the senior judiciary in subsequent years taking their lead from the House of Lords and pursuing a heavily welfare-based approach to dispensation. This was openly acknowledged by the Court of Appeal in the case of *Re H*, decided in 1977[28]. In that case, the county court judge had dispensed with the consent of a 20-year-old mother who had changed her mind only three months into the adoption placement (although the children had been with the adopters for eight months by the time of the court hearing). In dismissing the mother's appeal, Lord Justice Ormrod said this:

> The attitude of the court to the question of dispensing with consent, or holding that the consent is unreasonably withheld, has changed over the years…The relative importance of the welfare of the children is increasing rather than diminishing in relation to dispensing with consent. That being so, it ought to be recognised by all concerned with adoption cases that once the formal consent has been given or perhaps once the child has been placed with the adopters, time begins to run against the mother and, as time goes on, it gets progressively more and more difficult for her to show that the withdrawal of her consent is reasonable…In the present climate of opinion, it is misleading to say to a mother, having signed the form of consent, 'You can always withdraw up to the last minute before the court hearing'. Of course she can withdraw, but she runs the risk, as this mother has done, of the court finding that her withdrawal was not reasonable.

By 1992, the team responsible for the Adoption Law Review felt able to say that in this area the welfare of the child had in effect become the paramount consideration[29]. Despite the Review's concerns, the principle has now been codified by the 2002 Act.

The effect of the 2002 Act

Removing the child
When a relinquishing mother changes her mind about adoption, the immediate issue must be the security of the child's placement. Can the mother recover the child at will? If this can be done, then clearly it is liable to torpedo all adoption plans. If it cannot be done, and the child remains separated from the mother, the long-term issue will be the adoption proceedings themselves and the mother's prospects of successfully opposing an order. The two issues are linked, of course, because the longer the mother is separated from her child the more difficult it will be – on purely welfare grounds – for her to resist adoption (or some other order favouring the prospective adopters). The Adoption Act 1976 prevented a relinquishing mother from directly removing the child from prospective adopters once an adoption application had been lodged with the court[30]. It was a very simple provision and it applied even in cases where only a verbal consent to adoption had been given[31]. As with so much of the 2002 Act, the new provisions concerning removal are far more elaborate and in some respects more difficult to unravel. As far as relinquishments are concerned, the position is as follows:

▪ Where the child has been relinquished and placed within the first six weeks of his life and the mother within that period informs the agency that she wishes to have the child back, the agency must give written notice of the mother's wish to the prospective adopters, who must return the child to the agency within seven days (section 31(3) and (4)). As soon as the child is returned to the agency, the agency must return him to the mother (section 31(6)). None of this applies, however, if the agency is a local authority and an application to the court

for a placement order is made by the authority.

▪ The same rules apply if the child was placed within the first six weeks but no section 19 consent has been given by the mother by the time she changes her mind (section 31(3)).

▪ Where the mother has provided a section 19 consent to placement (as described earlier), she may withdraw that consent by giving written notice to the agency, unless an adoption application has already been lodged with the court (section 52(4) and (8)). If the mother then informs the agency that she wishes the child to be returned to her, the agency must give written notice of the mother's wish to the prospective adopters, who must return the child to the agency within 14 days (section 32(1) and (2)). As soon as the child is returned to the agency, the agency must return him to the mother (section 32(4)). None of this applies, however, if the agency is a local authority and an application to the court for a placement order is made by the authority. Furthermore, if *before* the agency gives notice to the prospective adopters they apply to the court for a residence order, a special guardianship order or an adoption order (or permission to apply for a residence order or a special guardianship order), the prospective adopters can hold on to the child unless the court orders otherwise (section 32(5)).

▪ Subject to her above-mentioned rights to ask for the return of the child, the mother has no right to remove the child from the prospective adopters (section 30(1)).

Opposing an adoption order at the final hearing
It follows from what has just been stated that some relinquishing mothers who undergo a change of heart will find it impossible to recover their child immediately. Others may well be in a position to try to recover the child but for some reason they will choose not to do so. In either case, any attempt by the mother to block an adoption order will be left until

the judicial stage of the process is reached. It is therefore necessary to turn to those provisions of the 2002 Act that deal with contested adoption applications. The bottom line here is that under section 47(2)(c) a court dealing with an adoption application can, as under the previous legislation, dispense with a protesting mother's consent. The unreasonableness ground has been abolished, however. Under section 52(1), the court can dispense with consent if it is satisfied that (a) the mother cannot be found or is incapable of giving consent (these grounds will rarely apply); or (b) the welfare of the child requires the consent to be dispensed with. In applying paragraph (b), the court's paramount consideration must be the child's welfare, throughout his life. This is laid down by section 1 of the Act. Section 52(1)(b) represents the logical statutory seal on the development in judicial policy initiated by the House of Lords in 1971 in the case of *Re W*, discussed earlier. Although it has been criticised as being unfair to parents, it should occasion no real surprise. It will enable the courts to carry on rejecting the late claims of relinquishing mothers where the child in question has become settled with capable prospective adopters and/or there are serious doubts about the mother's parenting capacity.

This is only part of the picture, however. In some circumstances, the scheme of the 2002 Act allows an opposed relinquishment adoption to go ahead without the court having to formally dispense with the mother's consent. One such situation is where the mother has provided advance consent to adoption under section 20. Section 47(2)(b) of the Act enables the court to make an adoption order if the mother has consented under section 20, has not formally withdrawn that consent, and does not oppose the making of the order. Section 20 consent cannot be withdrawn after an adoption application has been filed (section 52(4)). As for opposing the making of the order, section 47(3) provides that the mother may not oppose without the court's leave (i.e. permission) and section 47(7) provides that the court cannot give leave unless it is satisfied that there has been a

change of circumstances since the advance consent was given. It should be noted that even if the mother succeeds in showing a change of circumstances and obtains leave to oppose – and this may be difficult – her consent can still be dispensed with under section 47(2)(c).

A second situation is where the child was placed for adoption under section 19 with the consent of the mother and her consent to placement was given at least six weeks after the child's birth. As with section 20 cases, if the mother wishes to oppose the making of an adoption order she will need permission from the court and to get that she will have to show a change of circumstances[32].

A further point needs to be made. Even if the mother manages to persuade the court not to make an adoption order, she may still be denied day-to-day care of the child. Under section 10 of the Children Act 1989, the adoption court has the power to grant a residence order to the prospective adopters. This will have the effect of preserving the status quo.

It is clear from these rules – and indeed from the whole history of adoption law after 1971 – that relinquishing mothers, particularly those who confirm formally the relinquishment beyond the critical six-week point, need to receive the most thorough counselling about the consequences of their action. The law has shifted decisively against vacillating mothers. Recovering a child following a change of mind will not be impossible but it may be exceedingly problematic. As the team responsible for the 1992 Adoption Law Review put it: 'Once agreement has been given for the child to be placed for adoption, assumptions of good practice undermine for all practical purposes the birth parents' legal rights.'[33]

Birth Fathers who Oppose Relinquishment

A birth father may become aware of relinquishment arrangements through being told directly by the mother, or her relatives; through being told by the adoption agency;

through being contacted by the court to which the adoption application has been made; or simply by chance. However he learns of it, his formal consent to adoption is not required unless he has parental responsibility for the child, which is unlikely. This long-standing rule now appears in section 52(6) of the 2002 Act. Lacking parental responsibility, however, does not mean lacking all standing, and there are a number of options available to the father who wishes actively to oppose relinquishment. Which of these options is selected really depends on what the father's long-term plans actually are. It may be, for example, that he simply wishes to remain in some sort of contact with the child as the child grows up. It may be that he has in mind a different kind of placement (e.g. a placement with the paternal grandparents). Proposals such as these will require negotiation with the mother and the agency. The boldest form of intervention would consist of a bid by the father for outright care of the child, made either on his own or jointly with his current partner. Since 1991, when the Children Act 1989 came into force, a residence order application has been the appropriate mechanism for securing this and the father, as a legal parent (albeit one without parental responsibility) has been entitled to apply[34].

The case of *Re O*, decided by the Court of Appeal in August 1998[35], showed very clearly the anxieties and complexities inherent in such applications. In the words of the Court of Appeal, 'the judge was faced with, on one side, an impeccable father who, for reasons for which he has no responsibility, has had no contact with his child, and his fiancee…and, on the other side, impeccable and loving proposed adopters with whom S has lived since 7 March 1997. They clearly love him deeply and he is now securely bonded with them'. The father knew nothing about the child's existence, let alone the mother's relinquishment decision, until he was informed of the adoption application pursuant to an order of the county court. He and the mother had cohabited for three years and he was said to be deeply affronted that he had not been informed – either by the mother or by the

adoption agency – of his son's birth and that his claim to look after the child had been prejudiced by lapse of time. Although both the county court judge and the Court of Appeal expressed considerable sympathy for the father, and although the expert witnesses were divided in their opinions, the prospective adopters got their order. The critical factor was the timing of the father's intervention, which came too late due to his state of ignorance. As one of the expert witnesses put it: 'We are not starting with a new-born baby and saying 'Which of these two sets of parents would be better?' What we are starting with is a well-attached child who has had 18 months of his life and who would have to suffer what I think all of us agree would be pretty intense short-term distress in the hope that what he would go to would eventually turn out to be equivalent of what he is getting already in his adoptive home, plus that little extra bit of the immediate access to his genetic inheritance.' So it was that the blood tie, which the father not unnaturally was so keen to emphasise, was effectively trumped by other welfare-related considerations.

Although situations like this are bound to recur, it seems clear that after the implementation of the 2002 Act it will not be possible to resolve them under the auspices of a residence order application. This is because of section 28(1), which provides that where a child is placed for adoption under section 19 – viz. with the mother's consent – 'a parent or guardian of the child may not apply for a residence order'. This wording covers birth fathers. Whether the Department of Health intended birth fathers such as the one in *Re O* above to be caught by section 28(1) is unclear but the result is utterly bizarre. It means that the father will be forced into some other legal manoeuvre to stake his claim. At least three possibilities exist: an application for contact (section 26 of the Act allows this); an application to the High Court under its special inherent jurisdiction (an unlikely and artificial device in this context); and an application for a parental responsibility order under section 4 of the Children Act 1989. If the father chooses the last option (a course followed, incidentally, by the father in *Re O*) and gets the order, his consent to the placement is deemed to have been given[36] but he will still be in a position to oppose an adoption order. He will be joined as a party to the adoption proceedings as and when they arise, and he will be able to express his opposition to the court. The court will be in a position to grant him, and any partner of his, a residence order if it thinks fit.

Relinquishing the Child to the Birth Father

The case of *Re B*, decided by the House of Lords in December 2001[37], shows how it is possible for a relinquished baby to end up, with the mother's agreement, in the care of his father. Some of the facts of this case were described earlier[38]. The mother was set to relinquish to the couple who had adopted her first child but she agreed to a change of plan when the father intervened after a remarkable turn of events. A typist employed by the adoption agency recognised the father's name and revealed that his mother worked in the same building. In this way the father came to be contacted. Although the birth parents' relationship had long been over, the mother supported a placement with the father and the child was in due course handed over. In such circumstances, of course, the adoption agency's role came to an end but there remained the question of how to regularise the father's legal position. The parents decided to jointly register the child's birth (an act that under the 2002 Act would have the effect of giving the father parental responsibility). They also entered into a parental responsibility agreement under the Children Act 1989. There matters might have rested but in an attempt to maximise his security, the father launched adoption proceedings four months into the placement. Although both the mother, who of course stood to lose her status completely, and the local authority supported this application, the Official Solicitor, acting as the child's guardian ad litem, opposed it to the extent of taking the matter to appeal. The case

therefore sheds considerable light on the interesting question of sole adoptions by unmarried fathers and some of the prevailing judicial attitudes towards them.

As long ago as 1972 the Houghton Committee had expressed serious misgivings about these adoptions. 'The adoption of an illegitimate child by one of his natural parents alone,' it said[39], 'has one very important legal effect: it cuts out the other parent.' While not recommending a total ban on such outcomes (an idea floated in its earlier working paper) the Committee did suggest that the law should impose a special circumstances test. This suggestion was taken up in the ensuing legislation, so that under section 15(3) of the Adoption Act 1976 a court could grant adoption to a sole parent only if satisfied that the other parent was dead or could not be found or that there was some other reason justifying their exclusion. In *Re B*, the trial judge found that this last condition was satisfied: 'the mother has rejected A from birth and has played no part in her care or upbringing; the mother has consented to the adoption, and the mother wishes to play no part in A's life in the future, other than to have indirect contact.' Unhappily for the father, the Court of Appeal disagreed with this assessment of the case. It felt that in the legal and factual circumstances, there was no pressing social need to deprive the child of all legal relationship with one half of her birth family. The Court of Appeal agreed with the Official Solicitor that in this particular case 'it would not necessarily be to A's detriment if her mother at some time in the future were to display an interest in establishing a relationship with her'. It referred to the advantages to the child of the mother becoming involved again – however slightly – in the event of serious unexpected developments (e.g. the father's marriage to a woman who wanted to adopt, or the father's death). The father already had parental responsibility for the child ('just like any other parent') and his sense of security could be enhanced by restricting the mother's ability to seek Children Act orders[40]. It was, in fact, unlikely that this mother would ever seek to interfere with the father's upbringing of the child. The father was not prepared to accept this outcome. He remained anxious that at some point in the future the mother would get married and with her husband seek to recover her daughter. He therefore made an appeal to the House of Lords and in this he was successful. The House of Lords in effect declared that the Court of Appeal had not been entitled to overrule the exercise of what was a wide discretion possessed by the trial judge. Lord Nicholls stated that the father's argument, that an adoption order would safeguard and promote A's welfare, was wholly tenable. A residence order, which is what the Court of Appeal had given him, might not suffice to allay his genuine anxieties about the future conduct of the mother.

Clearly, this was an adoption application in which the decision could have gone – indeed, did go – either way. The language of the statute was, in the words of Lord Nicholls, 'open-ended' and the facts, inevitably in this class of case, were unusual. As long as the law permits sole adoptions by birth parents, difficult borderline applications such as this one are bound to occur from time to time, and it should be noted that no change in the law will take place by virtue of the 2002 Act because section 51(4) in effect repeats the wording of section 15(3) of the 1976 Act. A statutory ban, as originally suggested by Houghton, would produce more certainty but it would be liable to leave the caring parent (like the father in *Re B*) with a perception of reduced security.

Finding an Adoptive Family: Timescales

According to Standard A3 of the National Adoption Standards:

> Where a parent has requested that a child aged under six months be placed for adoption, a match with suitable adoptive parents will be identified and approved by panel within three months of the agency agreeing that adoption is in the child's best interest.

Like the other timescales contained in the National Standards, this is not a legal rule: there is no legal sanction for 'breaching' the standard in any individual case. It is true that a consistent pattern of missing deadlines would sooner or later be picked up but since baby relinquishments are now so rare it is difficult to see how a pattern of any sort could actually emerge within a particular agency. There will, of course, be cases in which there are very good reasons for an agency not identifying a suitable match within three months of a best interests decision. Health factors afford obvious examples.

Parental Responsibility after Relinquishment

As was explained in Chapter 2, one of the hallmarks of adoption is the transfer of parental responsibility from birth parent to adopters. The making of an adoption order, however, will necessarily have been preceded by a long period of care given by the adopters, and the issue of parental responsibility – including the 'right' to take significant decisions about the child – is clearly capable of arising during this period (indeed, as soon as placement begins). In a relinquishment case, where the birth mother usually starts off having exclusive parental responsibility, the fact that she is positively asking for an adoption placement should mean that no great problems occur in relation to decision-making or the obtaining of any necessary consents (e.g. to medical examinations or treatment). Nevertheless, it is not difficult to envisage situations in which the absence of formal legal power could cause difficulties or misunderstandings for agencies and prospective adopters, and the Adoption Law Review of 1992 recommended that steps be taken to fill the gap left by the legislation then in force. Under the Adoption Act 1976 prospective adopters in a relinquishment case would normally obtain parental responsibility only after the adoption order, and the agency would never obtain it unless it decided to use the freeing procedure, a course rarely followed.

The draft Adoption Bill produced by the Department of Health in 1996 contained provisions that would have required the relinquishing mother and the agency to enter into a written parental responsibility agreement before placement of the child. The effect would have been to give parental responsibility to the relevant prospective adopters during the placement and to the agency at any other time (e.g. following placement breakdown). The 2002 Act goes in for an altogether more direct approach. Under section 25, parental responsibility for the child is given to the agency as soon as it is authorised to place him under section 19. Furthermore, as soon as the child is actually placed for adoption, the prospective adopters also obtain it, and they will retain it for as long as the placement endures. None of this upsets the mother's parental responsibility, however, which means that pending the adoption order responsibility is shared between the mother, the agency and the prospective adopters. Section 25(4) establishes a hierarchy of decision-making by providing that the agency may determine that the parental responsibility of any parent, or of prospective adopters, 'is to be restricted to the extent specified in the determination'. This is reminiscent of a local authority's legal position following the making of a care order[41] but of course the two contexts are entirely different: the consensual nature of relinquishment, coupled with the mother's desire for early detachment from the child, should mean that conflicts over the day-to-day care of the child are rare. Section 25(4) probably reflects the reality of what has always been the case in relinquishments. Two specifically mentioned limits to the parental responsibility of prospective adopters should be noted. Under section 28(2), they may not cause the child to be known by a new surname or remove the child from the UK for more than a month unless they have the written consent of the mother or permission from a court. These limits will be removed when the adoption order is made.

The provisions of section 25 apply only where the agency has obtained a formal section 19 consent to placement from the mother. They do not, therefore, apply where a baby under six weeks old is placed without such consent (under section 18(1)). In such circumstances, the mother retains exclusive parental responsibility until she provides the section 19 consent. This is consistent with the enhanced removal rights given to mothers in six-week cases, which were described earlier.

Surrogacy

A surrogacy arrangement is an unusual form of relinquishment. For one thing, the relinquishment is planned even before the child is conceived. The mother's pregnancy is therefore not accidental but intended. For another thing, no adoption agency is involved: placement of the baby is not only immediate, it is direct, in favour of people with whom the surrogate will probably have negotiated at length on a face-to-face basis. Surrogacy arrangements vary in their nature but they usually involve insemination of the surrogate with semen from the infertile woman's husband[42]. In these circumstances, the surrogate is regarded as the child's first legal mother and so the commissioning parents, technically father and step-mother, will need a court order to regularise their position.

Until 1994 adoption was the only way in which commissioning parents could obtain full parental status but in November of that year there came into force section 30 of the Human Fertilisation and Embryology Act 1990. This section, together with a set of extraordinarily complicated regulations, enables married commissioning parents in a surrogacy case to apply for a parental order. Such an order is not the same as an adoption order but its consequences are more or less the same, which explains why the two are often confused. Parental orders were designed exclusively for surrogacy cases and it is therefore not surprising that most commissioning couples seem to prefer them to adoption in order to achieve legal parenthood[43]. One major difference that is worth noting relates to the timing of a court application: there is an absolute time limit of six months for section 30 applications, time starting to run from the date of the child's birth. It follows that if this deadline is missed, the commissioning parents will have to fall back on adoption. Such an adoption will proceed on a non-agency basis, in accordance with the rules described in Chapter 8 of this book.

Notes

1. Cmnd 5107, para 20.
2. *Meeting the Challenges of Changes in Adoption*, para 6.3.
3. *Adoption Now: Messages from Research*, page 1. The review noted that 'during the 1950s and 1960s around a fifth of all children who were born illegitimate were adopted by strangers, mostly as babies'.
4. For details of this Bill, see Chapter 1 of this book.
5. *Guardian*, 25 March 1996.
6. *Daily Mail*, 26 January 1999.
7. See, for example: *Daily Mail*, 27 January 1999 ('Is Jack Straw right to say that unmarried teenagers should give their babies away?'); *The Mirror*, 27 January 1999 ('Give up your child'); *Newcastle Journal*, 27 January 1999 ('The day they stole my baby'); *Northern Echo*, 27 January 1999 ('Are "real" families the best families?').
8. *Daily Mail*, 26 January 1999. See also the comments of Linda Grant in the *Guardian*, 28 March 1996: 'The experience of adoption has been so traumatic to a generation of women as young as those still in their forties today, that the moment there were other possibilities it was adoption itself that became stigmatised.'
9. Note 1 above, at para 84.
10. 'Relative' means a grandparent, brother, sister, uncle or aunt, whether of the full blood or half-blood or by marriage (section 144(1)).
11. Section 93.

12. A point confirmed by the High Court in the borderline case of *Gatehouse v R* [1986] 1 WLR 18.
13. See, for example, *Re G* [1995] 3 FCR 26 and *Re C* [1998] 2 FCR 641.
14. *Re G* (note 13 above).
15. Section 13(2) of the Adoption Act 1976.
16. Section 44. See further, Chapter 8 below.
17. Reported at [1977] 1 All ER 182.
18. [2001] 1 FCR 60. The case later went to the House of Lords on appeal.
19. Section 3(1)(a). See further, Chapter 4 above.
20. Regulation 7(1).
21. *Re S* [2001] 1 FCR 158 (Lord Justice Thorpe).
22. Illustrations may be found in the cases of *Re L* [1991] 1 FLR 171 and *Re P* [1995] 2 FCR 58.
23. [2001] 1 FCR 726.
24. Standard 4.
25. [2001] 1 FCR 238.
26. [1971] 2 All ER 49.
27. Emphasis added.
28. [1977] 2 All ER 339.
29. *Review of Adoption Law* (DH, 1992), para 12.3.
30. Section 27.
31. *Re T* [1986] 1 All ER 817.
32. Section 47(4), (5) and (7).
33. Inter-departmental Review of Adoption Law, *Discussion Paper Number 2* (DH, September 1991), para 63.
34. Section 10 of the Children Act.
35. Reported at [1999] 2 FCR 262.
36. Section 52(9) and (10).
37. Reported at [2002] 1 FCR 150.
38. See page 37.
39. Note 1 above, at para 100.
40. This can be done under section 91(14) of the Children Act.
41. See section 33(3) of the Children Act.
42. DH Circular LAC (94) 25, Annex G (The Clinical Aspects of Surrogacy).
43. *Surrogacy: Review for Health Ministers of Current Arrangements for Payments and Regulation* (Cmnd 4068, 1998), para 1.30.

CHAPTER 7

The Adoption of Looked After Children

Introduction

In May 2002 a remarkable advertisement appeared in a national newspaper. It had been inserted by the social services department of a London local authority and it invited applications for the job of Adoption Team Manager. In describing the work of its Children's Service, the department said this: 'We are aiming to build on the current success that has resulted in 21 orders granted last year with a further 40+ children placed for adoption.'[1] If evidence was needed of the way in which adoption has been forced onto the national social services agenda, it surely lies in statements like this, which suggest that 'success' in handling cases of children who are in the public care can be measured partly by the rate at which such children are adopted. It is unlikely that advertisements for adoption workers would have been couched in such terms ten or twenty years ago, even though the adoption of children from local authority care was by then a well-established process. That such a change of emphasis – and, indeed, policy – has come about is entirely due to pressure from central government. The Adoption and Children Act 2002 is designed to maintain that pressure.

In Chapter 1 of this book it was noted how, since 1998[2], adoption has come to be associated

in the Government's mind with the position and prospects of looked after children, even though the adoption procedure is also employed for other purposes in relation to other types of children. The strength of the association becomes very clear when the key documents and debates surrounding the Adoption and Children Bill are examined. As an example, one may take the words of the Prime Minister himself when writing the foreword to the report on adoption compiled by the Performance and Innovation Unit in July 2000:

> It is hard to overstate the importance of a stable and loving family life for children. That is why I want more children to benefit from adoption. We know that adoption works for children. Over the years, many thousands of children in the care of local authorities have benefited from the generosity and commitment of adoptive families, prepared to offer them the security and well-being that comes from being accepted as members of new families. But we also know that many children wait in care for far too long. Some of the reasons are well known. Too often in the past adoption has been seen as a last resort. Too many local authorities have performed poorly in helping children out of care and into adoption.

This determination to make 'much more use of adoption' in relation to looked after children came to be reflected in:

- The establishment in October 2000 of the Adoption and Permanence Taskforce, one of whose functions was to 'support local councils in improving their performance on maximising the use of adoption as an option for meeting the needs of looked after children'.
- The adoption white paper of December 2000, in which the Government set a national target (incorporated into the Department of Health's Public Service Agreement) of increasing by 40 per cent by 2004–2005 the number of looked after children adopted.
- The National Adoption Register, established in August 2001 as 'an extra resource for adoption agencies to use to help them identify matches for adoptive families and children'.
- The National Adoption Standards, also launched in August 2001 and containing the overarching principle that 'the needs and wishes, welfare and safety of the looked after child are at the centre of the adoption process'.

Nor was this emphasis lost when the Adoption and Children Bill was finally presented to Parliament. Introducing the Bill to the House of Commons, the then Minister of Health, John Hutton, said:

> Today, with this Bill, we are laying the foundations for a better future for thousands of young people in care. The Government firmly believe that adoption can often be the best solution for children in care who are unable to return to their birth families. Too often, it has been considered to be a last resort when it should have been considered as a first resort.[3]

Echoing this sentiment, a senior Conservative MP stated that the Bill's success would 'rely on resolving a number of major problems of children in care'[4]. These problems were said to include institutional abuse, drift, multiple moves, the disproportionate prospect of homelessness after leaving care, crime, jail, drugs dependency and pregnancy. This was a diagnosis with which the Government was not disposed to disagree. When it reintro-

duced the Bill after the 2001 general election, the minister then in charge told the House of Commons that the adoption system was letting down too many of the country's most vulnerable children. He went on:

> Children stay in the care system far longer than they should. Almost 30,000 have been in care continuously for two years or more, and, too often, despite the best intentions of all those involved in the care system, they end up being passed from pillar to post. Nearly one in five looked after children have three or more placements with different families in a single year. Some have six or more. These, remember, are precisely the children who already have a troubled history of family instability.[5]

At this point, one should perhaps pause to consider the role of the law – and more specifically, the 2002 Act – in this campaign to raise the profile of adoption in social services departments. The official government line, as expressed by the Secretary of State for Health, was that a change in the law was 'the necessary pre-condition' for the change in attitude or culture that had to be brought about[6]. This proposition is open to question. As was noted earlier, the Adoption and Permanence Taskforce, the National Adoption Standards and the National Adoption Register were all brought in before the 2002 Act, and therefore under the existing law. These non-statutory developments were clearly producing results, as the Government was keen to stress during the Parliamentary debates on the Bill. Even before all this, however, changes on the ground had been identified. In October 1999, at a time when the Government was still disputing the need for a new Adoption Act, the Department of Health issued a press release entitled 'Tide is turning on adoption'[7]. It recorded the Minister of Health as saying that 'a record rise in the number of children being placed for adoption shows that attitudes towards adoption are finally changing'. He expressed his delight that 'our concerted campaign to place adoption at the forefront of options for children in care is finally beginning to show results'. In an earlier Parliamentary debate, the same minister had stated that improvements in the adoption service would be secured through the *Quality Protects* initiative[8]. The argument that fresh legislation was needed to alter local authority attitudes must therefore be regarded as highly suspect.

One further important point needs to be made. Although the Government's criticisms tended to be made of the local authority sector as a whole, it is a fact that a considerable number of social services departments had long established very good records and reputations in the adoption field. Writing an introduction to the first annual report of the Adoption and Permanence Taskforce in October 2001, the Taskforce Chair and Director stated: 'At the heart of the Taskforce approach is the idea of having seasoned practitioners working alongside their peers, to learn from *the excellent work that many social services departments and voluntary adoption agencies undertake around adoption.*'[9] A year earlier, the Social Services Inspectorate had published a detailed survey of local authority adoption services. One overall conclusion was that: 'In many councils adoption practice is good. Looked after children who might benefit from being brought up in adoptive families are identified, made the subject of adoption plans as early as possible, and adoptive families are recruited and prepared for the task of taking on their care.' It acknowledged 'a great deal of skill, knowledge and commitment on the part of social work staff and their managers, and an enormous amount of commitment to meeting the needs of children'[10]. Even if, therefore, the Government was correct in saying that a change in the law was necessary to change attitudes, the attitudes in question were apparently to be found in only some of the country's social services departments.

This is not to say that the existing adoption law was entirely satisfactory. It dated from 1975, since when child care policy and practice had changed. It contained, in the freeing for adoption provisions, a procedure that had become largely discredited. It was not seen to deal adequately with the important issue of contested adoptions. It was also inconsistent

in significant respects with the Children Act 1989. These and other defects had been comprehensively exposed in the report of the Adoption Law Review of 1992, in which the case for reform was amply demonstrated. The 2002 Act, therefore, was a much-needed statute as far as looked after children are concerned, but not for the reasons articulated by the Government. Its role as a lever on local authority decision-making should not be exaggerated.

The Pool of Looked After Children

Although the pool of looked after children in England and Wales is frequently referred to as a single group of people, it is anything but homogenous. The same goes for those looked after children who are adopted. Variation can also be seen in the size and composition of the pools of children attached to individual local authorities. This diversity is very well documented, the most comprehensive account being found in the statistics published each year by the Department of Health. Although the figures fluctuate from year to year, the general pattern is reasonably clear. Children are looked after for a wide variety of reasons. 24,500 children started to be looked after by local authorities in England during the year ending 31 March 2001, and the recorded reasons for their entry into the care system were as follows[11]:

Abuse or neglect	10600
Disability	750
Parent's illness or disability	2300
Family in acute stress	3000
Family dysfunction	3500
Socially unacceptable behaviour	2100
Low income	280
Absent parenting	1900

The age distribution varies according to the category. Most of the 24,500 children noted above (10,500) were aged between 10 and 15. The child's legal status also varies. Of the 24,500, 4000 were the subject of an interim care order or full care order made under Part IV of the Children Act 1989. 16,900 entered local authority accommodation on a voluntary basis under section 20 of the 1989 Act. As far as ethnic origin is concerned, 19,600 were recorded as White; 1800 were Black or Black British; 610 were Asian or Asian British; 1500 were recorded as 'Mixed'. Needless to say, all of these children were placed in a wide variety of settings, including foster placements, children's homes and hostels, NHS facilities, family centres and residential schools. Many placements were outside the relevant local authority's boundary. Some would have been a long way away. 6,300 out of the 24,500 children had a previous care history with the local authority.

What the figures do not, and cannot, reveal is how long these particular children remained, or were destined to remain, in the care system. It is obvious, however, that the duration of care will vary dramatically, from a matter of days to the rest of the child's minority. Of the 25,100 children who ceased to be looked after during the year ending 31 March 2001, 5000 had been looked after for less than two weeks, while 1100 had been looked after for more than ten years[12]. Most children accommodated on a voluntary basis do in fact go home sooner or later[13]. Many care order children also go home, whether or not the order itself is formally discharged. Indeed, a number of such children may never actually enter local authority accommodation at all, staying at home while their parents share parental responsibility with the local authority[14]. For these reasons alone, it is inappropriate – indeed, absurd – to view the entire pool of looked after children as being in some way candidates for adoption. Remarkably, some politicians and commentators in recent years have come very close to doing this. The reality of the situation is better described in the report on adoption compiled by the Performance and Innovation Unit. The Unit made the key point that children being adopted from care form 'a distinct subset' of looked after children. They are, of course, children for whom rehabilitation with the birth family has been ruled out. Comparing those adopted in 1998/1999

with the overall looked after pool, the PIU reported the following survey findings[15]:

- The adopted children were more likely to be female and white.
- They were more likely to be part of sibling groups, but placed apart.
- They were younger and had an average age lower than that of the looked after pool as a whole.
- They had entered the care system at a younger age.
- They were more challenging.
- They had spent years in care before adoption (on average 2 years and 10 months).
- They were unlikely to have returned home before adoption.
- They had experienced more moves while in the care system.
- 80 per cent of looked after children adopted were subject to a care order when they were adopted.

As the Unit pointed out, 'adoption from care is not about providing couples with trouble-free babies. It is about finding families for children of a range of ages, with challenging backgrounds and complex needs'[16]. Simplistic approaches towards dealing with children in the care system need to be avoided, therefore. Only a proportion of looked after children need to be adopted. And of those who do need to be adopted, only a proportion will be easy to place.

Making a Plan for Adoption

The statutory framework

The overarching duty of a local authority in relation to its looked after children is contained in section 22(3) of the Children Act 1989. This provides that the local authority must (a) safeguard and promote their welfare, and (b) make such use of services available for children cared for by their own parents as appears reasonable. Under section 22(4), before making any decision with respect to a child whom it is looking after, the local authority must, so far as is reasonably practicable, ascertain the wishes and feelings of the child, the child's parents, any other person having parental responsibility for the child, and any other person whose wishes and feelings the authority considers relevant. Under section 22(5), in making any such decision the local authority must give due consideration to the wishes and feelings of the child and to the wishes and feelings of the other persons referred to in section 22(4).

The Arrangements for Placement of Children (General) Regulations 1991 require local authorities to draw up written plans for all looked after children. One of the considerations to which authorities must have regard when drawing up a plan is 'whether plans need to be made to find a permanent substitute family for the child'[17]. The Review of Children's Cases Regulations 1991 require local authorities to review, at prescribed intervals, the case of each child while he is being looked after. Again, one of the considerations to which authorities must have regard in reviewing each case is 'whether plans need to be made to find a permanent substitute family for the child'[18].

It will be noticed that this legislative framework, drawn partly from statute and partly from government regulations, does not mention adoption specifically. No timescales for decisions are laid down, except for the frequency of review meetings. There are no deadlines. Each local authority is free to go at its own pace in each case, exercising the widest of discretions based on its perception of the child's welfare. When one considers the astonishing variety of circumstances met in child care cases, this is entirely understandable.

Arriving at a best interests decision

Deciding to make an adoption plan for a looked after child can rarely be easy for a local authority, in view of the legally drastic and psychologically unpredictable consequences not only for the child himself but also for his birth parents, siblings (present and future) and other relatives. It is clear from the

provisions of the Children Act noted above that such a decision can be taken only on grounds relating to the welfare of the child concerned but what the law cannot do is prescribe a formula for working out the right time for taking it. It is a matter of professional judgment. This inescapable truth has been openly acknowledged by the Department of Health in its adoption circular of 1998:

> Time is not on the side of the child. Efforts to return a child to his or her family should of course be reasonable and will require intensive work; time spent in such work with families and children should be constructive and should be recorded in detail. A stage is reached in many cases, however, when it is apparent that rehabilitation is unlikely to be successful. *Experienced practitioners are aware that knowing when the time is right to plan for alternative forms of care is one of the many skills expected of social services staff;* that it includes an awareness of the importance of time in the rehabilitation process and of the damage which might be done to children where time is allowed to pass without any visible signs of their future being secured. Where it is clear that they can no longer live with their birth family, decisions about placing children with permanent families should be made as a matter of priority.[19]

The authors of this passage, which appeared under the heading 'Getting the balance right', wisely refrained from descending into specifics. It is true that some commentators have proposed the establishment of mandatory rigid timescales for looked after children, with adoption marked out as a high priority[20], but these are problematic and have been rightly discounted. Recognising that an adoption decision is a matter of judgment, however, must mean that different professionals can legitimately take differing views of the appropriateness of an adoption plan in a particular case. Furthermore, individual practitioners can quite properly undergo a change of mind during the consideration of a case. This is the price paid for giving decision-makers a discretion, and in the reported case law on adoption the superior courts have accepted it[21].

The National Standards

In the light of the preceding material, it is perhaps surprising to find the Department of Health venturing down the road of deadlines in its National Adoption Standards of 2001. According to Standard A2:

> Whenever plans for permanence are being considered, they will be made on the basis of the needs of each looked after child, and within the following timescales: (a) the child's need for a permanent home will be addressed at the four month review and a plan for permanence made...

Several points need to be made about this. First of all, there is no magic in the four-month point. Other times could with justification have been singled out. This is confirmed by the fact that the draft Standards (developed by an expert working group and organised by British Agencies for Adoption and Fostering) referred not to the four-month review but to a timescale of six months from the child's entry into the care system. (They also contained the significant word 'usually', thereby increasing flexibility.) Secondly, Standard A2 does not introduce a presumption of adoption after four months' care. The plan that is expected of the local authority is a plan for permanence, not a plan for adoption. In fact, most plans for permanence will not involve adoption at all (which makes the inclusion of this rule in Adoption Standards all the more awkward). This was made clear in the draft Practice Guidance on the Standards, published in 2001. It pointed out that a spectrum of options exists including returning the child home, care with wider family or friends and long-term fostering. 'For most children', it stated, 'the best prospect for a permanent family that meets their emotional, physical and legal needs will be with their own birth parents.'[22] Consequently, it was suggested, drawing up the permanence plan should not, of itself, be threatening to the child or his family. The draft Guidance went on to repeat the passage from the 1998 circular quoted earlier and to refer to *The Framework for the Assessment of Children in Need and their Families*. It recommended the making of a contingency plan where the family assessment indicated that the child's birth parents might be unable to make and sustain the changes in their parenting necessary to bring about rehabilitation. In such cases, two plans for permanence would be in existence. The result of all this is that professional discretion remains, though in a less unrestrained form. Thirdly, the four-month deadline is one of a number of deadlines fixed by the National Standards (the others are described later in this chapter). Like most deadlines, they are to some extent arbitrary and for that reason open to question. Their establishment is clear evidence, however, of the Government's determination to force the hand of those local authorities deemed to be under-performing in relation to child care planning. Figures published by the Department of Health suggested that some authorities would indeed have to modify considerably their decision-making practices in order to meet Standard A2: for those looked after children adopted during the year ending 31 March 2001, the average time between entry into care and a best interests decision was estimated at thirteen months[23].

A final question to consider here is the relationship between Standard A2 and the Government's decision, noted earlier, to set a national target of increasing by 40 per cent by 2004–2005 the number of looked after children adopted. Like the four-month deadline, the 40 per cent target was designed to concentrate the minds of local authority managers. Great store was set by it. However, it cannot possibly have been intended to detract from the overarching Children Act obligation to give dispassionate consideration to the particular needs of each looked after child. Such a policy would have been illegal. And yet it is not difficult to see how it could propel some social services staff, when carrying out reviews and making plans, into reaching premature decisions in favour of adoption at the expense of birth families who might have come up trumps given more time. A rush to adoption was the danger of this target, just as it was the danger of the separate target – described below – relating to matching a child with an adoptive family. This was quickly picked up during the passage of the 2002 Act. In written evidence submitted to the House of Commons, the Local Government Association stated:

> There are real concerns about targets which may rush agencies into placing children for adoption when the best plan, in accordance with the wishes of the child, may be to work with the birth family to enable them to care for their child.[24]

A particular danger was noted by Professor Audrey Mullender. In her written evidence, she sought to emphasise the adverse consequences of adoption for separated siblings. She pointed out that 'a headlong rush into increased adoptive placements will increase separations still further'. This was because prospective adopters were not coming forward in the required numbers for older sibling groups.

Perceived obstacles to adoption plans

During the period leading up to the 2002 Act, when the Government was talking of the 'step change' needed in local authority adoption work, it was only natural for politicians and commentators to speculate about the reasons why social workers in some authorities might be reluctant to regard adoption as a suitable outcome in child care cases. Clearly, this is an important question. If there is evidence of the existence of factors that are producing 'wrong' decisions, then they need to be addressed quickly and appropriately. Unfortunately, in this field the evidence is flimsy. A review of what was said and written during this period suggests that two factors in particular were being held up by critics as contributing significantly to the paucity of adoption plans. The first of these was the Children Act 1989. In its adoption circular of 1998, the Department of Health referred to the legal framework established by the 1989 Act for cases of looked after children and said that in that context 'there is a common

perception among too many in the field that efforts to rehabilitate a child should be constrained by no timetable: that every effort should be made and all possibilities exhausted to try to secure the return of the child to his family – no matter how long it might take'[25]. Confirmation of the existence of this perception came a year later in *Adoption Now*, the summary of adoption research studies undertaken for the Department of Health. This referred to the decline in adoptions from care over the period 1992–1998 and stated:

> This fall, it has been claimed, was attributable to the effect of the Children Act 1989 which was implemented in October 1991. It was reported that local authorities then became more hesitant to recommend adoption, believing that the courts would now only be prepared to grant an order if there was indisputable evidence that a child's rehabilitation with their family was impossible or unwise.[26]

This latter observation suggests that it was not only social workers who had extracted an anti-adoption message from the Children Act. Some judges and guardians ad litem had evidently done so as well. These professionals would have been in a position to influence child care plans through the medium of care order proceedings. The fact is, however, that the terms of the 1989 Act contain no such message. Nor were they ever intended to. It is true that section 23(6) of the Act requires a local authority which is looking after a child to make arrangements to enable him to live with his parents or relatives or other persons connected with him; and it is true that Schedule 2 paragraph 15 requires the local authority to endeavour to promote contact between the child and his parents and relatives. Both of these duties, however, are expressly made subject to considerations of practicability and welfare. By no stretch of the imagination can they be construed as anti-adoption. They do not, as one MP suggested, 'reinforce social workers' obsession with birth families'[27]. They were designed, in fact, to reflect existing good practice. The most obvious conclusion to draw is that something went wrong in some of the Children Act training and preparation programmes that were put on in the early 1990s. The mantra 'Partnership with Parents' may have been misused, following a misreading of the Department of Health guidance on the 1989 Act.

The second factor said to have held up the making of adoption plans is even more nebulous. The 1998 report of the House of Commons Health Committee on looked after children contained the following passage:'Several of our witnesses claimed that SSDs and individual social workers can display an irrational hostility to the concept of adoption. The Adoption Forum [a pressure group] told us that "the presumption that all children are better off with their birth families...is palpably lacking in common sense when so many children are mistreated, abused and neglected by those families". They claimed that "linked to this presumption is the practice of returning children time and again to their abusers, or those who have been seen to be unable to deal with life as a parent...". The Committee reported that a group of adoptive parents giving evidence to it had claimed that many social workers were biased against adoption[28].This proposition has surfaced regularly in recent years, in both Parliament and the press[29]. It is, of course, incapable of being disproved. Given the number of authorities and the number of child care social workers in the country, it would be surprising if there were not at least some individuals who – perhaps as a result of professional experiences – were not well disposed towards adoption as a matter of principle. The scale of the problem, however, is impossible to measure accurately. Nor do relatively low adoption rates for particular local authorities point inevitably towards an anti-adoption culture within them. Other explanations for such figures are possible. It should also be remembered that from time to time critical reports of social workers' alleged over-zealousness about adoption have appeared[30]. Perhaps the fairest conclusion on this difficult question was drawn by the Performance and Innovation Unit: 'Some commentators have suggested that...problems are the result of social workers' hostility to adoption. While there can be issues at an individual level, the study found little evidence of an institutional anti-adoption culture in social services departments. The more likely explanation for the limited use of adoption, on the basis of our visits and consultations, is that both social workers and their direct managers are (properly) highly committed to working to reunite children with their birth parents and the structures and procedures are not in place to ensure they think more widely than that. Social workers are also relatively untrained and inexperienced in adoption work.'[31]

Finding an Adoptive Family

The nature of the task

For those looked after children adopted during the year ending 31 March 2001, the average time between a best interests decision in favour of adoption and the matching of child and prospective adopters was six months[32]. Since this was an average, it is likely that in some cases the time spent making a match was considerably more than six months. Confirmation of this can be found in a survey report produced by the Social Services Inspectorate in 2000. Of 1000 children's cases considered, 190 involved a delay of twelve months or more before a suitable match was made[33]. There is nothing surprising about this. As far as looked after children are concerned, delay in finding adoptive families is caused largely by two factors:

- The particular needs of the child (or children in a sibling group).
- The shortage of adopters with the skills to assume the permanent, full-time care and parenthood over the child (or children).

The existence of these two factors is accepted on all sides of the adoption debate, even if the reasons behind the second one are disputed. The challenging nature of the local authority's task is encapsulated in the following passage from the SSI report referred to above:

> It is clear from the reasons for delay that local councils are trying to find adoptive families for many children with complex, special needs associated with medical problems, severe emotional difficulties, challenging behaviour, sibling group membership and particular racial/ethnic characteristics. Simply recruiting more prospective adopters, even if there is a potentially more extensive pool, does not address the problem of finding *appropriate* families for children some of whom will bring enormous challenges to their new families.[34]

In some cases the task proves too much, requiring the local authority to abrogate the plan for adoption altogether. A poignant example is afforded by the case of *Re J*, decided in April 2000[35]. This concerned a boy of eight, whose only consistent and affectionate family relationship was said to be his relationship with his 13-year-old half-brother (who was also in long-term care). He started being looked after by the local authority when aged five, following a chaotic and abusive home life. According to a court welfare report: 'In his short life, J has had four sets of carers offering different levels of care and experience and he has been led to believe that he has two different fathers, both of whom he dislikes. He has moved at least eight times and has lived in three different towns. He has also attended five different schools or nursery units. Most of J's moves will have been traumatic for him and accomplished with little planning or forethought. Naturally all these factors have had an impact on J's personality and social development. He finds it difficult to trust or to form attachments.' Following the making of a care order and a plan for adoption, J's case was advertised nationally. Two potential adoptive families came forward but then withdrew. Further publicity was put in place but there was a nil response. During this time, J's behaviour deteriorated. As the court observed, 'his distress has no doubt been compounded by his knowledge that other children have moved from his foster placement to permanent placements whilst he has been there and that, whilst he has been

made available too, no one has come forward for him'. The court accepted that adoption was no longer a realistic option for this child and assisted the local authority in extricating itself from an awkward legal position[36].

The statutory duty of the local authority

The Adoption Act 1976 contained two provisions relevant to the issue of matching. Section 6 required an adoption agency in reaching any decision relating to the adoption of a child to 'have regard to all the circumstances, first consideration being given to the need to safeguard and promote the welfare of the child throughout his childhood'. It also required the agency to ascertain the wishes and feelings of the child regarding the decision (so far as practicable) and give 'due consideration' to them having regard to the child's age and understanding. The second provision was section 7. This required an agency when placing a child for adoption to have regard (so far as practicable) to any wishes of the child's birth parents as to the religious upbringing of the child. Supplementary guidance on matching – containing far more detail than the provisions of the 1976 Act – was issued from time to time by the Department of Health, notably in the form of Circular LAC (98) 20 August 1998 and the National Adoption Standards, issued in 2001.

Section 1 of the 2002 Act contains the new statutory regime. Its features, so far as the matching function of local authorities is concerned, are as follows:

- The paramount consideration of the local authority must be the child's welfare, throughout his life[37].
- The local authority must at all times bear in mind that, in general, any delay in coming to a decision is likely to prejudice the child's welfare[38].
- The local authority must have regard to the following matters particularly: (a) the child's ascertainable wishes and feelings regarding the decision (considered in the light of his age and understanding); (b) the child's particular needs; (c) the likely effect

on the child (throughout his life) of having ceased to be a member of the original family and become an adopted person; (d) the child's age, sex, background and any of the child's characteristics which the authority considers relevant; (e) any harm which the child has suffered or is at risk of suffering; (f) the relationship which the child has with his parents, his relatives and others[39].

■ The local authority must give due consideration to the child's religious persuasion, racial origin and cultural and linguistic background[40].

A comparison of the two Acts shows that both give the local authority the widest of discretions when it comes to selecting adopters for a particular child. Although there is rather more detail in the new legislation it does not have the effect of imposing more restraints, not even in relation to ethnic matching, which is now mentioned in adoption law for the first time. Of rather greater significance in this context, as in others, are the Government's National Adoption Standards and associated practice guidance. These are considered below.

The National Standards

Pressure on local authorities to arrange adoption matches more quickly had been building up well before the National Standards were published in August 2001. In its adoption circular of 1998 the Department of Health stated:

> The Government is concerned about the length of time some children have to wait before being able to join an adoptive family. The social and emotional development of children is strongly influenced by their early childhood experiences, especially the quality and security of their attachment relationships with their birth family, relatives and carers. Allowing children to 'drift' is never in their best interests and is likely to make successful placements all the more difficult to achieve. It has to be recognised that certainty is rarely possible: professional judgment has to work with the balance of probabilities. The longer a child spends in temporary care before being placed with permanent carers, the more

difficult it is likely to be for that child to make the necessary social and emotional adjustments within the new family.[41]

At this time, it was agreed on all sides that insufficient numbers of appropriate prospective adopters were coming forward for looked after children with an adoption plan. There were at least two possible responses to this problem. The first was to make even greater efforts to recruit. The second, and more contentious, was to take a more flexible view of appropriateness in relation to matching, by considering for particular children (or sibling groups) prospective adopters who might not previously have been looked at favourably. The Labour Government has endorsed both of these responses. On the issue of recruitment, the Standards stated that the Government would 'provide support for local recruitment activity to find suitable families for looked after children including a range of national action which will raise the public awareness of adoption and the characteristics of children waiting and adopters needed'[42]. As for the appropriateness of adopters, Standard A8 states: 'Children will be matched with families who can best meet their needs. *They will not be left waiting indefinitely for a 'perfect' family.*'[43] The origins of this official concern about 'perfect family' syndrome seem to lie in the report of the Performance and Innovation Unit of July 2000. The Unit argued that delays and drift at the matching stage could occur 'both in terms of the lack of suitable adopters and by an insistence on finding the 'perfect' rather than the 'good enough' match'[44]. It went on to say that it had heard anecdotal evidence of local authorities turning down adopters who were 'suitable' and waiting for 'something better' to come along. The extent of this problem was, of course, impossible to quantify.

This commitment to more effective local and national recruitment strategies, coupled with a move towards a less rigid approach to matching and the advent of a national matching register (described below), meant that the way was clear for the introduction of what is clearly the boldest feature of the National Standards: a time limit for making a match. According to Standard A3:

The timescales below will be followed, taking account of the individual child's needs: (a) A match with suitable adoptive parents will be identified and approved by panel within 6 months of the agency agreeing that adoption is in the child's best interest; (b) In care proceedings, where the plan is adoption, a match with suitable adoptive parents will be identified and approved by panel within 6 months of the court's decision.

With a view to ensuring adherence to this, the Department of Health simultaneously imposed a requirement under section 7 of the Local Authority Social Services Act 1970 under which authorities had a duty to 'put in place systems to monitor their performance against the timescales set out in the Standards for matching children with adoptive families'[45]. The reference at the beginning of Standard A3 to the child's needs makes it clear that authorities are not expected to follow the timescale slavishly. It is a target. Matches may get delayed for all sorts of valid reasons and to that extent there is a measure of flexibility. When the Secretary of State for Health first announced this time limit in the House of Commons, he said that it would produce 'a major improvement on the current position'[46]. The reason for this was that it would reduce significantly ('halve the average time') the periods spent by looked after children waiting for new families. There is, of course, no disputing this view – provided always that the adoptive families selected are suitable to the needs of the children. In this connection, it will be observed that Standard A3 does not in terms discriminate in any way between different types of child. Children of all ages are covered by the same expectation. No allowance is made for any particular care history, disability or other special need.

The Adoption Public Service Agreement Target

In its white paper of 2000, the Government gave notice that, in addition to the target of a 40 per cent increase in the number of looked after children adopted, there would be estab-lished in due course a target to ensure that 'the adoption process takes place to timescales consistent with those set out in the National Standards'[47]. This target was set in December 2001 (evidently to mark the first anniversary of the white paper's publication). According to its terms, 'by 31 March 2005, at least 95 per cent of looked after children should be placed for adoption within 12 months of the decision that adoption is in the child's best interest, up from 81 per cent in 2001'[48]. Unlike the Standards, which impose timescales on each local authority, this target was national in character and was to be monitored through the annual adoption statistical collection, although in the press release announcing the target the Department of Health made it clear that it would be monitoring the performance of individual councils in relation to it. And although the focus of the target is placement for adoption, not matching as such, there is no doubt that the task of family finding was uppermost in the Government's mind. Perhaps conscious of the concerns expressed about the effects of those targets and timescales already laid down, the Department of Health went out of its way on this occasion to warn against a rush to adoption. A statement in the name of the Minister of Health read: 'We are clear that this target must not be met at the cost of quality and children must not be rushed into adoptive placements before they are ready. The target makes it plain that current levels of placement stability must be maintained.'[49] To this end, the Government stated that it would be monitoring stability levels through data on the proportion of placements for adoption ending in an adoption order. It also launched a consultation exercise on a revision of the looked after children statistics, with a view to estimating more accurately the number of children adopted from care whose adoptions break down after the making of an order (as opposed to the period before an order).

The National Adoption Register

The National Adoption Register, whose sole purpose is to assist agencies in the matching process, was set up on 7 August 2001. Like the National Adoption Standards (launched on the same day) the Register owes its existence to recommendations made in July 2000 by the Performance and Innovation Unit. A description of the position nationwide around this time in relation to the mechanics of matching can be found in the Social Services Inspectorate evaluation report on adoption services published a few months after the PIU review[50]. According to the SSI:

> The process of searching the available pool of prospective adopters for a likely match was a suitable source of some delay. Staff did not have access to databases of potential families, and tended to develop their own strategies for widening the search. Most began by considering adoptive families recruited by their own staff, though in several small councils there was an assumption that all children would be placed outside of the council's geographic boundaries. In those councils consortia arrangements provided the first pool of adoptive families. Where no appropriate match was identified, staff moved with varying speed, sometimes further delayed by the need to obtain permission to fund the purchase of an inter-agency placement, to trawl the resources available in the region. Sometimes staff singled out adoption agencies they had found helpful in the past, and used personal connections they had developed. Gradually they widened the net but the process could be a lengthy and time-consuming one, with individual workers trawling the same limited pool of colleagues for information on a limited pool of adopters. Systematic or simultaneous exploration of the whole range of placement sources was very rare.[51]

The PIU reported that it had identified a good deal of support for a database for matching children and adopters: 'A national level database would raise the profile of recruitment, enhance co-ordination and should be an invaluable tool for sharing information. Above all it should ensure improvements in the matching process and avoid unnecessary delay.'[52] The register would contain information on approved adopters and children with adoption as the plan. To work effectively – and this has become a distinctive feature of the Register – it would

require local authorities to contribute information on children and approved adopters and to keep this information up to date. It was for this reason that the PIU suggested a statutory base for the register, a suggestion now reflected in the 2002 Act.

The PIU recommendation for a national register came as no surprise because three months before it was made press reports were indicating that a register was under active consideration by Department of Health ministers[53]. The idea had been around for a few years but the key development appears to have been the publication by the SSI in April 2000 of an analysis of survey findings concerning the implementation of the Government's 1998 adoption circular. Buried within the analysis was the following paragraph: 'While almost 3000 adoptive placements were made in the year ending March 1999, there were approximately 2400 children for whom no adopters had been identified. At the same time there were a significant number of adopters who had been recruited but had no children placed with them (1297).'[54] In its report the PIU was careful to point out that it was impossible to know whether these figures represented a genuine mismatch. Indeed, a representative of the Association of Directors of Social Services wrote that it was 'simplistic to just compare numbers of adopters waiting with children waiting'[55]. Nevertheless, the SSI finding was persuasive and it formed the basis of a recommendation for a register that was immediately accepted by the Government, in advance of its adoption white paper. Not surprisingly, it also led to a recommendation of a rapid scrutiny of the apparent mismatch.

Details of the working of the Register were subsequently set out in two Department of Health circulars[56]. Local authorities were brought into the system in three stages. Forms were devised to cover children and approved adopters, these to be sent to the Register once a best interests decision was made (in respect of a child) or once approval to adopt had been given (in respect of an adoptive family). Following the submission of forms, agencies were to be given stipulated maximum periods (three to nine months, depending on the circumstances) to make a match using their own local resources. After these periods records would go live, enabling the Register and its staff to suggest a possible match for a child or for an adoptive family. In cases where the agency considered that a child should not be placed locally, it could ask for his record to go live at once. Provision was made for the obtaining of consents from approved adopters and from children or persons authorised to act on their behalf, and also for the updating of information.

It is important to note that the National Adoption Register is not a decision-making mechanism. Nor does it have any supervisory function. The decision to match a particular child with approved adopters remains a decision for the local authority which is looking after the child. In this way local authority autonomy is not compromised. The Register will, at most, suggest a link. The function of the local authority thereafter is, according to the relevant Department of Health circular, to 'actively consider' the link and report back to the Register whether the link will be pursued. Where the link is not being pursued, the local authority should tell the Register's staff why[57]. In the long term, the Register will operate on a statutory basis under the name of the Adoption and Children Act Register. Sections 125–131 of the 2002 Act provide the statutory underpinning that the PIU thought might be necessary – or, it should be said, some of the underpinning, because these sections are intensely skeletal in nature. As is so often the case with administrative machinery established by Parliament, the detailed rules relating to the operation of the Register were left to be worked out in the form of a government order. Very little indication of the content of such an order is apparent on the face of the Act, although it is likely to reflect the scheme of the circulars described above. The statutory Register will, however, be capable of covering voluntary adoption agencies as well as local authorities and may cover Scotland as well as England and Wales.

Race

The continuing debate

'I know of a couple who have successfully adopted a child of mixed parentage. A few years ago they saw an advert in either the *Observer* or the *Guardian* seeking a foster home, with a view to adoption, for a girl of mixed race who was then in a children's home in the care of the local authority. I believe that the couple did nothing at the time, believing erroneously that the child would soon be placed with a satisfactory couple and be well looked after. However, a year later virtually the same advert appeared in whichever newspaper it was. The child was still in care – still living in a children's home, with apparently no prospect of fostering or adoption. The couple wrote to the local authority concerned, expressing their interest and explaining their experience and background. They were astonished and astounded to receive a reply stating that they could not be considered because they were white and the authority's policy was to place such children with black families. The reaction of that family was unprintable…As far as is known the girl is still in the care of the local authority and still in a children's home.' This story was told to the House of Commons by a Labour MP in October 1989[58]. If the record is moved forward 11 years one finds the following observation being made by a Conservative MP on the day the Labour government published its white paper on adoption: 'Does the Secretary of State agree that probably the biggest cheer that he received for his excellent statement was for the passage in which he condemned blanket bans resulting from a form of reverse racialism that holds that loving, white potential adoptive parents should not be allowed to adopt black children? Can he throw some light on the puzzlement that Members on both sides of the House feel about how such attitudes ever came to be prevalent? Can he reassure us that the sort of people who held such disgraceful attitudes will not be in a position to inject more poison into the system?'[59]

Unhappily for government ministers, adoption practitioners and, of course, the children affected, the issue of same-race adoption placements continues to provoke the most heated debate, both inside and outside Parliament. It tends to crop up whenever adoption policy generally is discussed. It is extremely fertile territory for poignant anecdotal material such as the story described above. And it provides easy ammunition with which to attack the social work profession. As has been well said: 'Social workers are…left to deal with complexities which have not been sorted out by the rest of society, and then find themselves pilloried when decisions are made which other people either do not like or consider simplistic.'[60] Three principal arguments will be advanced here. First, government attempts during the 1990s to resolve the race issue through the medium of official guidance were doomed from the start. Second, the law itself (including the 2002 Act) has taken the matter no further. But third, the most likely instrument of resolution will be the National Adoption Standards.

One point should be disposed of at the outset: the relevance to the debate of 'common sense'. An appeal for the use of common sense in relation to ethnic matching in adoption cases first received official endorsement in the Conservative government's white paper of 1993. Following a widely publicised case in which a Norfolk couple were said to have been turned down as adopters for reasons connected with race, the white paper stated that in future there would be 'common sense values in such matters as the age of adoptive parents and issues of race and culture in considering the best option for the child'[61]. Announcing the white paper's publication in the House of Commons, the then Secretary of State for Health, Virginia Bottomley, said: 'There should be no place for ideology in adoption. We want common sense judgments, not stereotyping. There are, for example, no good grounds for refusing on principle to contemplate transracial adoptions.'[62] The Conservative Party maintained its advocacy

of 'a common sense approach' in this context right through to the publication of the Adoption and Children Bill in 2001. The underlying – and obvious – problem with this argument, however, is that common sense is just as capable of sustaining a policy of ethnic matching as it is of opposing it. For example, even one of the Conservative Party's most severe critics of social workers' adoption practice was forced to concede during debate on the Bill: 'Of course, if an Afro-Caribbean family is available for each Afro-Caribbean child, that is where such children should be placed.'[63] Other MPs made the same point. As one Labour MP (with a social work background) put it: 'Is it wrong in principle to try to find adoptive parents with physical similarities or common ethnic, cultural, religious or linguistic backgrounds? From my experience, I do not think that it is politically correct to suggest that, when appropriate, that should happen…It is not political correctness: *it is common sense.*'[64] The fact is that appealing to 'common sense' does not advance the same-race debate in any meaningful way. It serves only to obscure the real issues such as timescales for placements, the racial identity of the child and racial awareness on the part of prospective adopters.

The number of children affected

The focus of the adoption and race debate has been non-white looked after children. These children may of course be classified in various ways (classification itself being a matter of contention) but the labels used in Department of Health publications have tended to be 'black', 'minority ethnic background' and 'dual race heritage'. If these categories are accepted for present purposes, it becomes clear that in recent years between 10 and 20 per cent of the national pool of looked after children with a plan for adoption have fallen within them[65]. Although no detailed figures have been published, it must also be the case that the percentages vary considerably between individual local authorities.

Research evidence on delay

There is no doubt that the desire to achieve an appropriate ethnic match, coupled with a shortage of non-white approved adopters, has produced extra delay in the adoption process for many non-white children. This fact was confirmed by the Social Services Inspectorate in a survey carried out in 1999–2000. The survey found that delay occurred at the stage of taking a best interests proposal to an adoption panel (because the child's social workers anticipated difficulties in finding a suitable match) as well as the matching stage itself[66]. In 2000 the Government was working on the basis that the additional delay for black children amounted, on average, to five months[67].

Research evidence on outcomes

The research literature on transracial adoption is substantial and it has been reviewed on a number of occasions[68]. According to a review published in 1997, although the empirical evidence is inconclusive, it 'tends to give positive support for transracial placements'. The authors suggested that the balance of evidence was towards transracial placements having satisfactory outcomes in over 70 per cent of placements. They were careful to point out, however, that there were still many unanswered questions that could be resolved only by further research. They also argued that 'some questions about transracial placements can only be answered in a wider social and political context'. Accordingly, their own view was that, because the social context was a racist one, ethnically matched placements would be in the best interests of both the child and the community 'in most instances'[69]. The absence of conclusive evidence on this key issue of outcomes (a state of affairs apparently accepted in UK government circles) inevitably gives encouragement to both sides in the transracial adoption debate. Individual case histories – some positive, some negative – have emerged regularly in the media and there is no reason to think that these will dry up in the foreseeable future. They make good

newspaper copy. Like other adoption 'stories', however, they need to be treated with care.

Chronology of government guidance

The Department of Health has issued guidance to local authorities on the subject of adoption and race on three separate occasions: January 1990, February 1996 and August 1998[70]. The main features of these guidance documents were the same and they may be summarised in the following way:

- A child's ethnic origin is an important factor in the matching process.
- In the great majority of cases, placement with a family of similar ethnic origin and religion is most likely to meet the child's needs as fully as possible. This is because such a family is most likely to be able to provide the child with continuity in life and care, and a familiar and sympathetic environment in which opportunities will arise naturally to share fully in the culture of the child's ethnic group. In addition, such a family is usually best placed to prepare the child for life as a member of an ethnic minority group in a multi-racial society where he will encounter discrimination and racism.
- Consequently, sustained efforts are needed to recruit sufficient numbers of prospective adopters from appropriate ethnic minority groups. Specific recruitment campaigns directed at ethnic minority communities are required.
- Notwithstanding the above, ethnicity (like religion) is only one among a number of significant factors in the matching process. It must not be elevated into the decisive one.
- Consequently, where no matching family can be identified, the local authority must make diligent efforts to find an alternative family.
- Blanket bans on transracial placements are therefore unacceptable.
- Where a child is to be placed transracially, special care is needed. The local authority should ensure that the prospective

adopters are sympathetic to the race issues that will confront the child as he grows up, and that they understand those issues.

Although some newspaper headlines may have given the impression that this guidance would significantly affect local authority adherence to same-race placement policy, it is fairly clear that it did no such thing. Indeed, in 2000 some social workers still felt able to tell the Performance and Innovation Unit openly that they did not make transracial placements because 'they did not work'[71]. This is not surprising. Leaving aside adoption agencies' own experience with transracial adoption, and the sensitivity of race issues in social work generally, the fact is that each of the three guidance documents gave very strong support to ethnic matching. The emphasis on recruitment of ethnic minority adopters made sense only in the context of a same-race placement policy. Consequently, when government ministers complained about social workers being stuck in ideological and dogmatic mindsets that had no part in a multi-racial society[72], they gave the appearance of trying to face two directions at the same time. It was as if they were attempting to disown their own officials' advice. A further reason why these guidance documents were destined to have no great effect lies in their reliance on generalisations. This is particularly obvious in the 1998 circular. Although it directed local authorities to set 'agreed and realistic time limits' for ethnic minority children who could not be found an ethnically matched adoptive family, it failed to specify what these time limits might be. Leaving such a vital question unanswered merely served to reinforce local authority discretion.

Provisions of the law

The statutory provisions touching on the matching function of local authorities have already been noted[73]. Whereas the Adoption Act 1976 was silent on the question of race, section 1(5) of the 2002 Act provides that in placing a child for adoption a local authority must give due consideration to the child's religious persuasion, racial origin and cultural and linguistic background. This subsection mirrors a provision in the Children Act 1989 which covers children who are looked after[74]. It is certainly not a meaningless provision but it advances the same-race placement debate no further due to its open-textured language. This did not stop the Conservative Party opposing its inclusion in the Act without qualification. It was said that the subsection was too prescriptive and that it could be over-zealously interpreted by social workers. It was said that its lack of clarity would enable lawyers to have a field day in court, when in fact the provision bears on the much earlier matching stage of the adoption process when the courts are not involved. It was also suggested that the Government was introducing 'willy nilly' politically correct considerations into the adoption law, when in fact section 1(5) arises directly out of a recommendation made by the Adoption Law Review in 1992[75]. The rule contained in section 1(3) of the 2002 Act − that the local authority must bear in mind that, in general, any delay in coming to an adoption decision is likely to prejudice a child's welfare − is as mild as the section 1(5) principle. It demands no specific change in practice. The Government expressed the opinion during Parliamentary debates that taken together, section 1(3) and section 1(5) give effect to the policy set out in the National Adoption Standards. While this may be true in a general sense, the fact remains that the National Standards are far more prescriptive and are therefore more likely to bring about practice changes than the Act itself. These Standards are considered below.

The National Standards

The National Adoption Standards contain two key references to race. The first is to be found in the introductory section on 'values', which aims to explain 'the important principles' that underpin the Standards themselves. According to this, 'children's ethnic origin, cultural background, religion and language will be fully recognised and positively valued and promoted when decisions are made'. The second reference is more specific and refers to ethnic matching. In draft form the Standards provided that 'the family of choice for the looked after child is one that reflects his or her birth heritage, if this can be found without unnecessary delay'. This simple yet strong statement did not appear in the finalised Standards. Instead, the issue of matching was more closely integrated with the timescales laid down for all placements. Standards A8 and A9 read as follows:

A8. Children will be matched with families who can best meet their needs. They will not be left waiting indefinitely for a 'perfect family'.

A9. Every effort will be made to recruit sufficient adopters from diverse backgrounds, so that each child can be found an adoptive family within the timescales in 3) above, which best meets their needs, and in particular: a) which reflects their ethnic origin, cultural background, religion and language; b) which allows them to live with brothers and sisters unless this will not meet their individually assessed needs. Where this is the case, a clear explanation will be given to them and recorded.

It will be recalled that Standard A3 stipulates that a match with suitable adoptive parents will be identified and approved within six months of a best interests decision, 'taking account of the individual child's needs'. Standards A9 and A3, taken together, represent in theory the greatest threat to same-race practices out of all the statutory and non-statutory materials on this subject. Of course, if sufficient numbers of ethnic minority adoptive families are recruited nationally, then with assistance from the National Adoption Register the six-month deadline may be attainable in most cases. But suppose they are not? On the day the Standards were launched the chief executive of BAAF was reported as saying: 'We are very worried that unless more black families are actively encouraged to come forward, finding families who match

the ethnic and cultural background of the child will be incompatible with the timescale of the Standards.'[76] The alternative to incompatibility, of course, is a transracial placement. Much will hinge on the determination of social workers to make an ethnic match and their authority's willingness to go outside the deadline and rely, if challenged, on the 'individual child's needs' proviso. At the time of writing it is unclear how this aspect of the National Standards will work in practice. The draft Practice Guidance on the Standards, issued by the Department of Health in 2001, did not cast much light on the matter as it largely referred back to the 1998 circular. (It did, however, suggest that in transracial placement cases the agency should give the adopters training, advice and specific post-adoption support on how to foster the child's racial and ethnic identity.) Resolution of this long-running controversy seems as far away as ever.

Telling Adopters about Their Children

According to regulation 12(1) of the Adoption Agencies Regulations 1983 (made under the previous adoption statute), where an adoption agency has decided that a prospective adopter would be a suitable adoptive parent for a particular child, it must provide the prospective adopter with 'written information about the child, his personal history and background, including his religious and cultural background, his health history and current state of health, together with the adoption agency's written proposals in respect of the adoption, including proposals as to the date of placement for adoption with the prospective adopter'. The context in which this apparently straightforward legal obligation has been implemented is considerably different from the one that obtained when it was first created. As has already been emphasised, today's looked after children who are adopted tend to have backgrounds that are far more complex, and therefore more challenging, than the backgrounds of the

by the courts in two landmark cases: *Re KD* in 1988[87] and *Re B* in 1992[88]. Coincidentally, each case involved a birth mother who had herself grown up in the care system. *Re KD* was decided under the pre-Children Act legal framework. The child was a ward of court and was living with long-term foster carers who wanted to adopt, and in the words of one of the judges his welfare required that he should no longer see his mother 'because at the age of three years he could not cope with two competing mothers'. The point of law confirmed by the House of Lords was the primacy of the welfare consideration and the danger of using 'parental rights' language in this context. The court also made it clear that the European Convention on Human Rights (now formally incorporated in English law) added nothing to the domestic law. *Re B* arose out of a section 34(4) application in respect of two girls of two and four who had been effectively abandoned by their mother. The plan for adoption was made three months after the care orders. The local authority had identified suitable adopters but they were not prepared to offer continuing contact. The mother's case on the section 34(4) application was that she was now more mature and that she should not be written off as a future primary carer, a case that the children's guardian ad litem eventually came to accept. The Court of Appeal noted that the approach of the Children Act to contact with children in care is completely different from the approach of the previous legislation. The provisions of section 34, coupled with the welfare principle contained in section 1, mean that the court is in a position to override the wishes of the local authority and order contact between parent and child, even if that means delaying or upsetting a plan for adoption:

> The proposals of the local authority, based on their appreciation of the best interests of the child, must command the greatest respect and consideration from the court, but Parliament has given to the court, and not to the local authority, the duty to decide on contact between the child and those named in section 34(1). Consequently, the court may have the task of requiring the local authority to justify

their long-term plans to the extent only that those plans exclude contact between parent and child.

Placing a Looked After Child for Adoption

The position before the 2002 Act

The legal framework pertaining to placement for adoption of children in the care system has never been straightforward. One of the reasons for this has been the number of routes into care and the distinctions between voluntary and compulsory arrangements. Prior to the Children Act 1989 the position was particularly complex because of the multiplicity of compulsory care procedures. Some compulsory care orders, for example, were made by the juvenile court under the Children and Young Persons Act 1969 while others were made by the High Court under the wholly different wardship jurisdiction. Placement for adoption did not require the court's approval under the Children and Young Persons Act but approval was required where the care order had been made in wardship. Which care procedure was employed depended very often on local policy. Matters were simplified by the Children Act 1989, which introduced the 'looked after' terminology. Looked after children who were to be placed for adoption would either be accommodated by the local authority on a voluntary basis under section 20, or they would be in compulsory care under a care order made under section 31. Section 20 accommodation would nearly always have been provided with the birth parents' consent whereas a care order might well have been fiercely contested. Either way, the local authority in question had the legal authority to place the child in a suitable setting and this would include a home with prospective adopters. The decision-making framework was derived partly from the 1989 Act and its supplementary regulations and partly from the Adoption Act 1976 and its supplementary regulations, especially the Adoption Agencies Regulations 1983. In the case of a child in compulsory care, placement for adoption could take place only after consultation with the birth parents[89]. If the parents objected to the placement, they had the right to apply to the court for a discharge of the care order but such an application would not automatically stop the placement going ahead. As was noted earlier, if the local authority wished to terminate parental contact it would need the court's permission. Placement for adoption could, however, be effected whatever the contact arrangements. Even if contact litigation was pending in the courts, placement for adoption could go ahead[90]. In the case of an accommodated child the position was different. Prior consultation with the birth parents was still required but because the provision of section 20 accommodation is a wholly consensual arrangement, parents who objected to an adoption plan could remove the child from the accommodation at once unless the local authority took preventive steps under the compulsory care or emergency protection provisions.

Criticisms of the position before the 2002 Act

The arrangements described above – especially those arising out of compulsory care orders – came to be seen as fundamentally flawed. The flaw detected related to the position of the child's parents and their inability to contest an adoption placement in court *at the time the placement was effected*. It was summarised by Jane Rowe as long ago as 1989, when the Children Bill was before Parliament. Looking back at developments in child care following the Houghton Report and the Children Act 1975, she wrote:

> Agencies developed the dubious practice of placing children with prospective adopters, choking off parental access and then claiming that parents would be 'unreasonable' in refusing consent to adoption because the child was now emotionally bonded to new parents. Many children benefited, but injustices were also done.[91]

The point being made here concerns the timing of the court's involvement in contested adoptions of children in care (which account for well over half of the total). The effect of the legislation outlined above was that the local authority was frequently able to proceed with an adoption placement against the wishes of one or both birth parents, secure in the knowledge that by the time the child's case came before a court, the placement would have lasted some considerable time[92]. Although the birth mother (and the father, if he had parental responsibility), was entitled to withhold consent to adoption at the final hearing of the adoption order application, she would by then be vulnerable to an application to have that consent dispensed with. Only if the local authority sought termination of contact, or if it chose to use the freeing for adoption procedure, would the court become involved at an earlier stage. The fact that adoption had not specifically featured in the authority's original care plan was irrelevant. This sequence of events became known as the 'fait accompli adoption' after the issue was picked up by the Adoption Law Review in 1992:

> The lack of consideration generally given to the importance of parental agreement is sometimes attributable in part to the late stage in the process at which the court is asked to resolve the question of parental agreement. This has frequently been the case where a child is in care and the local authority has decided that there is no prospect of rehabilitating the child with his or her birth parents and has placed the child for adoption…It is…open to the local authority to place the child for adoption without having the court address the question of parental agreement until the adoption application is heard several months later. Even if the parents have had some contact with the child during the placement (which is perhaps more likely to be the case following implementation of the Children Act 1989), the strength of the relationship between the child and the prospective adopters at the time of the hearing may present the court with what it regards as a fait accompli.[93]

It was this concern about injustice to birth parents that led the Review to recommend that 'where an agency is planning to place a child with prospective adopters (i) a placement order must be granted by the court before a placement is allowed to proceed and (ii) a placement order is not made without a prior full hearing if the adoption (or any related matter, such as the level of contact) is contested by the child, anyone with parental responsibility, or any member of the child's family'[94]. The need to have better regard for the birth parents' interests was accepted by the Labour government although philosophically it sits rather awkwardly with its determination to increase the rate of adoptions from care.

The debate about placement orders

What the Adoption Law Review recommended was a new essential stage in the adoption process. It is true that the proposed placement order bore a resemblance to the existing freeing order (recommended for abolition by the Review) but there were significant differences between the two, not least the fact that freeing was always optional for local authorities. If this novelty was going to be introduced, many basic questions would have to be addressed. Who, for example, would make the application for a placement order? Who would be the judge of whether the application was contested? What would be the legal position in the period between introductions and the making of an order? What would be the legal effect of a placement order on the birth parents, the prospective adopters and the local authority? What would be the effect on a care order or a contact order? What would happen to a placement order in the event of the placement breaking down? In what circumstances might a placement order be discharged? Should there be any exceptions to the placement order requirement? These were only some of the questions that were raised in 1992. Answering them has haunted the Department of Health ever since. The Review's detailed proposals got off to a bad start when British Agencies for Adoption and Fostering declared that they would not work[95]. Consequently, in its 1993 white paper on adoption the Conservative government announced that there would have to be

further examination and discussion of the matter. This led to the publication in 1994 of a separate consultation document entitled *Placement for Adoption* (which also generated controversy[96]) and a further set of proposals two years later when the draft Adoption Bill was published. That Bill afforded the Department of Health its first opportunity to translate the idea of placement orders into concrete legislation. Further opportunities arrived when the Adoption and Children Bill was presented to Parliament in March 2001 and then re-presented in October of that year. On each occasion the legislative drafting was different, which clearly shows the difficulty of the task. The subject matter, though of considerable practical importance, is technical and legalistic and a far cry from the politically controversial areas of race, unmarried adopters and intercountry adoption. The difficulty that MPs and ministers experienced on the issue during 2002 was exacerbated by the fact that the proposed scheme was based on a review carried out nearly ten years earlier.

The scheme of the 2002 Act

The provisions of the 2002 Act regarding placement are contained in sections 18 to 29. In attempting to unravel them, it is important not to lose sight of their overall objective: to prevent fait accompli adoptions. The first point to note about them is that although they do apply to baby relinquishments, they are not primarily aimed at such cases. The history of the provisions makes this clear. The underlying facts and issues in relinquishment cases are very different from those found in looked after cases and the relevant law has been dealt with separately in this book. Readers are accordingly referred to Chapter 6 for a description of the placement provisions of the Act in the relinquishment context. The focus here is on children – whether babies or not – in the care system. These are children who will have arrived in the system either on the basis of voluntary accommodation or on the basis of compulsory care.

A further point to note is that the provisions reflect a fundamental distinction between agreed adoption placements and contested adoption placements. Both types of placement are regulated by the Act but, crucially, the second type requires a court order.

Agreed adoption placements

The Adoption Law Review of 1992 proposed that even where the child's birth parents consented to an adoption placement, a formal placement order from the court should be obtained following a joint application made by the local authority and the prospective adopters and an investigation of the case by a guardian ad litem. This proposal was rejected by the Department of Health, partly because of the fear of delay. Instead, section 19 of the 2002 Act permits agreed placements to occur without the involvement of the courts. Section 19(1) provides: 'Where an adoption agency is satisfied that each parent or guardian of a child has consented to the child (a) being placed for adoption with prospective adopters identified in the consent, or (b) being placed for adoption with any prospective adopters who may be chosen by the agency, and has not withdrawn the consent, the agency is authorised to place the child for adoption accordingly.' It will be noticed that section 19(1)(b) allows the birth parents to provide a general consent, i.e. one that is not tied to particular prospective adopters (and section 19(2) allows a specific consent under section 19(1)(a) to be combined with a general one, to be used if the identified placement breaks down). This, too, represents a departure from the regime envisaged by the Adoption Law Review, which expressed concern about freeing for adoption cases under the Adoption Act 1976 in which children had effectively been left without any family because suitable adopters could not be found.

The providing of parental consent to an adoption placement is regulated, confusingly, by later parts of the Act:

■ According to section 52(6), 'parent' for these purposes means a parent with parental responsibility. All mothers are therefore 'parents', as are fathers who are married to the child's mother. Unmarried fathers may or may not have parental responsibility depending on the circumstances. If any such 'parent' objects to an adoption placement, section 19 cannot be used and the local authority will have to apply to the court for a placement order.

■ According to section 52(5), 'consent' means consent given unconditionally and with full understanding of what is involved. The word 'freely' was in the original draft of this subsection, just as it was in the equivalent provision of the Adoption Act 1976. However, the Government agreed to drop it after sustained pressure from voluntary organisations. It was said to be 'unacceptable to most birth parents who whilst recognising the need for their child to be adopted only accept that plan with regret and sorrow'[97].

■ According to section 52(7), consent must be given in the form to be prescribed by government rules.

■ Section 102 requires the government to draw up rules under which CAFCASS officers are appointed to witness parental consent forms. This process of witnessing forms was at one point described by the Government as amounting to 'court consideration of the nature of consent'[98]. Such a description is an exaggeration although it is true to say that the introduction of CAFCASS into consensual placement arrangements constitutes a safeguard for birth parents. The immediate consequences of giving consent to placement – and its role in the adoption process as a whole – will need to be carefully and fully explained to them, first by the local authority and then by CAFCASS. These are described below.

Once parental consent has been obtained, the child can be placed with prospective adopters (introductions may already have taken place). Other consequences follow:

- The child continues to be 'looked after' by the local authority (section 18(3)). This means that the various welfare and review obligations imposed on the authority by Part III of the Children Act are maintained. It is likely, however, that government regulations made under section 53 of the 2002 Act will have the effect of modifying the authority's duties in relation to consultation with parents and the promotion of parental contact.

- Parental responsibility for the child is acquired by the local authority if it did not already have it (section 25(2)). This will be the case only if the child was previously being accommodated on a voluntary basis under section 20 of the Children Act. When the child is actually placed for adoption, the prospective adopters also acquire parental responsibility (section 25(3)). The relevant birth parents do not lose their parental responsibility at this stage which means that responsibility is shared three ways. Section 25(4) gives prime parental responsibility to the local authority during the adoption placement by providing that 'the agency may determine that the parental responsibility of any parent or guardian, or of prospective adopters, is to be restricted to the extent specified in the determination'. These provisions have had a mixed reception. The automatic acquisition of parental responsibility by the prospective adopters from the commencement of the placement was recommended by the Adoption Law Review on the grounds that the adopters 'are effectively responsible for the child's day-to-day upbringing'[99], although as explained earlier the Review would have required the adopters to obtain a placement order from the court. Some groups, however, questioned whether adopters would actually want parental responsibility right from the start. Furthermore, the three-way allocation of responsibility was said by some critics to be a recipe for confusion. The automatic acquisition of responsibility by the local authority in voluntary accommodation cases was

also contentious – indeed, even the need for it was questioned by some organisations (including BAAF).

- No person may cause the child to be known by a new surname unless they obtain the written consent of each parent or permission from the court (section 28(2)).

- There is a similar restriction on taking the child out of the country for more than one month (section 28(2)).

- The right of the birth parents to apply for a residence order under Part II of the Children Act is removed (section 28(1)).

- Any contact order previously made under the Children Act is terminated (section 26(1)). In the case of a looked after child with an adoption plan, such an order is most likely to be one made in care order proceedings under section 34 of the 1989 Act. If formal provision for post-placement contact is felt to be desirable (and in an agreed adoption this may be unlikely) an application can be made to the court by, among others, the local authority and the parents. The application is made under section 26 of the 2002 Act, not the 1989 Act. The rationale offered for disapplying contact orders under the Children Act and having free-standing provisions in the 2002 Act was that the arrangements set out in a previous contact order might well be inappropriate in the light of the plan for adoption.

- Restrictions apply in relation to the removal of the child by a birth parent who undergoes a change of mind and signals a withdrawal of consent to placement. These bear primarily on the parents of children who arrived in the care system on a voluntary basis under section 20 of the Children Act. Parents of children who arrived under a compulsory care order will never have had the right to remove in the first place but in section 20 cases that right is absolutely central, and expressly provided for in section 20(8). It was one of the most notable features of the 1989 legislation. It has now been modified, however. The principal modification is effected by section 30 of the 2002 Act, which makes it a criminal offence for any person other than an agency worker to remove a child once he has been placed with prospective adopters under section 19 or once the agency has been authorised to place him under that section. By way of qualification, limited rights are given to birth parents by sections 31 and 32. If the child is not actually in an adoption placement, a parent is entitled to the return of the child within seven days unless the local authority initiates placement order proceedings (section 31). If the child is in placement, a parent is entitled to the return of the child within 14 days unless the local authority initiates placement order proceedings, or unless the prospective adopters have already filed an application for an adoption order, a special guardianship order or a residence order (section 32). The general parental right to remove an accommodated child, enshrined in section 20(8) of the 1989 Act, is expressly disapplied by section 30(6) of the 2002 Act. Not surprisingly, these provisions attracted criticism from those concerned about the erosion of the voluntary accommodation principle. There was particular anxiety about their operation in cases where the child has not yet been placed – why should there be any restriction on removal in such circumstances? In response the Government made a concession, reducing the maximum retention period from 14 days to seven (section 31 above) but even this will not apply if the local authority applies for a placement order. Of course, one can argue in defence of these provisions – and all the other provisions that impinge on a birth parent's parental responsibility – that they become operative only after the parents have provided an initial consent to an adoption placement, duly witnessed by CAFCASS. A full explanation of the legal consequences would therefore have been supplied to them at the outset and they would have gone into the procedure with their eyes open. That, at any rate, is the theory.

■ The birth parents can choose to provide formal consent to the making of a future adoption order – 'advance consent to adoption', as section 20 calls it. This consent may be geared to specific prospective adopters or it may be general; and it may be accompanied or followed by a notice that the parent does not wish to be informed when an application for an adoption order is eventually filed. Like initial consent to placement, advance consent to adoption is subject to safeguards prescribed by sections 52 and 102: it must be given unconditionally and with full understanding and the document signifying it must be witnessed by CAFCASS. The provision of this consent will not remove the parent's parental responsibility or parental status – that will happen only when the adoption order is made, perhaps many months (or years) later – but if it is maintained it will necessarily have the effect of curtailing their participation in adoption order proceedings. Section 20(3) allows a parent to withdraw an advance consent although section 52(4) renders such a withdrawal ineffective if it comes at a time when prospective adopters are on the scene and they have already filed an adoption application with the court. (In such circumstances, the dispute will be left for the adoption court to resolve.) A parent who does withdraw an advance consent will usually wish to withdraw their consent to adoption placement as well. This may well trigger an application by the local authority for a placement order in which the authority seeks to have parental consent dispensed with (as described later in this chapter).

Contested adoption placements

If a parent (with parental responsibility) of a looked after child cannot be persuaded to provide consent to an adoption placement, or if such a parent having previously given consent withdraws it before prospective adopters have made their adoption application, the local authority cannot proceed with a placement unless it obtains a placement order from the court. This rule, which applies irrespective of the strength of the parent's case, is laid down by section 18(1) of the 2002 Act. For those parents who maintain their opposition to losing their children from the start of compulsory intervention, it means that the local authority's adoption proposal – and more specifically, the issue of parental agreement – will be brought before a court at an earlier point than would have been required under the previous legislation. As was mentioned earlier, this was the key change in the placement law advocated by the Adoption Law Review in 1992. For the local authority concerned, it means a delay in the execution of its long-term plan for the child until such time as the dispute with the parent has been disposed of by the legal system.

The procedure under the Adoption Act 1976 for freeing a child for adoption did allow a local authority to test an opposed adoption plan in the courts at an early point but freeing suffered from at least two related defects. First, it was not compulsory and some local authorities steered clear of it. Second, even where it was used the authority was entitled to place the child with prospective adopters well in advance of the freeing proceedings. In fact this was done in a significant proportion of freeing cases. The placement order under the 2002 Act can be regarded as a revised version of freeing which addresses these two defects (as well as others) and which is tailor-made for contested cases. Its principal features are set out below.

- The application is made by the local authority (section 22). Voluntary adoption agencies are not involved in this procedure.
- An application can be made if the child is subject to a care order, if care order proceedings are pending, if the child is being accommodated on a voluntary basis, or if the child is already placed for adoption but parental consent to the placement under section 19 has been withdrawn (section 22).

- As one would expect, an application can be made only where the local authority is satisfied that the child ought to be placed for adoption (section 22). Government regulations will provide for appropriate input to this decision by the authority's adoption panel.
- Where the local authority's application relates to an accommodated child, only a person who has the court's permission may remove the child (section 30(2)). The birth parent's right to remove under section 20(8) of the Children Act is therefore brought to an end.
- Unless the child is already subject to a care order, the local authority will have to satisfy the court that the so-called threshold criteria for care orders, contained in section 31(2) of the Children Act, are met (section 21(2)). The Department of Health stated that linking the making of placement orders with section 31(2) was intended to deliver on the Government's undertaking to align adoption law with the Children Act but this reasoning is not convincing because the provision was missing from the version of the Bill first presented to Parliament. The reality is that this part of the Bill was redrafted in order to deal with powerful criticisms made by a number of organisations, including the National Foster Care Association and the Family Rights Group. They pointed out that an enforced adoption placement in respect of an accommodated child is a form of compulsory State intervention and should accordingly attract stringent criteria. They also argued that without such criteria, parents of children in need would be even more fearful of accepting an offer of accommodation under the Children Act in case it led to a placement order application that hinged purely on welfare considerations.
- Whatever the child's legal status, the welfare considerations contained in section 1 of the Act will be applied by the court when hearing the application for the placement order. These are as follows:

1. The paramount consideration is the welfare of the child, throughout his life (section 1(2)).
2. In general, any delay in coming to a decision is likely to prejudice the child's welfare (section 1(3)).
3. The court must have regard to the following matters (among others): the child's ascertainable wishes and feelings regarding the application (considered in the light of his age and understanding); the child's particular needs; the likely effect on the child (throughout his life) of having ceased to be a member of the original family and become an adopted person; the child's age, sex, background and any of the child's characteristics which the court considers relevant; any harm which the child has suffered or is at risk of suffering; the relationship which the child has with parents, relatives and any other relevant person (including the likelihood of any such relationship continuing and the value to the child of its doing so; the ability and willingness of any parent or relative to provide the child with a secure environment in which the child can develop and otherwise to meet the child's needs; and the wishes and feelings of any parent or relative regarding the child) (section 1(4)).
4. The court must consider the whole range of powers available to it, whether under the 2002 Act or the Children Act (section 1(6)). In this connection, it should be noted that placement order applications are classed as 'family proceedings' for the purposes of the Children Act and the court can therefore in principle make one or more section 8 orders (including a residence order).
5. The court must not make a placement order unless it considers that making it would be better for the child than not doing so (section 1(6)).

■ The child will be a party to the application and his interests will be additionally safe-guarded through the appointment of a CAFCASS officer (section 102).

■ The court may give directions for the medical or psychiatric examination or other assessment of the child (section 22(6)). A child of sufficient understanding has a veto, however.

■ The court has the power to – and in a contested case will need to – dispense with parental consent (section 21(3)). The circumstances in which this can be done are described below.

■ The main effect of a placement order is that it authorises the local authority to place the child for adoption with any prospective adopters who may be chosen by it (section 21(1)). This means that the local authority is not required to have identified any particular adopters for the court to scrutinise. It may have done so – indeed, it may even have commenced introductions – but it is under no duty. This is contrary to what the Adoption Law Review recommended. The Review considered it undesirable for the court to deal with contested adoption plans in a vacuum. It suggested that there was a danger that 'courts may contrast the readily apparent shortcomings in the care offered or likely to be offered in future by a child's parents with the care likely to be offered by hypothetically perfect adoptive parents'[1]. The scheme embodied in the 2002 Act resembles more closely the one put forward by BAAF, which argued strongly that in many cases it would be pointless for the local authority to seek to identify a specific placement before the court's approval of an adoption plan.

■ The local authority has parental responsibility for the child while the placement order is in force (section 25(2)). Where the child was already subject to a care order or interim care order, parental responsibility will have been acquired previously. The relevant birth parents do not lose their parental responsibility (unlike the position under the previous law relating to freeing orders).

■ When the child is placed with prospective adopters, they too acquire parental responsibility (section 25(3)). In this three-way sharing situation, it is for the local authority to determine how parental responsibility is to be exercised (section 25(4)). Prospective adopters are not, however, entitled to change the child's surname or remove the child from the UK for more than a month unless they obtain written consent from each parent or permission from the court (section 28(2)).

■ If the child is already subject to a care order, that order lapses while the placement order is in force (section 29(1)). The child remains looked after within the meaning of the Children Act (section 18(3)) although government regulations made under section 53 are likely to modify the local authority's usual Children Act obligations (e.g. in relation to the promotion of parental contact). The suspension of the care order means an end to the local authority's duty to allow the child reasonable contact with the parents under section 34 of the Children Act. Any contact order made under section 34 is also terminated (section 26(1)). As mentioned in relation to agreed placements, the thinking behind this is that it is right at this stage for the parties to take a fresh look at contact arrangements when the existing order may well have been drawn up at a time when adoption was not on the agenda. This leads on to section 27, considered next.

■ Section 27(4) provides that before making a placement order the court must (a) consider the arrangements which the adoption agency has made, or proposes to make, for allowing any person contact with the child, and (b) invite the parties to the proceedings to comment on those arrangements. Linked to this is section 26(2) which enables the court to make an order requiring 'the person with whom the child lives, or is to live' – this could include prospective adopters – to allow the child to visit or stay with the person named in the order, or for the person named in the order

and the child otherwise to have contact with each other. Such an order can be made subject to specially crafted conditions (relating to timing or supervision, for example) and can be sought at any time following the making of the placement order. It can be varied or revoked but will in any event come to an end when an adoption order is made (section 27(1)). It would be unwise to expect section 26 contact orders to be made liberally. As is explained later in this chapter, the courts exercised caution under the Adoption Act 1976 in relation to formal contact provision, for fear of destabilising adoption placements, and there is no reason to think that this will change under the new legislation, even at the placement order stage. This was certainly the approach of the Department of Health in 1994 when its consultation document on placement orders was written:

> The making of an order endorsing a general adoption plan would indicate that the child's paramount need is for successful placement with a new family. The court has judged that the birth family is unable to take responsibility for the child's upbringing. Once the court has decided in favour of an adoption plan it should grant other orders only when it considers these would increase the chances of a future adoption being successful. A contact order for example should only be made when a court believes such contact would help rather than hinder the child to settle permanently with a potential new family. Guidance would emphasise the need for court decisions to support the potential new family relationship once the adoption plan has been generally endorsed by the court.[2]

■ Once the placement order is made, nobody (other than the local authority) may remove the child from prospective adopters (section 34(1)).

■ A placement order will have the effect of automatically revoking any previous section 8 order or supervision order (section 29(2)). No application for a section 8 order can be made and the same goes for supervision orders and child assessment orders (section 26(2) and section 29(3)).

- It was noted earlier that a placement order application can be made if care order proceedings are pending. Where this happens there will be two sets of proceedings running side by side in the same court. If both applications succeed, the court will make the two separate orders but the care order will immediately be superseded by the placement order (section 29(1)(b)). Although some disquiet was voiced about these concurrent applications, the procedure has long been accepted by the courts in the context of freeing for adoption. Clearly, it will be relevant only in those cases where the local authority is convinced of the need for adoption at the outset of compulsory intervention.

- A placement order will continue in force until the child is adopted, or until the child marries or attains the age of majority, or until the order is revoked by the court (section 21(4)). Revocation, which is regulated by section 24 of the Act, is an important matter. It could be sought for a number of reasons. One possible reason is that the local authority is unable to find suitable adopters and wishes to abandon the adoption plan. Another possibility is that a birth parent or relative wishes to make a fresh bid for the child, perhaps after a series of abortive adoption placements. A further possibility is that the child himself becomes set against adoption. The equivalent provision in the Adoption Act 1976 dealt with the revocation of freeing orders and lessons have clearly been learned from the fiascos generated by its faulty drafting. Anyone can apply under section 24 but an application may not be made by a person other than the child or the local authority unless the court has given permission *and* the child is not currently placed with prospective adopters (section 24(2)). The court cannot give permission unless it is satisfied that there has been a change of circumstances since the placement order

was made (section 24(3)). If an application is made and the child is not currently with prospective adopters, the local authority is barred from placing the child pending the hearing of the application without the court's consent (section 24(5)). The court hearing the revocation application will apply the welfare considerations previously described. If revocation does take place, any previous care order will be revived, so maintaining the local authority's prime parental responsibility for the child and public law protection for him.

- The making of a placement order will have a significant bearing on the ability of the birth parents to participate in future adoption order proceedings. If the local authority's plan proceeds smoothly, the child will be put into an adoption placement shortly after the placement order is made and in due course the prospective adopters will file their application with the court. During the Parliamentary proceedings on the 2002 Act, the Government made it clear that regulations would require the birth parents to be notified of the prospective adopters' application. This will provide the parents with an opportunity to seek the court's permission to oppose the application. Section 47(5) of the Act requires such permission to be obtained and section 47(7) requires the relevant parent to demonstrate a change of circumstances since the date of the placement order. If permission is granted and the opposition is maintained, the adoption order cannot be made unless the parent's consent is dispensed with under section 47(2) (see below). This small window of opportunity for the protesting birth parent is in fact an advancement on the parent's position under the previous law relating to freeing because under the Adoption Act 1976 a parent was not involved in any way in adoption proceedings when their child had already been freed. The new provisions in section 47 are conceptually consistent with the fact that a placement order does not remove the parent's parental responsibility.

Placement of orphans

The 2002 Act makes special provision for children who are accommodated by a local authority but who have no parent with parental responsibility. If the local authority constructs an adoption plan for such a child it will be unable to effect an agreed placement under section 19 of the Act because that procedure is confined to situations in which the parents (not other relatives) signify their consent to adoption. Consequently, a placement order from the court will be needed. Sections 21(2) and 22(1) expressly refer to children who have no parent or guardian and they permit the court to make a placement order in respect of an accommodated child without the local authority having to prove the threshold criteria for a care order. These proceedings will almost certainly be uncontested but of course the court will still have to take into account the welfare considerations mentioned in section 1 of the Act, including 'the relationship which the child has with relatives'. As noted earlier, the effect of a placement order will be to give the local authority parental responsibility for the child.

Dispensing with Parental Consent

Introduction

In the context of looked after children, there are three sets of circumstances in which an application to the court to dispense with parental consent will prove necessary if an adoption order is to be made:

1. Placement for adoption is opposed by the relevant parent from the start and the local authority seeks a placement order so that it can arrange such a placement. In this type of case, prospective adopters will not be directly involved.
2. The parent withdraws consent to placement under section 19 before prospective adopters have made an adoption application. (Section 19 consent cannot be withdrawn once an adoption application has been made.) The local authority seeks a placement order in order to arrange or maintain a placement. In this type of case, prospective adopters may well be directly involved – indeed, the child may have been living with them for a very considerable period.
3. The parent is given permission by the court to oppose an adoption application at the final hearing in the light of a change of circumstances since the giving of section 19 consent or the making of a placement order. In this type of case, it is the prospective adopters who seek to have parental consent dispensed with. The child will have been living with them for at least ten weeks, in accordance with section 42(2) of the Act.

The previous legislation

Section 16(2) of the Adoption Act 1976 set out the grounds on which a parent's consent could be dispensed with on the hearing of an adoption application or a freeing application. These were that the parent:

- could not be found or was incapable of giving consent
- was withholding consent unreasonably
- had persistently failed without reasonable cause to discharge parental responsibility for the child
- had abandoned or neglected the child
- had persistently ill-treated the child
- had seriously ill-treated the child.

These six grounds were examined by the Adoption Law Review in 1992. The last four, though apparently seldom used, were said by the Review to be unsatisfactory 'in that they relate exclusively to shortcomings in parental care rather than to the needs of the child'[3]. The first ground was found to be satisfactory. This left the unreasonableness ground, the one used most frequently. This ground caused difficulties for judges for many years. Delivering judgment in 1970, a senior judge remarked that 'it is, unfortunately, not...clear to what sort of circumstances the [ground] is intended to relate, for the Act does not specify what standard or degree of unreasonableness is envisaged'[4]. Thirty years later, another senior judge commented that 'the difficulty lies not in the language of the section, which could hardly be more straightforward, but in applying it to what are usually agonising situations'[5]. In Chapter 6 of this book it was noted how, in the 1971 case of *Re W*, the House of Lords came to deliver authoritative guidance on the nature and scope of the unreasonableness ground in the context of baby relinquishment and the position of the vacillating mother[6]. In subsequent years, however, when the nature of adoption changed, *Re W* was taken to be the leading authority in relation to *all* types of application, including the adoption of looked after children. As recently as June 2000, it was being described as 'the classic case' in this field[7]. The emphasis placed by the House of Lords on welfare considerations that 'the reasonable mother' would take into account had the inevitable effect of making it easier for courts to dispense with parental consent in looked after cases, where episodes of neglect or maltreatment of the child, or instability or a chaotic lifestyle on the part of the birth parents, not infrequently formed part of the background. Even where this was not the case and the reason for the local authority's intervention lay ultimately in the parents' poor intellectual capacity, the *Re W* approach facilitated forced adoption, which led one judge to voice anxieties about social engineering[8].

The Adoption Law Review did not support the retention of the unreasonableness ground. Its view was that the test used by the courts after *Re W* had tended to give paramount weight to the child's welfare 'which we consider unsatisfactory when dealing with parental wishes and feelings in relation to so important a step as adoption'[9]. The Review recommended that in future there should be only two general grounds for dispensing with consent:

- The parent cannot be found or is incapable of giving agreement (repeating the existing law).

- The advantages to the child of becoming part of a new family and having a new legal status are so significantly greater than the advantages to the child of any alternative option as to justify overriding the wishes of the parent.

Although the Review's proposed second ground was worded very differently from the 1976 Act, the difference in substance was more difficult to pin down. For in assessing the 'reasonableness' of the protesting parent's position, were not the courts already weighing the advantages for the child of adoption? Had not this always been the reality of contested adoption? Support for this view can be found in a decision of the Court of Appeal in October 2000 in which the court overruled a county court judgment and dispensed with the consent of both parents on the unreasonableness ground. Lord Justice Judge stated that if the county court judgment stood, everything about the parents' history predicted an utterly bleak future for the child. He went on:

> He will in reality spend most, if not the whole, of his childhood and his youth in care, and his mother and father will drift in and out of his life as their own lives ebb and flow…Adoption represents an incalculably better prospect. Even relying, as one always should, on the profound natural bond between a mother and her child or a father and his child…it seems to me that *the advantages of adoption are so obvious that the views and interests of the parents ought to be set aside. For either to withhold consent in this case is in my judgment unreasonable.*[10]

The effect of the 2002 Act

Dispensing with consent under the 2002 Act is governed by section 52(1), which provides two separate grounds:

a) The parent cannot be found or is incapable of giving consent.
b) The welfare of the child requires the consent to be dispensed with.

Ground b) does not reflect the form of words recommended by the Adoption Law Review and, as was probably inevitable, it attracted adverse comment. On the face of it, it is a peculiar provision. According to section 1(2) of the Act, the paramount consideration in all placement order and adoption order proceedings is the welfare of the child. This is the case whether the proceedings are contested or uncontested. It is not surprising, therefore, that critics argued that the test in section 52(1)(b) – enabling a parent's opposition to be rejected simply on welfare grounds – failed to add anything of substance to what was already required of the court. As BAAF put it in its evidence to the House of Commons: 'There is nothing special about what the court has to do if it is actually going to override the parent's disagreement to adoption.'[11] As a matter of analysis, it is not easy to refute this argument. On the other hand, it could be argued that the Act does probably reflect the trend of the case law since the House of Lords decision in *Re W*, which in the context of parents said to be unreasonably withholding consent placed so much weight on the child's welfare. Furthermore, since – in the words of Lord Reid – 'adoption cases depend so much on general impression rather than the ascertainment of particular facts'[12], it could be said that any linguistic permutation would lead the court ultimately to rely on welfare factors, unless of course the law were to revert to a state in which specific acts of wrongdoing by a parent were required before their consent could be overridden.

The Department of Health was evidently not impressed by the Adoption Law Review's recommendation on this question. A senior official told the House of Commons that the Department was concerned that the inclusion of the expression 'significantly greater' would create confusion by opening up a large vein of debate about its meaning. He sought to emphasise the duty of the court in contested cases to have regard to the welfare considerations set out in section 1(4) of the Act, especially the relationship which the child has with his parents and relatives, and he suggested that

the 'significantly greater' test would not add anything to those considerations.

Unmarried Fathers

Background

In Chapter 6 of this book the legal position of unmarried fathers in baby relinquishment cases was considered[13]. It was noted there how the substantive adoption law and the family courts of this country have in recent years given greater recognition to the interests of such men. Not surprisingly, the same has happened in relation to looked after children. After all, in looked after cases the claims of the birth father are likely to be considerably stronger: the child is far less likely to be an infant and consequently he may well have lived with the father for a significant period. Even if this is not the case, the father may well have had substantial contact with the child, in contrast to fathers in relinquishment cases. He is not, therefore, a peripheral figure in the present context.

Both the Children Act 1975 and the Family Law Reform Act 1987 secured advances in the position of the unmarried father in adoption proceedings but the provisions in question were absurdly complicated. As with other areas of child law, it took the Children Act 1989 to bring a measure of clarity to the situation. The position after the 1989 Act was as follows. Where a child was being looked after by a local authority, whether under a care order or on a voluntary basis, the authority had a duty to consult the birth father prior to making any decision with respect to the child, if this was 'reasonably practicable'. In making any such decision the local authority was bound to give 'due consideration' to the father's wishes and feelings[14]. These duties embraced decisions about adoption. Where a child was being looked after under a care order the local authority was obliged to allow the child reasonable contact with the birth father, whatever the father's circumstances. This duty could be disapplied only by court order[15]. Similarly, the

National Adoption Standards, published in 2001, drew no distinction between married and unmarried fathers in the context of looked after children: the Standards imposed obligations in relation to birth parents generally. In the adoption legislation, however, distinctions were apparent. A 'parent' for the purposes of the Adoption Act 1976 meant any parent who had parental responsibility under the 1989 Act. If, therefore, an unmarried father had acquired parental responsibility, either by court order or by entering into a parental responsibility agreement with the mother, his consent to an adoption order or a freeing order was needed (subject to dispensing by the court). Granting parental responsibility to the father was accordingly a method by which his participation in future adoption or freeing proceedings could be guaranteed and this was expressly recognised by the courts as a legitimate factor to consider in parental responsibility order applications[16]. It was also confirmed that a local authority holding a care order was unable to prevent the child's parents from entering into a parental responsibility agreement[17].

If the father lacked parental responsibility, his formal consent to adoption or freeing was not required. However, if he wished his voice to be heard, he could apply to be joined as a party to adoption or freeing proceedings. In any event, his position would be brought to the attention of the court via a welfare report on the child and the court had an unfettered discretion to order him to be joined as a party or notified of the proceedings. Furthermore, before making a freeing order the court was under an obligation to satisfy itself 'in relation to any person claiming to be the father' that he had no intention of applying for a parental responsibility order or a residence order, or that if he did make any such application it would be likely to be refused[18]. The courts also took a liberal approach in care order cases under the Children Act where a father without parental responsibility applied to be joined as a party to the proceedings in order to argue against the local authority's plan for adoption. Research into the adoption of looked after children indicated that about 75

per cent of birth fathers lacked parental responsibility[19].

The father's position under the 2002 Act

The adoption provisions of the 2002 Act maintain the law's discrimination against unmarried fathers who do not have parental responsibility. The key provision is section 52, which deals with parental consent. According to section 52(6), 'parent' means a parent having parental responsibility and section 52(2) applies this restrictive definition to all references within sections 18 to 65 to 'any parent giving or withdrawing (a) consent to the placement of a child for adoption or (b) consent to the making of an adoption order (including a future adoption order)'. Consequently, the definition applies to agreed placements under section 19, advance consents to adoption under section 20, contested placement orders under section 21 and opposed adoption applications under section 47 (for the avoidance of doubt, those sections specifically refer to section 52 as being applicable). In none of the procedures regulated by those sections will the local authority or the court have to obtain, or dispense with, the consent of the unmarried father who lacks parental responsibility. The father's legal entitlement relates merely to consultation, under the Children Act provisions.

Three other sets of provisions should be noted, however. First of all, section 52(9) and (10) make special provision for the case where the child is placed for adoption under section 19 with the unmarried mother's consent and at a later date the father acquires parental responsibility. In these circumstances, the father (now, of course, a 'parent') is treated as having given his consent to the arrangement in the same terms as the mother. This deeming provision assists the local authority by making it unnecessary for it to go through the formal CAFCASS signification procedure. Secondly, section 1(4)(f) of the Act – part of the new welfare checklist – requires both the court and the adoption agency, when coming to a decision relating to the adoption of a child, to have regard to the relationship which the child has with relatives. This includes the value to the child of the relationship continuing and the wishes and feelings of relatives regarding the child. According to section 1(8), references to a 'relative' here include the child's mother and father. Since the discriminatory provisions of section 52 do not apply to section 1, the result is that all unmarried fathers fall within the scope of the checklist. This mirrors the non-discriminatory approach of the Children Act provisions relating to looked after children and the National Adoption Standards, noted earlier. Finally, there should be noted the provisions relating to the parental responsibility of unmarried fathers contained in section 111. These have the effect of amending the Children Act by conferring parental responsibility automatically on all those men who become registered as the father under the Births and Deaths Registration Act 1953. These fathers, who will acquire parental responsibility whether or not they know it or like it, will accordingly be 'parents' for the purposes of the adoption consent provisions. The practical effect of this important – if logically flawed – reform will therefore be to draw more fathers into the mainstream of the adoption process, a development that must surely be welcomed.

The Extended Birth Family

Background

Until the Children Act 1989 was implemented, grandparents and other adult relatives had little or no legal standing when it came to challenging the adoption plans of local authorities. The existence of this glaring defect in the law was amply demonstrated by a case which was appealed to the House of Lords in 1985[20]. The case concerned a four-year-old girl who had been effectively rejected by her parents (the mother suffering from a psychiatric condition). The local authority removed the child from the family home at the parents' request and decided to institute care order proceedings with a plan for adoption. When the child's aunt and uncle and the paternal grandparents learned of this plan, they vigorously opposed it and made their own bid to take over the care of the child. However, they felt frustrated by what they saw as the local authority's unhelpful attitude. They claimed that the child was being whisked away from her family and that the local authority was not properly considering their offer to take over her care. They were incensed that they were refused contact with her. They also became aware that as relatives they would have no right to be heard in either the care proceedings or any subsequent adoption proceedings (which would not be contested by the birth parents). In these circumstances they attempted to make the child a ward of court so that the High Court could give appropriate directions to the local authority. Unfortunately, they were prevented from doing so by both the Court of Appeal and the House of Lords on the grounds that the absence of consultation and participation rights for relatives in the care order and adoption legislation then in force had been deliberately brought about by Parliament. 'For better or for worse', said one of the judges, 'the only check which the legislature has thought fit to impose on the process is that of either obtaining consent from the parents, or satisfying the court that the case is one where the consent of the parents can be dispensed with.' This decision, which in policy terms was thoroughly retrograde, put the onus squarely on government to bring about necessary change and this was eventually achieved through the passage of the 1989 Act. The advances secured by the Children Act were as follows:

- A local authority looking after a child was now under a duty to make arrangements to enable the child to live with a parent *or relative*, unless that would not be reasonably practicable or consistent with his welfare (section 23(6)).
- Such a local authority was under a duty to endeavour to promote contact between the child and any relative, unless it was not

reasonably practicable or consistent with his welfare (Schedule 2, paragraph 15).

▪ Relatives were enabled to apply for contact orders and residence orders in respect of looked after children (sections 10 and 34). Permission to apply would normally have to be obtained, however, and where a relative sought permission to apply for a residence order, the court was required to have particular regard to the applicant's connection with the child and the local authority's plans for the child's future. This is the procedure that the relatives in *Re W* (above) would have used had the Children Act been in force in 1985.

Official guidance on the Children Act issued by the Department of Health sought to emphasise the role of the child's wider family in relation to care planning. Local authorities were told that 'the child's family, parents, grandparents and other relatives involved with the child should be invited to participate actively in planning and to make their views known'[21]. Possibilities for a child to be cared for within the extended family should, it was said, be investigated and considered as an alternative to the provision of accommodation by the authority and even where it became necessary for an authority to arrange the provision of accommodation, 'placement with a relative will often provide the best opportunities for promoting and maintaining family links in a familiar setting'[22]. The extent of the change brought about by the 1989 Act was illustrated by a case decided by the High Court in 1994, in which a maternal grandparent successfully applied for residence orders in respect of her two grandchildren, following the institution of care order proceedings by the local authority. The authority had planned adoption for the children. Mr Justice Hollis expressed the view that adoption should be regarded as a last resort (a view the Department of Health has come to reject, of course) and said that 'if there is a reasonable alternative within the family it should be taken'[23].

All of these developments were encouraging, and no doubt they had some effect on the ground. In some quarters, however, there remained serious doubts about the willingness of social services departments to work with relatives of looked after children, particularly in the context of adoption. For example, writing in 1994 the National Secretary of the Grandparents' Federation stated: 'Ours is a perspective which is rarely heard and we represent a group which is largely ignored by professionals as a placement resource or source of help for its children and young people when things go wrong in their immediate families.'[24] For its part, the Department of Health reiterated the need to have regard to the extended family's contribution to children's welfare. In its adoption circular of 1998, it addressed the issue of adoption plans within care order proceedings and declared that before reaching a decision that adoption should be the principal aim of a care plan, 'local authorities and approved adoption agencies must be satisfied that sufficient assessment has taken place to rule out rehabilitation or placement with relatives, for example, under a section 8 residence order'[25]. Three years later, in its draft Practice Guidance on the National Adoption Standards, the Department sought to convey a similar message:

> Before reaching a decision that adoption should be pursued councils should have considered, and if possible provided, services that would enable reunification with the birth family and made positive efforts to identify and support any relative or friend of the child's family who is a fit person to care for a child and can provide a permanent home.[26]

The effect of the 2002 Act

In its evidence to the House of Commons committee considering the Adoption and Children Bill, the Family Rights Group proposed that the new legislation should contain an explicit statement that 'kinship placements ought to be the placement of first choice for children who cannot live with their birth parents'. Such a provision, by virtue of its legal standing, would have considerably strengthened the messages already contained in the Department of Health's guidance documents. Finding an appropriate form of words would not have been easy, however, and it is not surprising that the proposal was not taken up. Instead, section 1(4)(f) of the Act directs agencies and courts, when coming to an adoption decision, to have regard to the child's relationships with relatives. (As was pointed out earlier, this provision also applies to unmarried fathers.) Also of significance is section 1(6), which requires agencies and courts to consider the whole range of powers available to them in the child's case, whether under the 2002 Act itself or the Children Act. One particular power which might be useful where a relative is fighting an adoption plan is the power of the court to make a residence order in the relative's favour. Section 10 of the Children Act enables the court to do this in adoption (or care) proceedings on its own initiative in the absence of a formal application by the relative in question. It goes without saying, however, that before a court can take this sort of initiative, someone needs to inform it of the existence of the relative and their willingness to assume permanent care of the child. It cannot be assumed that relatives will always push themselves forward in children's litigation in which the birth parents are the principal parties. They may well be reluctant to interfere, hoping perhaps that the local authority's application for a care order or a placement order will fail on other grounds. They may not even have thought through alternative care proposals while the parents are engaged in their own legal contest. Provided it is taken seriously by practitioners, section 1(4)(f) of the 2002 Act should help in bringing the wider family perspective to the court's attention.

A rather different problem may arise where a looked after child is placed with parental consent under section 19. No court order is needed for this and there is a danger that the voice of concerned relatives will go unheard. Section 1(4)(f) does apply to adoption agencies as well as courts, so agency workers should be looking at the position of relatives even in cases where an adoption placement is agreed with the birth parents. But what if the parents are opposed to the involvement of relatives? What if they object to relatives even being told of the adoption plan? In Chapter 6 of this book there is described the case of Re R[27], in which a mother was flatly opposed to her siblings being contacted either by the local authority or by the child's guardian ad litem. The High Court declined to order disclosure of the freeing proceedings to them. However, the case was one of baby relinquishment and the court emphasised that its ruling turned very much on the facts. It is not therefore directly transferable to the more typical looked after case where a child has entered the care system as a result of shortcomings in the standard of parental care. Given the court's acknowledgement in Re R that 'it is clearly an especially grave matter to interfere with the right to respect for family life without first informing the extended family of [the child's] existence and investigating whether they could care for [him]', and its declaration that 'there should normally be wide consultation with, and consideration of, the extended family', it is suggested that the scope for a parental veto in looked after cases is very small.

The Making of the Adoption Order

An adoption order in respect of a looked after child can be made by a court only following an application made by the prospective adopters. Such an application can be made only after the child has been living with the prospective adopters for ten weeks (section 42(2)). Throughout that so-called probationary period, the prospective adopters will have had parental responsibility for the child (section 25(3)) and this will have been shared with the local authority and the relevant birth parents. The local authority is required to submit to the court a report on the suitability of the applicants and on any other matters relevant to the operation of the section 1 welfare considerations (section 43). Those welfare considerations have to be taken into account by the court when arriving at its decision. If a birth parent with parental responsibility wishes to oppose the making of the adoption order, they will need to show a change of circumstances since the making of the placement order or the giving of consent to placement (section 47(7)). Even if they are given permission to oppose, their consent to adoption can be dispensed with (section 47(2)).

The Adoption Law Review of 1992 floated the idea of adoption orders being made in certain circumstances without a full court hearing:

> Where no relevant person is contesting an adoption and there are no other disputed issues relating to it, we consider it an inappropriate use of court time, whether or not there has been a pre-placement hearing, to require a hearing before an adoption order can be made. The court must still consider the written evidence and reach a decision as to whether an order can be made, but without the parties being invited to attend. Consideration should be given to providing for some other means of marking the occasion for the child and the adopters.[28]

There was a further proposal that birth parents should not be parties to an adoption order application when their consent had previously been dispensed with at a placement order hearing. Two separate issues are at stake here. One relates to the opportunity to be given to birth parents and relatives to voice their opinions at the point when their legal relationship with the child is being extinguished. These opinions will not necessarily concern the making of the adoption order itself – the birth family may be resigned to that. They may, however, concern future contact provision. It is unrealistic to expect contact plans made at the beginning of an adoption placement (perhaps following a contested placement order application) to remain viable for all time in every case

because the child's needs may well change, particularly when the probationary period is lengthy. The views of the child himself may change. Dispensing with a court hearing at the final stage of the adoption process would make it more difficult for these important matters to be ventilated. Linking the need for a hearing with the existence of a disputed issue, as the Adoption Law Review recommended, would give rise to potentially difficult questions, such as the meaning of 'disputed' in this context and the allocation of responsibility for detecting a 'dispute'. Fixing a hearing in every case avoids these problems and gives birth family members an opportunity as well as a deadline. A second issue relates to the ceremonial aspect of the process: the marking of the transfer of parenthood, and everything that flows from that, by the physical presence of the new legal family in the courtroom at the critical point.

Both of these considerations point firmly towards the retention of the requirement of a proper court hearing, and the 2002 Act has been drafted on this basis. Although the detailed procedure for the making of adoption orders will be regulated by government rules (just as it was under the Adoption Act 1976), the Act itself contains two sets of provisions that bear on this matter. Firstly, section 141 (the section that authorises the government to make procedural rules for adoption) states in subsection (3) that in the case of an application for an adoption order the rules must require a range of persons (including birth parents with parental responsibility) to be notified 'of the date and place where the application will be heard' and of the fact that they 'need not attend' unless the court requires it. The implication is that there will be a hearing in every case. The second set of provisions – contained in sections 26 and 46 – concern contact orders made at the same time as an adoption order. It is difficult to see how these provisions, which are examined below, could operate properly in the absence of a hearing.

Contact after Adoption

Introduction

Adoption with contact has become much more common. There has been little research into the extent but it is believed that at least 70 per cent of adopted children have some form of contact with members of their birth families. Contact may be direct, involving meetings and phone calls, or indirect, involving the exchange of occasional letters or information. Research evidence on the impact of contact on the outcomes of adoption is at present mixed and inconclusive.

These general – but very fair – observations on contact after adoption were made by the Performance and Innovation Unit in its report on adoption published in July 2000[29]. The Unit highlighted two key problems affecting local authorities: inconsistent practice ('the management of contact arrangements has developed on an ad hoc basis over the years and many local authorities depend upon the collective memories of social workers') and lack of expertise ('most social workers do not have sufficient skills or knowledge to be able to provide guidance to birth parents about what might be the most positive way to communicate'). Recommendations designed to rectify these and other problems followed.

The literature on contact after adoption and other forms of openness is formidable, and no attempt to review it will be made in this book. Detailed accounts of the various developments, and analysis of the arguments and counter-arguments, can be found elsewhere[30]. The emphasis here is on the legislation and related guidance.

Birth parents, grandparents and siblings

Although open adoption is often understood as involving contact between the child and a birth parent, it is important not to lose sight of the fact that contact with other birth relatives also occurs on a significant scale. Many combinations are possible in this context, ranging from contact with just one relative to contact with a large group. Sibling contact

has been a matter of particular concern. In its 2000 survey of local authority adoption services, the Social Services Inspectorate noted that many adoptive families were involved in contact, both direct and indirect, between siblings placed separately. The majority of children placed for adoption had siblings. According to the SSI 'this was an area poorly covered by policy, procedure and practice guidance'[31].

Formal and informal arrangements

It has always been possible for a court, when making an adoption order, to make a further order containing provisions for birth family contact. Prior to the Children Act 1989 this was done by attaching a special condition to the adoption order (a device created by section 12(6) of the Adoption Act 1976). After the 1989 Act, it was done by making a contact order, an outcome made possible by section 10 of that Act. These were formal arrangements, enforceable (in theory, at any rate) by heavy sanctions. They would be binding on the adoptive parents until such time as the court was persuaded to vary or revoke its order. In practice, formal contact provision was rarely made. As Triseliotis and his colleagues observed in 1997, 'the impression so far is that most contact arrangements in Britain are negotiated between the parties without resort to the courts'[32]. Informal arrangements have the obvious advantage of flexibility. They can be entered into, changed and cancelled at a moment's notice at the parties' discretion, with the adopters having the final say in cases involving young children. And it should be noted that once an adoption order is made, neither the court, nor the local authority, nor any other public agency has the power to stop the parties from making these contact arrangements, no matter how undesirable they are thought to be by the professionals.

The position of the local authority

Reference has already been made to Schedule 2, paragraph 15 of the Children Act, which requires a local authority looking after a child to endeavour to promote contact between the child and his parents and relatives, unless it is not reasonably practicable or consistent with his welfare. While this is an admirable provision, it has never made sense in cases where an adoption plan is being formulated by the authority. Although a child ceases to be looked after once an adoption order is made, paragraph 15 could be read as creating a presumption in favour of some form of openness *after* adoption. There is evidence to suggest that such an interpretation was indeed drawn by some adoption practitioners. This, however, was never the intention of the framers of the Act. What seems to have happened is that in the course of drafting paragraph 15 they simply overlooked the position of children who were being prepared for adoption (and, of course, the position of prospective adopters). This anomaly has finally been addressed in the 2002 Act. Section 53 enables the government to make regulations that will relieve local authorities of the paragraph 15 duty in relation to all looked after children whom they are authorised to place for adoption. 'Authorised to place' means authorised under section 19 (i.e. where the birth parents consent to an adoption placement) or authorised by a placement order. At these points in time, the general statutory obligation to promote family contact will cease. Instead, according to the Department of Health, guidance will be given to local authorities to deal with the contact issue on a case by case basis[33].

In fact, DH guidance on post-adoption contact has been around for some time. The issue was addressed, alongside other adoption matters, in a Social Services Inspectorate letter in 1996 and again in a circular in 1998[34]. The guidance contained in these documents was couched in suitably general, and therefore cautious, terms. It was emphasised that the purpose of contact is primarily for the benefit of the child, and that consequently contact should not be used as a bargaining tool to extract parental consent to adoption. It was pointed out that arrange-ments that tend to have the best chance of success are those which are mutually agreed between the parties and have the details set out and confirmed in writing. Authorities were reminded that sibling contact arrangements require very careful attention; and that some children find it difficult to express their desire for no contact through guilt or a misplaced sense of responsibility for their birth parents. A further opportunity to influence agency practice in this area arrived with the publication in 2001 of the National Adoption Standards. The document containing these Standards included a summary of a consultation exercise undertaken with 82 children and according to this, contact arrangements were identified as among the most important things that could be improved about adoption. Birth family contact was covered by Standards A10, A11, C4 and D7:

A10. The child's needs, wishes and feelings, and their welfare and safety are the most important concerns when considering links or contact with birth parents, wider birth family members and other people who are significant to them.

A11. Adoption plans will include details of the arrangements for maintaining links (including contact) with birth parents, wider birth family members and other people who are significant to the child and how and when these arrangements will be reviewed.

C4. Adoptive parents will be involved in discussions as to how they can best maintain any links, including contact, with birth relatives and significant others identified in the adoption plan.

D7. Where it is in the child's best interest for there to be ongoing links, including contact, with birth parents and families (including siblings separated by adoption), birth families will be involved in discussions about how best to achieve this and helped to fulfil agreed plans, e.g. through practical or financial support.

The draft Practice Guidance to Support the National Standards contained eight paragraphs devoted to planning and managing contact. Like the guidance of 1996 and 1998, its terms were neutral in so far as they suggested no presumption one way or the other: contact could be 'reassuring to give a child a strong link with their past by providing information about family members and their well being' but it could also be 'unsettling or even disturbing'.

The position of the adopters

The legal position of adoptive parents in relation to post-adoption contact is clear: in the absence of a formal contact order or a formal undertaking given by them to the court, they are under no obligation to allow the child contact with anyone. This is the inescapable result of the adopters receiving exclusive parental responsibility for the child. The fact that the adopters were recruited by the local authority on the understanding that some sort of contact would be facilitated by them is irrelevant; so is the fact that an understanding (including a written understanding) with the birth family was reached during their probationary period. These factors may heavily influence the way in which the adopters behave towards the birth family but as a matter of law they do not detract from the authority and discretion vested in them by the adoption order. Should the adopters renege on a pre-adoption agreement reached with a birth relative, the relative's legal remedy is to apply to the court for a contact order. Preliminary permission will be needed from the court, however (because after adoption the relative will in law be a stranger) and this will not be a straightforward matter. As is explained below, contact orders in adoption cases are not favoured by the judiciary.

Contact orders made by the court

As far as formal post-adoption contact provision under the 2002 Act is concerned, the starting point is section 46(6). This states that before making an adoption order the court must consider whether there should be arrangements for allowing any person contact with the child. For that purpose, the court must consider any existing or proposed arrangements and obtain any views of the parties to the proceedings. These obligations were not to be found in the previous legislation. Indeed, they were not contained in the original draft of the Adoption and Children Bill. However, they had been recommended by the Adoption Law Review in 1992, which pointed out that they would flow naturally from the proposed duty of the court (now effected by section 1(6) of the 2002 Act) to consider the whole range of powers available to it in the child's case. Because adoption proceedings are classed as 'family proceedings' for the purposes of the Children Act, section 8 contact orders under Part II of that Act can be made in those proceedings. Such orders are therefore clearly within the range of powers available to the adoption court.

It is important to note the limitations of section 46(6). It requires the court only to listen to the views of the parties regarding contact and to *consider* whether there should be 'arrangements' (which in this context must mean formal orders or else undertakings given to the court). It certainly does not require the court to make formal contact provision – not even at a minimal level. The court's discretion remains absolute, with no presumption in favour of an order. This is the case even where formal contact provision has been made by the court under section 26 of the Act to cover the prospective adopters' probationary period. If anything, there is a presumption of no order because under section 1(5) of the Children Act, the court is not to make a contact order unless it considers that doing so would be better for the child than making no order at all. Although it is impossible to be sure how section 46(6) will operate in practice, it is likely that the courts will pursue the same cautious approach to contact orders as they did under the Adoption Act 1976. The senior judiciary were acutely aware of the need to provide support to people who are adopting, especially in cases where the child has already experienced damaging episodes in his life. They stressed – as one judge put it – 'the importance of not interfering with the rights of the adopters, not placing constraints upon the adopters, not fettering them in the difficult task they have in integrating a child into their family'[35]. Whatever else a contact order does, one thing is certain: by imposing obligations on the adopters, it serves to limit their exercise of parental responsibility. Their autonomy is not total. Furthermore, and crucially, the limitation will remain in place until the child is 16 unless the contact order is varied or revoked by the court. Although the child may express clear views about birth family contact as the final adoption hearing approaches, those views are liable to change significantly as the months and years go by. If this happens, and the original contact arrangements have been embedded in a court order, the adoptive parents may find it necessary to return to court to obtain a formal variation. Such a variation application could be contested vigorously by the birth relative whose contact rights stand to be reduced or extinguished. For all these reasons, the courts refused to embrace post-adoption contact orders with enthusiasm. They were firmly disinclined to impose them on unwilling adopters. Few were therefore made. None of the considerations that led to this sceptical approach has been invalidated by the passage of the 2002 Act. Consequently, it is unlikely that section 46(6) will bring about a significant increase in the number of orders. It must be emphasised that this does not mean that birth relatives will be marginalised – their position in the legal proceedings has actually been enhanced by section 46(6). Rather, it means that their 'entitlement' to contact will usually have to flow from informal arrangements negotiated (or re-negotiated) with the local authority and the adopters against the background of the National Adoption Standards. Section 46(6) – like section 27(4) which deals with contact after placement orders – may result in more such negotiations taking place.

Support for Adoptive Parents and Grandparents

Introduction

Giving evidence to the House of Commons during proceedings on the Adoption and Children Bill, a Department of Health official offered this view of the Bill's adoption support provisions:

> One of the strong messages to come through our consultation was the need to provide adoptive families with effective support in helping them to cope with their multiple needs, and also a mechanism to try and join up the various public services who could be relevant in the situation. Adoptive families told us they are almost having to fight against the system to get access and assessment. The Bill helps to tackle that.[36]

The less than perfect picture of existing support services provided in this statement would have occasioned no surprise within adoption agencies because alarming variations in the levels of service provision had been widely documented[37]. To a government anxious to increase the number of adoptions from care, to increase the recruitment rate of prospective adopters, and to reduce the rate of placement breakdown, the need to address the issue of support services was therefore both obvious and substantial. Although resources and training are the most important factors here, the legal framework clearly has a role to play and while the Adoption Act 1976 was not silent on adoption support, its provisions were regarded as weak. Consequently, new statutory rules have been introduced to operate alongside the National Adoption Standards.

The National Adoption Standards

Children interviewed in connection with the Standards identified post-adoption support as one of the most important things that could be improved about adoption. According to the Department of Health, they said that more clearly defined support should be provided, including continuing social worker contact, a chance to meet with other adoptive families and children, a telephone helpline and counselling, help with finding out life history, financial support, family support and help with school-related issues (particularly bullying). With this in mind the Government issued the following Standards:

A12. Children are entitled to support services that meet their assessed needs. These include advice and counselling, health, education, leisure and cultural services, and practical and financial help when needed. Information from agency records will be made available to the child when they are of an age and level of understanding to comprehend it.

C3. There will be access to a range of multi-agency support services before, during and after adoption. Support services will include practical help, professional advice, financial assistance where needed and information about local and national support groups and services.

C6. Adoptive parents whose adopted child has decided to explore their birth heritage will be supported to deal with the impact of this decision.

C7. Where there are difficulties with the placement or the adoption breaks down the agencies involved will co-operate to provide support and information to the adoptive parents and the child without delay.

The draft Practice Guidance to Support the National Adoption Standards addressed the implications of these provisions. It pointed out that 'the complexity of children's needs, the impact of any previous neglect or maltreatment, and the interaction with the adoptive parents' patterns and ways of managing these difficulties, may threaten placements whatever services have been made available'[38].

Provisions of the 2002 Act

In its white paper of December 2000, the Government promised to support a 'better deal' for adopters. It undertook to introduce new legislation as follows[39]:

- Give all families adopting children, especially those who have been looked after, a new right to an assessment by their council for post-placement support. They will be able to request an assessment at any stage after the placement has been identified.
- Place a clear duty on local social services authorities to provide post-adoption support, including financial support, planned jointly with local education authorities and the NHS, and any other relevant agencies. This support will be available from the time a placement is made, for as long as it is needed.

It has been questioned whether the terms of the 2002 Act actually reflect this undertaking. The key provisions on adoption support, which are to be found in sections 3 and 4, have already been described in Chapter 4 of this book. As is explained there, these sections create only a bare framework for service provision with the detail to be added by government regulations. What is clear, however, is that while section 4 implements the white paper undertaking to give adoptive parents a right to an assessment – and the importance of this new entitlement should not be underestimated – it conspicuously fails to give them a right to receive support. Section 4(4) states that where, as a result of an assessment, a local authority decides that a person has needs for adoption support services, it must then decide *whether to provide* any such services to that person. The local authority therefore retains a discretion in the matter. It is not difficult to see why the Act is framed in this way. Creating an absolute statutory duty to provide support services could have significant resource implications for some authorities and it would place adopted children (and adopted adults) and their adoptive and birth families in a special position compared to others seeking help from authorities. On the other hand, leaving authorities with a mere discretion could be said to devalue the new right to an assessment and to run the risk of perpetuating what has been described, by the Government itself, as the postcode lottery in service provision. This point was forcefully put to the Government throughout the passage of the Bill. Adoption UK, representing the interests of adoptive families, said: 'Our 30 years experience of supporting adoptive families has shown us that they need access to the actual provision of support post-placement and post-adoption, not simply an assessment to determine the nature of that support. This aspect of the Bill will not encourage potential adoptive parents to come forward to be considered for the range of children who most need new families here and now.'[40] It was said that the terms of section 4 were baffling and illogical, and that they would provide local authorities with an easy get-out; it was argued that from a purely economic point of view it was well worth forcing local authorities to spend relatively small sums up front in order to support adoptive placements, when the failure to provide support might mean placement breakdown and a (very expensive) return of a child to the care system; indeed, it was suggested that the 'unique public service' performed by adoptive parents justified the imposition of a duty. The Government, however, remained unpersuaded by these arguments. 'The problem of a statutory duty,' said one Department of Health minister, 'is that it would or could mean that adoption support services would be given priority over almost every other service provided by a local authority social services department.'[41] This was not to say that section 4 would be ineffective: according to the Government, 'it provides an extremely important step forward in enabling families and adopted children to access the necessary adoption support'[42]. It did not believe that local authorities would simply ignore assessments that were carried out. It drew attention to the increased funding supplied to local authorities to be used to expand post-adoption support services. And it pointed out that adopters who were dissatisfied with an authority's response to an assessment could invoke the authority's social services complaints procedure.

Regulations and guidance

The 2002 Act provides for the making of regulations covering the following matters:

- ▪ The meaning of 'adoption support services' (over and above counselling, advice and information).
- ▪ The range of people for whom support services must be provided.
- ▪ The range of people who are entitled to an assessment.
- ▪ The circumstances in which an adoption support plan is to be prepared.
- ▪ The assessment procedure.
- ▪ The procedure for preparing and reviewing an adoption support plan.
- ▪ The imposition of conditions on the adoptive parents.
- ▪ Out-of-area provision of support services.

In June 2002 the Department of Health began this secondary law-making process by issuing a consultation paper entitled *Providing Effective Adoption Support*. Although it gave very little away, the paper did contain some significant pointers:

- ▪ In relation to cross-authority support provision, the DH stated that as a general starting point it considered that it would be sensible for the placing authority to assess the child's needs and provide support services until the date of the adoption order. Thereafter, responsibility should, as a general rule, be transferred to the receiving authority.
- ▪ In relation to financial support, an overhaul of the adoption allowances arrangements was signalled. The DH said that authorities should be empowered to stipulate that financial support should be spent on specified items or services.
- ▪ Guidance and directions would be issued to education and health agencies to ensure co-ordinated planning and service provision.

However, those agencies would have to decide whether to provide services 'in accordance with the statutory framework under which they operate'. As with social services departments, no absolute duty to provide support would be imposed.

The paper also emphasised the need to place adoption support in a wider context, including the general 'children in need' provisions of the Children Act 1989. As it pointed out, 'there are very few services that are only applicable to adoption'[43]. Those affected by adoption must be assisted in accessing mainstream services.

Foster Carer Adoptions

According to government statistics, 432 children in England were adopted by their foster carers in the year ending 31 March 2001, 14 per cent of the total of adoptions from care. The average age of the children at the time of adoption was 5 years 10 months and the average duration of the final period of care preceding the adoption was 3 years 10 months[44]. As one would expect, these figures differ significantly from those pertaining to non-foster carer adoptions.

Where foster carers and their local authority jointly seek to turn a long-term foster placement into an adoptive one, the 2002 Act requires normal procedures to be followed. No special provision is made in the law, even though many of the features of these cases will be special (for example, the foster carers will have received professional training and will have established a close relationship with the local authority, no matching process or introductions will be needed, extensive information on the child and his history will already be known to the foster carers, and considerable birth family contact may well be ongoing). Although there is no 'placement' for adoption in the usual sense – because the child is in situ when he is 'matched' with the prospective adopters – the scheme of the 2002 Act requires there to be a placement and this has been achieved by giving that notion an extended meaning. Under section 18(5), references in the Act to an agency placing a child for adoption 'include, where it has placed a child with any persons (whether under this Act or not), leaving the child with them as prospective adopters'. Accordingly, once the local authority officially notifies the foster carers that the child is being 'left' with them as prospective adopters (rather than as foster carers) the adoption placement begins. However, because normal placement procedures have to be followed, this notification can occur only if the local authority has obtained formal parental consent under section 19 (witnessed by CAFCASS) or if it has obtained a placement order from the court (in a contested case). Until this point is reached, the placement is a foster placement under the Children Act 1989. Once it is reached, the foster carers/prospective adopters gain parental responsibility for the child in accordance with section 25 of the 2002 Act.

According to Standard B5 of the National Adoption Standards, foster carers who make a formal application to adopt children in their care will be entitled to the same information and preparation as other adopters and be assessed within four months. Where foster carers wish to adopt but fail to obtain the support of the local authority, any application they make to the court will necessarily be on a non-agency basis. The relevant rules are described in Chapter 8 of this book.

Notes

1. *Guardian*, 1 May 2002.
2. DH Circular LAC (98) 20.
3. *Hansard* (House of Commons), 26 March 2001, col 698.
4. David Davis MP, *Hansard* (House of Commons), 26 March 2001, col 735.
5. Alan Milburn MP, *Hansard* (House of Commons), 29 October 2001, col 649.
6. Alan Milburn MP, note 5 above, col 650.
7. Press Release 1999/0617 of 18 October 1999.
8. *Hansard* (House of Commons), 16 June 1999, col 352.
9. Emphasis added.
10. *Adopting Changes: Survey and Inspection of Local Councils' Adoption Services.* (DH, 2000), paras 1.3 and 1.12.

11. *Children Looked After by Local Authorities Year Ending 31 March 2001, England* (DH, 2002). The figures exclude agreed series of short-term placements.
12. Note 11 above.
13. Performance and Innovation Unit, *Prime Minister's Review of Adoption* (2000), para 3.9.
14. A reported example of such a case, concerning a child of six months, is *Re T* [1994] 1 FCR 663.
15. Note 13 above, paras 2.10 and 3.12. See also *Adopting Changes*, note 10 above, Chapter 3.
16. Note 13 above, para 2.11.
17. Schedule 1.
18. Schedule 2.
19. Note 2 above, para 8 (emphasis added).
20. Patricia Morgan, *Adoption and the Care of Children* (Institute of Economic Affairs Health and Welfare Unit, 1998), Chapter 15, arguing for 'controls to overcome the inertia and discretion of local authorities'. See also David Davis MP, 'Adopt them', *Guardian*, 20 October 1999.
21. Examples include *Re B* [1993] 1 FCR 363 and *F v Lambeth LBC* [2001] 3 FCR 738.
22. Chapter A, para 5.
23. *Children Adopted from Care in England 2000/2001* (DH, 2001), Table 2.
24. Memorandum submitted to the Select Committee on the Adoption and Children Bill (April 2001).
25. Note 2 above, para 7.
26. *Adoption Now: Messages from Research* (DH, 1999), page 3. See also *Adopting Changes*, note 10 above, para 3.9.
27. David Davis MP, *Hansard* (House of Commons), 26 March 2001, col 740.
28. HC (1997–1998) 319, paras 148–9.
29. See, for example, Julian Brazier MP, *Hansard* (House of Commons), 16 June 1999, col 350: 'the evidence points to the overriding need to break the anti-adoption culture among social workers in many local authorities' and 'A policy to adopt' (editorial), *Daily Telegraph*, 24 March 1998, referring to 'local authorities' hostility to adoption, which is seen as a cynical method of redistributing children from the poor to the middle class'.
30. See, for example, Frances Rickford, 'For all they care', *Guardian*, 11 May 1994.
31. Note 13 above, para 3.33.
32. Note 23 above.
33. Note 10 above, para 7.13.
34. Note 10 above, para 7.24.
35. [2002] 2 FCR 133.
36. This was brought about by the local authority's original strategy of freeing the child for adoption.
37. Section 1(2).
38. Section 1(3).
39. Section 1(4).
40. Section 1(5).
41. Note 2 above, para 21.
42. National Adoption Standards, Response to the consultation exercise. See also the white paper *Adoption: a new approach*, Cmnd 5017 (December 2000), paras 6.3–6.5; and DH Circular LAC (2001) 33, paras 14–18 (the Adoption Recruitment Toolkit).
43. Emphasis added.
44. Note 13 above, para 3.108.
45. Circular LAC (2001) 22, para 3.
46. *Hansard* (House of Commons), 21 December 2000, col 581.
47. Note 42 above, para 4.16.
48. DH Circular LAC (2001) 33, para 4.
49. DH Press Release of 21 December 2001.
50. Note 10 above.
51. Para 7.15.
52. Note 13 above, para 5.10.
53. See, for example, 'Blair to help parents adopt', *Guardian*, 10 April 2000.
54. CI (2000) 7, para 3.9.
55. *Guardian*, 12 April 2000.
56. LAC (2001) 21 and LAC (2002) 5.
57. Circular LAC (2002) 5, para 9.
58. Robert Hughes MP, *Hansard* (House of Commons), 23 October 1989, col 566.
59. Julian Lewis MP, *Hansard* (House of Commons), 21 December 2000, col 589.
60. Barbara Tizard and Ann Phoenix, *Black, White or Mixed Race?* (Revised edition, 2002), page 77.
61. *Adoption: The Future,* Cmnd 2288 (November 1993), para 2.6.
62. *Hansard* (House of Commons), 3 November 1993, col 343.
63. Julian Brazier MP, *Hansard* (House of Commons), 26 March 2001, col 726.
64. David Hinchliffe MP, *Hansard* (House of Commons), 26 March 2001, col 725 (emphasis added).
65. Annex to SSI letter CI (2000) 7 (April 2000), paras 3.6 and 4.2; *Adopting Changes*, note 10 above, para 3.8.
66. *Adopting Changes*, note 10 above, paras 7.6 and 7.16.
67. *Adoption: a new approach*, note 42 above, para 6.4.
68. See, for example, June Thoburn, *Review of Research Relating to Adoption* (DH, 1990), Section 5; Alan Rushton and Helen Minnis, 'Annotation: Transracial Family Placements', *Journal of Child Psychology and Psychiatry*, Vol 38 No 2 (1997), page 147.
69. Rushton and Minnis, note 68 above.

70. SSI letter CI (90) 2; SSI letter CI (96) 4; Circular LAC (98) 20.
71. Note 13 above, para 3.114.
72. Paul Boateng, Health Minister, quoted in the *Times*, 29 August 1998.   He called for local authorities to show a more common sense approach.
73. Page 60 above.
74. Section 22(5)(c).
75. *Review of Adoption Law* (DH, 1992), para 27.2.
76. *Guardian*, 8 August 2001.
77. *Adoption Now*, note 26 above, pages 28–30; Susan Oliver, *Supporting the Adoptive Parents of Special Needs Children* (UEA Social Work Monograph No 183, 2000), pages 19–21.
78. *Hansard* (House of Commons), Special Standing Committee on the Adoption and Children Bill, 18 December 2001, col 720.
79. Note 2 above, para 42.
80. Chapter C, para 5.
81. *W v Essex County Council* [2000] 1 FCR 568.
82. *A and another v Essex County Council* [2002] EWHC 2707 (QB).
83. *Adoption Now*, note 26 above, pages 30–32.
84. Note 2 above, para 56.
85. *Adoption Now*, note 26 above, page 49.
86. *R v Legal Aid Board, ex parte W* [2000] 3 FCR 352.
87. [1988] 1 All ER 577.
88. [1993] 3 All ER 524.
89. Section 22(4)(b) of the 1989 Act.
90. This happened in the case of *Re U(T)* [1993] 2 FCR 565.
91. 'Caring concern', *Guardian*, 2 June 1989.
92. A case typifying the courts' unwillingness to interfere with placement for adoption is *Re W* [1979] 3 All ER 154, involving care orders made under the Children and Young Persons Act 1969.
93. Note 75 above, para 12.2.
94. Para 14.8.
95. *The BAAF Response to the Review of Adoption Law* (1993), page 6.
96. See, for example, Mary Ryan, 'Contested proceedings: justice and the law' in Murray Ryburn (Ed.) *Contested Adoptions: Research, Law, Policy and Practice* (1994), page 19.
97. Memorandum submitted by the National Organisation for the Counselling of Adoptees and Parents (NORCAP) to the House of Commons Select Committee on the Adoption and Children Bill (May 2001), para 4.7.
98. Jacqui Smith MP, *Hansard* (House of Commons), 16 May 2002, col 959.
99. Note 75 above, para 17.1.

1. Note 75 above, para 14.4.
2. *Placement for Adoption* (DH, 1994), para 4.30.
3. Note 75 above, para 12.5.
4. Lord Justice Cross in *Re W* [1970] 3 All ER 990.
5. Lord Justice Thorpe in *Re S* [2001] 3 FCR 375.
6. See page 43 above.
7. Lord Justice Thorpe in *Re F* [2000] 3 FCR 337, a sexual abuse case.
8. Lord Justice Balcombe in *Re C* [1994] 2 FCR 485.
9. Note 75 above, para 12.4.
10. *Re D* [2001] 1 FCR 501 (emphasis added).
11. Evidence given to the House of Commons Special Standing Committee on the Adoption and Children Bill, 20 November 2001 (Deborah Cullen).
12. *O'Connor v A and B* [1971] 2 All ER 1230.
13. See pages 38 and 46 above.
14. Section 22(4) and (5).
15. Section 34.
16. *Re H* [1991] 2 All ER 185.
17. *Re X* [2000] 1 FCR 379.
18. Section 18(7) of the Adoption Act 1976.
19. BAAF press release, 7 October 2000.
20. *Re W* [1985] 2 All ER 301.
21. *The Children Act 1989 Guidance and Regulations, Volume 3* (1991), para 2.49.
22. Para 3.33.
23. *Re H* [1994] 3 FCR 183.
24. Noreen Tingle, 'A view of wider family perspectives in contested adoptions' in Murray Ryburn (Ed.) *Contested Adoptions: Research, Law, Policy And Practice* (1994), page 175. The whole article repays reading.
25. Note 2, page 95 above, para 30.
26. Page 43.
27. [2001] 1 FCR 238. See page 40 above.
28. Note 75 above, para 15.6.
29. Note 13, page 96 above, para 3.141.
30. See, for example, the materials cited in Chapter 3 of this book.
31. Note 10, page 95 above, para 8.18.
32. John Triseliotis et al., *Adoption: Theory, Policy and Practice* (1997), page 90.
33. *Explanatory Notes on the Adoption and Children Bill* (2001), para 133.
34. CI (96) 4 and LAC (98) 20.
35. Lady Justice Butler-Sloss in *Re T* [1995] 2 FCR 537.
36. James Paton, oral evidence to the Select Committee on the Adoption and Children Bill, 24 April 2001.
37. See, for example, *Adoption Now*, note 26, page 96 above, Chapter 7; *Prime Minister's Review of*

Adoption, note 13, page 96 above, paras 3.117–3.135; *Adopting Changes*, note 10, page 95 above, Chapter 8.

38. Chapter C, para 20.
39. *Adoption: a new approach*, note 42, page 96 above, para 6.27.
40. Memorandum submitted by Adoption UK to the House of Commons Select Committee on the Adoption and Children Bill, para 4.5.4.

41. Lord Hunt, *Hansard* (House of Lords), 27 June 2002, col CWH 76.
42. Jacqui Smith MP, *Hansard* (House of Commons Special Standing Committee), 13 December 2001.
43. Para 6.
44. Note 23, page 96 above.

CHAPTER 8

Non–agency Domestic Adoption

Introduction

This chapter is concerned with all those adoption applications made in respect of UK-born children who have not been placed for adoption with the applicant(s) by an adoption agency. Such applications can be broken down into the following categories:

1. Applications by step-parents and other partners of birth parents.
2. Applications by relatives.
3. Applications by local authority foster carers in respect of a looked after child where the local authority has not supported the application.
4. Applications by private foster carers.

Several general comments may be made about these 'non-agency cases' (this expression now appears in the legislation itself, as a heading to sections 36–40 of the 2002 Act). Firstly, they received remarkably little attention during the passage of the 2002 Act. Debate was largely concentrated on the adoption of looked after children by people selected by an agency, and on intercountry adoption of children born abroad. These preoccupations may be contrasted with the situation preceding the enactment of the Children Act 1975, in which step-parent

adoption featured prominently. The low profile of non-agency adoption in 2001/2002 cannot be attributed to numerical insignificance: orders in favour of step-parents and relatives account for nearly half of all adoptions. Rather, it was a natural consequence of the Government's determination to improve the performance of local authorities (and their social workers) and to improve the life prospects of damaged children in care.

Secondly, non-agency cases tend to involve children whose profile is very different from the profile of children placed by an agency. With the exception of local authority foster children, they are very unlikely to have experienced significant shortcomings in care offered by their birth parents. Indeed, step-parent applications will by definition concern children who are still living with one parent (invariably the mother). These children will in all probability never have been in the care system. Their parents will not be 'known' to the social services department (a factor that has on occasion provoked antagonism towards social workers who have the job of preparing a welfare report for the court). Thirdly, the overwhelming majority of step-parent and relative adoptions are – like baby relinquishments – uncontested. It was probably this factor that led the Performance and Innovation Unit to describe step-parent adoptions as 'straightforward' and 'simpler'[1]. Fourthly, the failure of the prospective adopters to secure an adoption order does not mean that they will lose the child. On the contrary, the child will probably stay put. As the Adoption Law Review put it in 1992: 'In a non-agency application, the main question at issue is not whether the child will continue to live in the family of the would-be adopters but whether he or she will live there as an adopted child, as a child subject to a different order, or under the existing arrangements.'[2]

Residence Orders and Special Guardianship Orders under the Children Act 1989

The object of an adoption application in a non-agency case is to create a secure legal relationship between the applicant and a child for whom the applicant has been caring for a considerable period. It needs to be borne in mind, however, that an adoption order is not the only court order which will have this effect. Under Part II of the Children Act 1989, step-parents, relatives and foster carers are able to apply for a residence order in respect of the child they are looking after. Such an order will have the effect of conferring parental responsibility on the applicant and a legal relationship with the child will accordingly arise. To this extent, therefore, a residence order is an alternative to an adoption order in all non-agency cases (just as it is in agency cases) and it is perfectly legitimate to consider whether such an order would be more appropriate to the child's circumstances. The legal consequences of an adoption order are described in Chapter 2 of this book and the statutory provisions and reported cases cited there make it very clear that in terms of security and permanence the benefits flowing from a residence order fall considerably short of those offered by adoption. This is not to say that a residence order will always be a poor second best in a non-agency adoption application. Rather, its limitations need to be appreciated and weighed in the balance. What is most important is that applicants are provided with

a complete explanation of what is available to them under the legislation. When the draconian nature of adoption is spelt out, and the possible effects on the child are considered, it may be possible to persuade them that a residence order, or perhaps a special guardianship order as described in the Appendix below, would be more suitable and realistic. This will be a key issue for local authority social workers when compiling – as they have to do – a report for the court.

The Role of the Local Authority

Where the child is being cared for by foster carers, the local authority will already have supervisory obligations under the Children Act. In all non-agency adoption cases, however, there is an obligation on the part of the proposed adopters to serve on the authority notice of intention to adopt. This is governed by section 44 of the 2002 Act, which largely repeats the previous law. The notice must be given not more than two years, or less than three months, before the adoption application is filed with the court. On receipt of the notice, the local authority must arrange for the investigation of the matter and submit to the court a report of the investigation. The investigation must, so far as is practicable, address the suitability of the proposed adopters and any other matters relevant to the operation of the section 1 welfare considerations.

Removal of the Child before the Adoption Hearing

In cases involving relatives, local authority foster carers and private foster carers, it is possible that the initiation of adoption proceedings (e.g. the serving of notice of intention to adopt on the local authority) will trigger vigorous opposition on the part of a birth parent. Such a parent may attempt to frustrate the adoption plan by removing the child from the placement. The special provisions on this issue, contained in sections 36–40 of the 2002 Act, are considered below in relation to each type of applicant.

Applications by Step-Parents

Although one would never guess it from recent government literature or the debates surrounding the 2002 Act, step-parent adoption remains a problematic issue for many people. Concerns have been expressed over the years by members of the judiciary, by the Adoption Law Review of 1992[3] and by British Agencies for Adoption and Fostering[4]. These concerns relate not to the creation of a secure legal relationship between step-parent and child, which is seen as generally beneficial, but to the extinguishment of the child's legal relationship with one half of his birth family. According to the Adoption Law Review: 'There may be circumstances in which this is appropriate, for instance where the other parent has never acted in a parental capacity and the child has never really known any member of that side of the birth family. But where the child has some relationship with the parent, or with his or her relatives, it is unlikely to be in the child's interests for their legal relationship to be extinguished.'[5] The Review went on to say that in many circumstances a residence order was likely to be a better way of confirming a step-parent's responsibility for a child. It also suggested that fewer inappropriate adoption applications might be made if step-parents were able to acquire parental responsibility through a written agreement made with the birth parents, a recommendation taken up by the Government and now enshrined in section 112 of the 2002 Act. In fact section 112 goes further, by enabling a step-parent to apply for a parental responsibility order from the court. This is designed for cases in which the non-residential birth parent refuses to join in an agreement. It follows from all this that step-parents who wish to obtain some sort of legal recognition of their role now have the following options:

1. A parental responsibility agreement.
2. A parental responsibility order.
3. A residence order.
4. An adoption order.

It remains to be seen whether these legislative changes bring about a reduction in the number of adoptions by step-parents. In those cases where adoption is pursued, some special rules will apply:

- The application cannot be lodged with the court until the step-parent has looked after the child for six months (section 42(3)).
- The application will be made in the sole name of the step-parent. It is no longer necessary for the step-parent's spouse to join in the application.

Most step-parent applications are made by step-fathers rather than step-mothers. Whether or not the formal consent of the non-residential birth father is required will depend on whether he holds parental responsibility for the child. However, even an unmarried father who lacks parental responsibility will be entitled to put forward his views on adoption. It has been said that in the context of step-parent applications, the position of such a father must be evaluated on a wide spectrum: 'There will be cases in which the natural father will have very little merit and, accordingly, very little entitlement to consideration. At the other end of the scale, there will be cases in which the natural father should be given what will be something akin to the statutory right [of veto].'[6] If the father is determined to play a central role in the adoption proceedings, he should apply for a parental responsibility order and/or a contact order under the Children Act. If he does this, it is likely that all the applications will be consolidated and heard by the same court at the same time. If the father is granted a parental responsibility order, an adoption order cannot be made unless the court is prepared to dispense with his consent on one of the statutory grounds. In a 1998 case the Court of Appeal noted that where a father with parental responsibility opposes adoption by a step-parent, it is 'comparatively unusual' for an adoption order to be made[7].

Applications by Other Partners of Birth Parents

The 2002 Act has brought into existence the legal category of 'a partner of a parent'. Step-parents, of course, meet this description but so do partners who are not married to a child's birth parent. Following Parliament's decision to allow unmarried couples to make a joint application to adopt (a matter explored in Chapter 9 of this book) the Government concluded that it was appropriate to follow through the logic of that decision in relation to step-parent applications. The result is that the 2002 Act enables adoption applications to be brought by persons who are, in effect, unmarried step-parents, on the same basis as true step-parents. These are 'partners of parents'. According to section 144(7), a person is the partner of a child's parent if the person and the parent are a couple but the person is not the child's parent; and according to section 144(4), a couple means (a) a married couple, or (b) two people (whether of different sexes or the same sex) living as partners in an enduring family relationship. In this rather convoluted fashion, the notion of a 'step-parent adoption' has been extended. This is a remarkable development, given the fact that at one time the prohibition of step-parent adoption was on the agenda. It should be noted, however, that although the rules for step-parents, described earlier, apply to other 'partners of parents', the parental responsibility provisions of section 112 do not. They apply only to true step-parents.

Applications by Relatives

Adoption by relatives has also been controversial. The Adoption Law Review identified two major concerns: the prospect of the child suffering as a result of losing his legal relationship with one half of his birth family, as in step-parent adoptions, and the distortion of natural relationships (for example, birth mother becoming sister of the child when a maternal grandparent adopts). This second factor, which is peculiar to relative adoptions, was considered liable to cause identity problems for the child, particularly if he discovers the truth about his parentage late in the day. The Review acknowledged the need of some relative-carers to obtain legal confirmation of their relationship with the child but it thought that a residence order would usually suffice for this purpose. Cases where adoption might be appropriate were said to include those where the child's birth parents were dead and those where the parents were living abroad in circumstances which made it unlikely that they would be able to exercise parental responsibility in the future. The Review was clear that adoption should not be used merely to protect a relative against removal of the child by a birth parent. Since the publication of the Review, and under Part 2 of the 2002 Act, special guardianship orders, described in the Appendix below, have become available to relative-carers and these too will need to be considered as alternatives to adoption orders. The following special rules apply to adoption applications made by relatives:

- The application cannot be lodged with the court until the relative has looked after the child for three years out of the last five, unless the court grants permission for an earlier application (section 42(5) and (6)). This represents a major change in the law: under the Adoption Act 1976, relatives needed to show a minimum care period of only 13 weeks. Where the three-year condition is not met, any notice of intention to adopt under section 44 will be ineffective unless the court has granted permission for an early adoption application (section 44(4)).
- If a birth parent wishes to frustrate the proposed adoption by removing the child from the relative's care, the restrictions contained in sections 36–40 will need to be borne in mind. Under section 37, once an adoption application has been lodged with the court, the parent cannot remove

the child without the leave of the court. Under section 40, the same restriction applies once the relative has given notice of intention to adopt to the local authority (or has sought the leave of the court to make an early adoption application). The protection to the relative afforded by the notice of intention to adopt lasts for four months and there are special provisions preventing the giving of repeated notices as a device to retain care of the child (section 36(2)). Breach of these rules by a parent will result in criminal liability (section 36(6)). Quite apart from these provisions, security of the child's placement can be achieved by a relative-carer in the period prior to adoption through a residence order under the Children Act 1989. A residence order will automatically have the effect of prohibiting removal of the child by a parent; it will also confer parental responsibility on the relative.

If the adoption application is opposed by a birth parent who has parental responsibility, the relative will have to invite the court to dispense with the parent's consent on one of the statutory grounds.

Applications by Local Authority Foster Carers

Two features of these applications need to be noted at the outset. First, they relate to children in the care system. These children will be 'looked after' by the local authority either under a care order or on a voluntary basis under section 20 of the Children Act 1989, and their placement with the foster carer will be tightly regulated by the 1989 Act and the regulations made under it. Second, these applications are 'non-agency' because the local authority is not prepared to support an adoption application made by the foster carer (even if it would support an application made by someone else). Indeed, the local authority may be on the point of terminating the foster placement and removing the child. This leads on to a further point: allowing foster carers a

wide open route to adoption could undermine the basis on which support services (including accommodation) are provided to birth families by social services departments. For these reasons, it is thought right to erect appropriate obstacles in the path of local authority foster carers who choose to go it alone by making a bid for adoption. Exactly the same thinking was behind the restrictions imposed by the Children Act 1989 on residence order applications by foster carers.

The following special rules apply to adoption applications made by local authority foster carers:

- The application cannot be lodged with the court until the foster carer has looked after the child for one year, unless the court grants permission for an earlier application (section 42(4) and(6)). Where the one-year condition is not met, any notice of intention to adopt under section 44 will be ineffective unless the court has granted permission for an early adoption application (section 44(4)).
- Removal of the child from the foster carer after adoption has been signalled is a complex matter. This is for two reasons. First, removal may be desired either by a birth parent or by the local authority. Second, the legal positions of the parents and the local authority will vary depending on whether the child is in compulsory care or accommodated on a voluntary basis (section 20(8) of the Children Act gives a parent with parental responsibility the right to remove an accommodated child from the accommodation without notice). Under section 37, once an adoption application has been lodged with the court, lawful removal of the child can be effected only by a person who has the leave of the court or by a local authority (or the police) acting in pursuance of a statutory power (e.g. on child protection grounds under an emergency protection order). The parental right to remove an accommodated child is taken away in these circumstances. Section 38 deals with the earlier period, following the giving of notice of intention to adopt

to the local authority. If the foster carer has cared for the child for at least five years, the restrictions on removal are the same as under section 37 (above). If the foster carer has cared for the child for at least one year, the restrictions on removal are also as under section 37, except that in addition a parent with parental responsibility may remove an accommodated child. Finally, section 38 also deals with cases where the foster carer has to apply to the court for permission for an early adoption application under section 42(6) (i.e. before the one-year point). Here, the restrictions on removal pending the disposal of the application are as under section 37. Where, in accordance with these provisions, a local authority applies to the court for leave to remove a child from a foster carer, the court will have to take account of the welfare considerations contained in section 1 of the 2002 Act. These are made applicable by section 1(7)(b). In a case decided under the equivalent provisions of the Adoption Act 1976, the Court of Appeal stated that on an application for leave to remove, the judge should consider – among other things – the prospects of the foster carer ultimately obtaining an adoption order[8].

■ If the adoption application is opposed by a birth parent who has parental responsibility, the foster carer will have to invite the court to dispense with that parent's consent.

■ If the application is opposed by the local authority that opposition will be brought to the attention of the court through the authority's welfare report.

Applications by Private Foster Carers

The special rules applicable to private foster carer applications are the same as those applicable to relatives' applications.

Notes

1. *Prime Minister's Review of Adoption* (2000), paras 7.21 and 8.11.
2. *Review of Adoption Law* (DH, 1992), para 24.1.
3. Note 2 above, Chapter 19.
4. *The BAAF Response to the Review of Adoption Law* (1993), page 26.
5. Note 2 above, para 19.2.
6. Lord Justice Thorpe in *Re G* [1999] 1 FCR 482.
7. *Re B* [1999] 3 FCR 522.
8. *Re C* [1994] 2 FCR 839.

CHAPTER 9

Eligibility to Adopt

Introduction

Legal rules on eligibility tend to be absolute. There is little room for discretion. Either one is eligible for something or one is not. Adoption, of course, is a highly discretionary process but the discretion – both at agency level and court level – arises only after eligibility has been established. A person who is caring for a child but who is not eligible to adopt is obliged to look at other devices (orders under the Children Act 1989, for example) in order to give the placement a measure of security. A person who is eligible to adopt, and who wishes to adopt, is faced with the task of convincing the court – and an adoption agency – of their suitability. The rules relating to eligibility to adopt in England and Wales have always been fairly straightforward. The relevant legislation has been brief. This was set to be the case with the Adoption and Children Act too, because the initial text of the Bill, presented to Parliament in the autumn of 2001, largely repeated the previous law. The eligibility provisions, however, proved to be the most fiercely contested, and the most misunderstood, parts of the Bill and the final text of the 2002 Act contains a new code that can legitimately be described as revolutionary.

The Position Prior to the 2002 Act

Before the 2002 Act, eligibility to adopt was governed by sections 14 and 15 of the Adoption Act 1976. These sections drew a distinction between single adopters and joint adopters. All adopters had to be over 21 (except in step-parent cases) and domiciled in a part of the UK or the Channel Islands or the Isle of Man. Joint adopters had to be married. Single adopters could be unmarried or married, but if they were married the court would have to be shown that the applicant's spouse could not be found or that the two spouses were living apart or that the applicant's spouse was incapable of adopting for reasons of ill-health. These provisions, which originated in the Children Act 1975, were completely uncontroversial when they were enacted. In the years that followed, however, developments occurred that served to expose what some saw as gaps:

- Cohabitation, and therefore birth, outside marriage increased. By the year 2000, 39 per cent of children born in England and Wales were born outside marriage. 63 per cent of births outside marriage were registered by both parents who were recorded as living at the same address[1].

- Social attitudes towards homosexuality were transformed.
- The adoption of children from local authority care was promoted.

The confluence of these factors had the following results. People living together outside marriage – whether in a heterosexual or in a homosexual relationship – came forward in increasing numbers expressing an interest in adopting a child from care. They had to be told that, while one of them could apply for an adoption order, they could not make a joint application. If adoption was pursued, they would both go through the approval and matching process arranged by the agency, but when it came to the filing of an application with the court, only one of them would proceed. That party, and that party alone, would obtain an order and emerge as the child's (sole) legal parent. The other party would no doubt become a psychological parent to the child, but not a legal one. The most that the non-adopting party could expect was a residence order under the Children Act 1989, held jointly with the adopter. Such an outcome became available in 1995, following a decision of the High Court[2]. A residence order did have the beneficial effect of giving parental responsibility to the non-adopting party but in the circumstances it was a limited and artificial device. Inevitably, it served to bring the law into disrepute.

The law's discrimination against unmarried couples was felt by local authorities anxious to recruit adopters for looked after children. In evidence to the House of Commons during the passage of the Adoption and Children Bill, the Local Government Association stated as a fact that 'unmarried couples are deterred from adopting because they cannot apply jointly'[3]. And in relation to the adoption order/residence order arrangement referred to above, BAAF stated as a fact that 'children's organisations tell us that children find it difficult to perceive the logic by which they have got a real mum and a dad who has got, if you like, some kind of custody order…rather than a legal and forever adoption'[4].

The Labour Government's Original Position

When the initial draft of the Adoption and Children Bill was published in March 2001, it was clear that the Government intended to make no great changes in the eligibility rules. Provision was now made for sole applications by step-parents, and habitual residence in Britain was made an alternative qualification criterion to domicile. But there was to be no alteration in the rules governing joint applications. Introducing the Bill to the House of Commons, the Minister for Health said:

> We are not making any changes to who may adopt. As now, single people may adopt and, as the Adoption Law Review recommended, only married couples may adopt jointly. That is absolutely right.[5]

As this statement indicates, the Government in proposing no change on joint applications was faithfully following the recommendations made in 1992 by the Adoption Law Review. That Review had argued for continued discrimination against unmarried couples on three policy grounds[6]:

- Unmarried parents do not have the same legal obligations to one another as a married couple have. Should the relationship break down, the caring parent may be less financially secure than if they were married.
- However great the commitment of unmarried adoptive parents to a child might be, it is open to question how far their wider families would be willing to accept that child as part of their family.
- The security and stability which adopted children need are more likely to be provided by parents who have made a publicly recognised commitment to their relationship and who have legal responsibilities towards each other.

This argument was made in the full knowledge that adoption orders would continue to be made in favour of sole applicants who were cohabiting with a partner. It may be the case that even by 1992, British society was not yet ready to accept a liberalisation of the law in this area. In any event, the Adoption Law Review's recommendation chimed with the 'family values' being promoted by the Conservative government and in that respect it was scarcely surprising. By 2001, however, it was more difficult to defend, especially now that there was a drive to increase the number of adoptions from care. Critics (led by BAAF, which had never agreed with the Adoption Law Review on this issue) were able to point to the serious anomalies inherent in the existing law:

■ Unmarried partners were already allowed to look after a child under an adoption order made in favour of one of them.
■ They were already allowed to look after a child under a joint residence order.
■ They were already allowed to look after a child as local authority foster carers.
■ They were already allowed to look after a child as private foster carers.

In addition, they would in future be allowed to look after a child under a joint special guardianship order. On top of this was the wave of evidence now coming from child care organisations to the effect that the existing law was deterring suitable adopters from coming forward. This last factor appears to have been crucial and by the time the second draft of the Adoption and Children Bill emerged in October 2001, the Government's line had softened. What had been 'absolutely right' seven months earlier was now only 'broadly right', according to the Secretary of State for Health[7]. The Labour Party ended up giving its MPs a free vote on the issue. Most of them voted for change.

The Provisions of the 2002 Act

In examining the new provisions on eligibility, it is important to bear in mind their provenance. They are based on amendments to the Adoption and Children Bill proposed in May 2002 not by the Department of Health, but by

a backbench MP, David Hinchliffe. These amendments were designed to establish the principle of joint adoption applications made by unmarried couples. The Government's line was that if the House of Commons voted in favour of the amendments (which it did) it would propose a further batch of consequential amendments so as to make the rest of the Bill compatible. Its intention was to do this when the Bill reached the House of Lords. The House of Lords, however, voted to delete the Hinchliffe amendments and preserve the status quo, which rendered consequential amendments irrelevant. This led to the Bill being returned to the House of Commons – at the very end of the 2001–2002 Parliamentary Session – where the Hinchliffe amendments were restored and the Government's consequential amendments were finally proposed and made. The significance of this chronology is that the full details and effects of the new eligibility provisions were never debated, either in Parliament or outside. These provisions had not, of course, been in the Conservative government's draft Bill of 1996 (because the Conservative Party consistently opposed a change in the rules); and they were not in the Labour government's initial draft of the Adoption and Children Bill. The Parliamentary debates in 2002 – like the debates in the media – focused on the principle of the proposed code, not the detail. If the Labour government had been more decisive on this issue and made proposals of its own at an early stage, there would have been ample time for the thorough examination that was so obviously called for. In the event, the execution of this important reform was botched.

The eligibility provisions are contained in sections 49–51 of the 2002 Act. They are based on a distinction between applications made by 'a couple' and applications made by 'one person'.

Applications made by 'one person'

The rules are as follows:

■ The applicant must be domiciled in a part of the British Islands or, alternatively, must have been habitually resident in a part of the British Islands for at least one year (section 49).

■ The applicant must be over 21 (section 51(1)).

■ If the applicant is married then, unless it is a step-parent application, the court will have to be satisfied that the applicant's spouse cannot be found or that the spouses have separated on a permanent basis or that the applicant's spouse is incapable of making an application due to ill-health (section 51(3)).

Applications made by 'a couple'

The rules here are as follows:

■ One of the applicants must be domiciled in a part of the British Islands or, alternatively, both of the applicants must have been habitually resident in a part of the British Islands for at least one year (section 49).

■ Both of the applicants must be over 21 except where one of them is the child's birth parent, in which case the age limit for that applicant is 18 (section 50).

■ The expression 'a couple' means (a) a married couple or (b) – and this is the major change effected by the Hinchliffe amendments mentioned earlier – 'two people (whether of different sexes or the same sex) living as partners in an enduring family relationship' (section 144(4)). Part (b) of the definition does not include two people one of whom is the other's parent, grandparent, sister, brother, aunt or uncle, whether of the full blood or half blood (section 144(5) and (6)).

There is no explanation in the Act of the expression 'enduring family relationship'. Nor does the expression occur in any other piece of legislation. Consequently, it will be for adoption agencies, CAFCASS and the courts to use their discretion in every case in which an unmarried couple wish to adopt jointly. If it is ruled that such a relationship does not exist (and the court will be the final arbiter of this) an application in the name of only one of the couple can still proceed. The exclusion of close relatives from the definition of 'a couple' was apparently based on the proposition that relationships between such people – who are not able to marry – may not be stable and lifelong. A Department of Health minister put it this way: 'It would be very difficult for two sisters to demonstrate that they have an enduring family relationship and are able to offer a secure environment for a child throughout his childhood. One or both sisters could at any stage meet a partner, and the nature of the sisters' relationship would immediately change.'[8]

A point made at the beginning of this chapter should be repeated: establishing eligibility to adopt is not the same thing as establishing suitability to adopt. Eligibility is simply a gateway to assessment, approval, matching and placement. Failure to appreciate this distinction lay at the root of many of the flawed contributions made by politicians and commentators during the debates on the unmarried couples issue.

Notes

1. Annual Update: Births in 2000 and Conceptions in 1999 in England and Wales, *Population Trends 106* (2001), page 69.
2. *Re AB* [1996] 1 FCR 633.
3. Memorandum submitted to the House of Commons Special Standing Committee on the Adoption and Children Bill (November 2001).
4. Oral evidence by Felicity Collier, House of Commons Select Committee on the Adoption and Children Bill, 1 May 2001.
5. John Hutton MP, *Hansard* (House of Commons), 26 March 2001, col 709.
6. Paras 26.10 and 26.11.
7. Alan Milburn MP, *Hansard* (House of Commons), 29 October 2001, col 654.
8. Lord Hunt, *Hansard* (House of Lords), 4 July 2002, col CWH 220.

CHAPTER 10

Assessment of Adopters

Introduction

Adopter assessment is in the hands of social workers. Although adoption orders are made by the courts, it is unreal to view the adoption process as being controlled by them. For an adoption order to be made an applicant is needed and as far as children in the care system (and relinquished babies and children adopted from overseas) are concerned, people do not get to be applicants until they have been assessed and approved by an agency's social workers. Those workers therefore hold the key. There is plenty of scope for both unintentional and wilful media distortion of the truth in this area of adoption practice. Making judgments about potential adopters is not straightforward and inevitably misjudgments will be made. Personality clashes between social workers and applicants are also bound to occur from time to time. Unfortunately, it takes only one or two highly-publicised cases where things have gone wrong to create a general assumption of agency insensitivity or malevolence. (Child protection work is, of course, bedevilled by the same problem.) Perversely, even cases where things have, from a child welfare perspective, actually gone right can give rise to such an assumption, especially when the agency concerned has to remain silent in the face of criticism in order to preserve the confidentiality of information. The remarkable case of the Bramleys, noted in Chapter 1

of this book, is a very good example of the difficulties confronting adoption agencies – and especially local authorities – in this respect. On the basis of an extremely meagre set of facts, newspaper pundits rushed in to condemn 'unaccountable power', the 'unchallengeable professional mystique' of the social work service, social workers who were 'sometimes eager to rule out good adoptive parents on a whim', and 'the arbitrary rejection of prospective adoptive couples for spurious reasons'. Amid this nonsense, however, was to be found a serious and important proposition: that rejected applicants should be given a right of appeal against their rejection. This idea has been taken up and finds expression in the provisions of the 2002 Act.

The Legislation Prior to the 2002 Act

The provisions of the Adoption Act 1976 concerning adopter assessment reflected the distinction between agency placements and non-agency applications. In non-agency cases (e.g. step-parent and relative applications) assessment was in the hands of local authorities but work with the prospective adopter was undertaken only after the local authority had been notified of the intention to apply to the court. Once notification occurred, the local authority was required by section 22 of the

1976 Act to 'investigate, so far as is practicable, the suitability of the applicant' and report to the court. By the time this investigation took place, of course, the prospective adopter would have been looking after the child for a considerable period, possibly several years. As far as agency placements were concerned, section 23 required the agency to submit to the court 'a report on the suitability of the applicants'. Since the applicants would have been selected by the agency to care for the child, the section 23 report would inevitably be favourable to them. Under section 1, local authorities were obliged to provide, as part of the statutory adoption service, 'arrangements for assessing prospective adopters'. These arrangements could be provided directly by an authority or by a voluntary agency on its behalf. The broad terms of section 1 were supplemented by the Adoption Agencies Regulations 1983 (which also applied to assessments done by voluntary agencies). These regulations required agencies to provide a counselling service for enquirers. Where suitability to adopt seemed possible, agencies were required to obtain specified particulars about the applicants (including the stability of their relationship, their personalities, their ability in respect of child care and their understanding of the nature and effect of adoption) to obtain medical reports and to obtain referees' reports. The regulations required an agency to prepare a written report 'which shall include the agency's assessment of the prospective adopter's suitability to be an adoptive parent'. This report was then passed to the agency's adoption panel, together with any written observations made by the prospective adopters. The role of the panel was to make recommendations to the agency, which would take the final decision to approve or reject. If the agency decided to reject applicants, it was required to give advance notice to them and invite them to make representations which, if submitted, would be considered. The regulations did not seek to limit agency discretion during this decision-making process, except in relation to applicants with specified criminal convictions.

Research Findings and Proposals for Change

During the 1990s local authority adopter assessment processes were examined by the Social Services Inspectorate on two occasions. On each occasion the examination formed part of a wider study of adoption services. The overall picture presented by the SSI was encouraging. 'Much practice with enquirers and adoptive applicants,' it stated in its first report, 'was positive. Initial responses made to enquirers were often prompt. Preparation and approval processes were generally sound and delivered by competent staff. Applicants found approval processes generally relevant and helpful, with assumptions about adoption usefully challenged.'[1] In its second report, the SSI reported: 'A great deal of skilled and professional input goes into the preparation of adoptive families. There is little or no evidence of any over-zealousness in the criteria being applied in the recruitment of adopters, and the vast majority of those who have gone through the recruitment and preparation process are very satisfied that they have been thoroughly and appropriately prepared for the challenging task.'[2] One significant problem that was identified, however, was delay in assessment.

One dimension missing from the SSI studies was the perspective of people who had not made it through the approval stage. Although it is not surprising that such people might be unwilling to discuss the reasons for their withdrawal or rejection, the absence of their viewpoint meant that questions could still be raised about the way in which recruitment teams and adoption panels across the country went about their work. This point was picked up by the Performance and Innovation Unit in its report of July 2000:

> What was clear from our discussions with agencies was whatever effort was put into advertising, there was a huge drop-out rate from initial enquiries to the number of approved adopters. As a general rule of thumb, 1 in 10 of initial enquiries would result in an approved adopter... The reasons for this are not clear. It could simply be that enquirers have an expectation which is

different to the reality i.e. still expect healthy babies, or they simply apply to a number of adoption agencies. Another possibility, which was raised during our discussions, was that potential adopters are 'put off' at an early stage in the process by the general response they receive. This can either be in the time taken to receive the information requested... or in the general manner in which the enquiry had been received. We received a number of reports of unfriendly, unsupportive or even insensitive reactions to people making enquiries.[3]

The PIU, having observed that 'the recruitment and assessment of adopters has received intense and widely publicised criticism'[4], made the following recommendations:

- Recruitment and assessment should be covered by the proposed National Standards. These Standards, which would include appropriate evidence-based criteria for assessment, would produce a more open, transparent and consistent assessment system.
- The assessment process should be reviewed to promote best practice and innovative approaches.
- The assessment for 'second time round' adopters should be streamlined.
- The composition and function of adoption panels should be reviewed to ensure they do not contribute to delay.
- An appeals mechanism for potential adopters should be put in place in all local authorities. Under this mechanism, applicants rejected by an adoption panel could have their case reviewed by the panel of a neighbouring authority. If the second panel disagreed with the first, its authority would be empowered to place children with the applicants without compensating the first authority.

These recommendations were broadly endorsed by the Government in its white paper of December 2000, although the nature of the independent review mechanism was to change. People turned down by an adoption panel would now be able to appeal to 'a review panel' convened by an independent body appointed by the Department of Health. The review panel would make its own recommendation to the local authority, which would have to take it, together with the recommendation of the authority's panel, into account when making its final decision.

The National Adoption Standards

Prospective adopters are covered by Section B of the National Standards. The overarching principles are as follows:

> People who are interested in becoming adoptive parents will be welcomed without prejudice, responded to promptly and given clear information about recruitment, assessment and approval. They will be treated fairly, openly and with respect throughout the adoption process.

In addition to general statements about the provision of information, there are more specific rules. According to Standard 3(a), people will not be automatically excluded on the grounds of age, health or other factors, except in the case of certain criminal convictions (a reference to the Adoption Agencies Regulations 1983). Standard 4 prescribes timescales for each stage of the assessment process. And Standard 6 makes it clear that applicants should be given the opportunity to attend the meeting of the adoption panel in which their application is being considered and address the panel.

Draft Practice Guidance to Support the National Standards was published in 2001. This reminded agencies that members of the public do not have the right to be assessed. They have no right, therefore, to attend a preparation course for adopters. 'Agencies,' it was suggested, 'should have clearly identified priorities for recruiting adopters to meet the needs of the children waiting for families, and should use these to determine whether to proceed with an application.' The document suggested that *The Framework for the Assessment of Children in Need and their Families*, published by the Department of Health in 2000, provided a practical, evidence-based tool which could be used to inform the preparation and assessment process.

The Review of the Assessment Process

In October 2002, as the Adoption and Children Bill was nearing the end of its passage through Parliament, the Department of Health published a consultation paper entitled *Adopter Preparation and Assessment and the Operation of Adoption Panels: A Fundamental Review*. This was done in response to the PIU report two years earlier. The consultation paper was a curious document. Although changes in assessment procedures were certainly proposed, much of the text resembled a piece of practice guidance, and of course such guidance had already been issued in draft in connection with the National Standards. Unless the reader was an adoption novice, the issues covered would have seemed all too familiar. So, for example, the paper stated: 'Prospective adopters should expect to be asked to discuss their relationship history with assessing social workers. Where the prospective adopter has parented children jointly with a former partner it is likely to be appropriate for the social worker, with the prospective adopter's consent, to seek further information in writing from the former partner.' Then it was said: 'It is unlikely that asking ill-thought through questions about a prospective adopter's sex life will provide information pertinent to the assessment. Such questions should only be asked if they have a clear purpose which has been explained to the prospective adopter.'[5] It is not clear why such remarks were thought to belong to a 'fundamental review' of the assessment process. What, however, clearly *did* belong to the review were three proposed changes in procedure:

■ In order to establish a level playing field for all adopters, a standard menu of 'issues to be explored' should be produced for use in all agencies. The importance of consistency of approach was emphasised, especially in the light of the establishment of the National Adoption Register ('agencies are increasingly being asked to have confidence in the quality and appropriateness of assessments carried out by other agencies when exploring placements for the children in their care').

■ There should be 'a degree of consistency' between agencies over the content and scope of preparation courses. The objective here was to ensure that all prospective adopters, wherever they seek approval, receive adequate preparation.

■ There should be clarification of the range of checks to be carried out on prospective adopters.

It was proposed that these matters should be dealt with by a combination of regulations and guidance.

The Provisions of the 2002 Act

The 2002 Act contains no substantive rules concerning adopter assessment and yet the topic was extensively discussed in Parliament during the Act's passage. The explanation for this is that, firstly, there will be Department of Health regulations on the subject (these will replace the Adoption Agencies Regulations 1983 and will take their place alongside the National Standards and Practice Guidance) and secondly, the power to make those regulations is conferred by the Act. Two sets of regulations affecting assessment are signalled. The first set, on the so-called independent review mechanism for rejected applicants, is referred to in section 12. The second set, on agency criteria for judging suitability to adopt, is referred to in section 45. The inclusion of these two empowering provisions in the Adoption and Children Bill (especially section 12) provided an opportunity for the Government to set out its thinking and an opportunity for critics to attempt to influence that thinking. It is important to note, however, that nothing in the Act constrains the Government in the framing of its regulations because the wording of sections 12 and 45 is open-ended.

As far as section 12 and the independent review mechanism are concerned, even after more than 18 months of deliberation the Department of Health had still not managed to finalise its blueprint by the autumn of 2002. This became clear when the Fundamental Review of Adopter Preparation and Assessment, noted above, was published. Part B of that Review was devoted to the operation of adoption panels and it contained a number of ideas – not fixed conclusions – about the new mechanism. The mechanism, it was suggested, could be triggered at the request of prospective adopters when they were told that the agency was minded not to approve them. The agency would then notify the IRM governing body, which would arrange for a new panel to consider the case papers. If this forms the basis of the scheme that finally emerges from Whitehall, the practical impact will probably be modest. This is because about 95 per cent of people whose application gets as far as the adoption panel are recommended for approval. The independent review mechanism will be available for use by the small number who are rejected at panel. It will not, however, be available to those who are steered away from the assessment process prior to panel. This was seen as a significant gap by some commentators.

Section 45 was not in the original draft of the Adoption and Children Bill. It reads as follows:

(1) Regulations under section 9 may make provision as to the matters to be taken into account by an adoption agency in determining, or making any report in respect of, the suitability of any persons to adopt a child.

(2) In particular, the regulations may make provision for the purpose of securing that, in determining the suitability of a couple to adopt a child, proper regard is had to the need for stability and permanence in their relationship.

Contrary to what was suggested by some MPs, this is not the first piece of adoption legislation to refer expressly to the relationship between prospective adopters. The Adoption Agencies Regulations 1983 required an agency that had decided to assess an applicant to obtain specified particulars, one of which was 'marital status, date and place of marriage (if any) and comments on stability of relationship'. The 1983 regulations also referred to other issues touching on suitability to adopt. This is, therefore, hardly virgin legal territory. Viewed in this light, section 45 seems a peculiar provision, and indeed it was technically unnecessary. However, it appears to have been regarded as tactically necessary by those who sponsored the amendments relating to the eligibility of unmarried couples. It was, in other words, part of a wider package that was offered to, and ultimately accepted by, Parliament. Its purpose was to reassure critics who were concerned that widening the eligibility rules would cause children to be placed by social workers with unstable, unmarried couples. As has already been noted, however, eligibility and adopter assessment are very different matters, which made those concerns misplaced. Section 45 is best viewed as a political device employed to satisfy those who could not appreciate the difference and those who were unaware of the existing legal safeguards.

Notes

1. *For Children's Sake: An SSI Inspection of Local Authority Adoption Services* (1996), para 8.48.
2. *Adopting Changes: Survey and Inspection of Local Councils' Adoption Services* (2000), paras 1.13 and 1.14.
3. *Prime Minister's Review: Adoption*, paras 3.76 and 3.77.
4. Para 3.69.
5. Paras 5.13 and 5.36.

CHAPTER 11

Adoptions with a Foreign Element

Introduction

This chapter is concerned with two types of adoption: first, cases in which UK residents obtain a foreign adoption order in respect of a foreign child and then bring the adopted child back to the UK to live with them; and second, cases in which UK residents bring a foreign child into the UK to live with them and then seek to obtain an adoption order from a British court. These types of adoption have been discussed and debated in recent years under the umbrella term 'intercountry adoption'. The issues arising out of them cut across the debates over purely domestic adoptions in a variety of interesting and complex ways:

- A significant number of intercountry adoptions concern infants relinquished by their mothers. The existence of this class of case is attributable in part to the decline in the supply of UK-born relinquished babies, as noted earlier in this book. It is clear that market forces have driven some people who are desperate to have a baby to look abroad for a way of completing their family. The use of the expression 'market' is not out of place here. Intermediaries with varying degrees of expertise and integrity have been active in this field for many years and considerable sums of money have changed hands. Intercountry

adoption can be both expensive and lucrative[1].

- A significant number of intercountry adoptions are transracial. These cases tend to generate the same arguments and concerns that arise in relation to UK local authority policies favouring same-race placements.

- Some intercountry adoptions concern children (both infants and older children) whose development has been hindered by maltreatment or neglect. For many commentators, the so-called Romanian 'orphans' (many of whom in fact had parents who were alive) who were brought to the UK in the aftermath of the 1989 revolution have come to represent the adoptees in this category. Adoptive parents in such cases frequently act out of altruistic motives. The burden they take on increases the likelihood that specialised support services will be needed as the child grows up and the local social services department may be called upon to devote some of its resources to providing some of them.

- Even though intercountry adoptions are – like domestic relinquishments – generally unopposed, the existence of a foreign element in the case necessarily renders the procedure more complicated. Emigration and immigration formalities, coupled with initial vetting and approval requirements, mean that substantial delays are likely rather than possible. The temptation for prospective adopters to by-pass official bureaucratic procedures is both obvious and real.

■ The number of intercountry adoptions is not high. During debates on the 2002 Act it was said that the Department of Health processes fewer than 300 applications a year, in contrast to the 3600 cases processed in France. One consequence of this is that individual agencies' experience of intercountry adoption work is limited and therefore social work expertise is thinly spread. In this respect, intercountry adoption resembles domestic baby relinquishment.

In its adoption circular of 1998, the Department of Health stated that 'it is not acceptable for an applicant to be denied the opportunity to be assessed by an agency on the grounds that the agency does not agree with the notion of intercountry adoption'[2]. This was an official acknowledgement of the very strong views held by many social work practitioners about the validity of intercountry adoption. There is no secret about this. When it was said during the Parliamentary consideration of the Adoption and Children Bill that such adoptions have acquired 'a negative connotation'[3] and that adopters 'have often had a lot of negative vibes from the local authority about their wish to adopt from overseas'[4], it could have occasioned little surprise. Indeed, in view of the particular problems sometimes seen in these adoptions – including the commodification of children and adopters' lack of insight into difficult racial and cultural issues – and the need to divert scarce social services resources into child care work that should arguably be done in countries of origin, it would be surprising if there were not professional reservations about this phenomenon.

These reservations have not, of course, gone unchallenged. Stories in the press, about the obstacles encountered by able and willing prospective adopters wishing to rescue a child from neglect or abandonment, can make for compelling reading, and these have duly appeared in considerable numbers. They mirror the stories of people turned down by agencies for domestic adoption. Some, indeed, have concerned journalists' own trials and tribulations[5]. Perhaps sensing the electoral benefits to be gained, successive ministers in relevant government departments have, in their public statements at any rate, appeared keen to agree with these criticisms and to promote a more positive approach to intercountry adoption by local authorities. This political trend first emerged during the Romanian orphans episode in 1990, when a Foreign Office minister told the House of Commons:

> It is understandable that many couples in Britain, where the number of babies available for adoption has fallen sharply in recent years, want to adopt a child from overseas. Their wishes can only have been intensified by knowledge of conditions in Romania. I want to make it quite clear at the outset that all British government departments concerned… are committed to helping all suitably qualified couples…to adopt from Romania without unnecessary bureaucracy and as quickly as possible.[6]

Similar sentiments were expressed by a Department of Health minister in January 1993 in relation to the adoption of babies yet to be born to Muslim women in Bosnia as a result of rape perpetrated by Serbian soldiers[7]. And in November of that year, the Secretary of State for Health, introducing the Conservative government's white paper on adoption, said that people who wanted to adopt children from abroad should have their wishes respected. 'In all suitable cases,' she said, 'such adoptions should be facilitated.'[8] For its part, the Labour government has endorsed this approach. In its 1998 adoption circular, noted earlier, it stated that it recognised and understood the humanitarian and altruistic response of people who wish to adopt children living overseas, particularly those described as orphaned or abandoned. Local authority policies, it said, should reflect the positive view of adoption referred to in legislation and government guidance and not support policies and attitudes of their own[9].

At the same time, however, the Department of Health has been very careful to qualify its generally supportive statements with directions to local authorities to maintain proper vetting standards for prospective adopters. It has also sought to address the issue of unofficial intercountry adoption, in which government-prescribed procedures are circumvented by people who would not necessarily be approved by an agency for domestic adoption (and by people who have actually been rejected). These concerns were highlighted in the most intense manner in 2001 following the most heavily publicised adoption case ever to occur in the UK: the case of the so-called internet twins. Indeed, such was the level of official concern about this case and its implications (which are described below) that the Government was induced into the premature introduction of the Adoption and Children Bill[10].

The Legal Position Before the Adoption (Intercountry Aspects) Act 1999

The Adoption Law Review of 1992 identified four main categories of intercountry adoption:

1. Children adopted overseas in circumstances where the foreign adoption order would be recognised as valid under UK law. No adoption proceedings in the UK were necessary in these cases.
2. UK adoptions arranged through a governmental or officially authorised agency overseas, with the assistance of a local authority in the UK, including home study report, and official authorisation of the child's entry into the UK under the Immigration Acts.
3. UK adoptions arranged privately by the adopters overseas but with the assistance of a local authority in the UK, including home study report, and official authorisation of the child's entry into the UK under the Immigration Acts.

4. UK adoptions arranged privately by the adopters overseas with no official intervention in the UK, probably with a home study report from a private social worker and with the child being brought into the UK without entry clearance under the Immigration Acts.

Countries whose adoption orders would be recognised as valid in the UK for the purposes of category 1 above were listed in a 1973 statutory instrument[11]. Procedures for the entry of children under categories 1, 2 and 3, including the preparation of home study reports on prospective adopters by local authorities, were contained in Home Office and Department of Health publications[12]. Cases in category 4 – unofficial intercountry adoptions – were by far the most problematic. In some of these, deception by the prospective adopter as well as technical infractions of the criminal law would be identified; in others, the suitability of the prospective adopter would seriously be questioned. In all of them, however, the UK authorities, including the immigration service, the local authority and the court that ultimately heard the adoption application, were liable to be faced with a fait accompli due to the difficulty of prising apart the child and the prospective adopter by the time those authorities became involved. Many of these factors came together in *Re C*[13], a 1998 case which exemplified the problematic nature of unofficial intercountry adoption. The prospective adopter was a 39-year-old woman said to be 'both desperate and determined to become mother of a child'. She had been rejected by three UK adoption agencies, for medical and other reasons, but she nevertheless managed to acquire (with the help of a privately-commissioned home study report) an eight-month-old baby from Guatemala, collecting him at Amsterdam airport from a paid intermediary. These exotic circumstances formed the background of an adoption application made in the unlikely setting of the Eastbourne County Court. Following transfer to the High Court in London, an adoption order was made but with no enthusiasm. The judge noted that 'the applicant has sought to achieve her objective in disregard of the legal processes laid down by Parliament for the protection of children'. Criminal offences under the Adoption Act 1976 had been committed in relation to the commissioning of the home study report and the instruction of Guatemalan lawyers. The judge posed the question: 'If it was not proper for this applicant to adopt a British child is there to be one set of criteria for the British child and another and lower set for this brown Mayan Indian child?' He acknowledged, however, the fait accompli element (by the time of the hearing, the applicant had been looking after the child for 14 months) and stated that 'the present application does require the court to apply a lower standard and to recognise the reality that a two-tier system does operate'. It was against this background that the Adoption (Intercountry Aspects) Act 1999 was enacted.

The Effect of the 1999 Act

The Adoption Law Review of 1992 was well aware of the widespread dissatisfaction with the existing arrangements for intercountry adoption and made a variety of recommendations for reform. It was hampered in this task by the fact that negotiations for a new international treaty on intercountry adoption had not been finalised. Nevertheless, it was clear that a far tighter regulatory framework was needed in the UK. Its principal proposal was that children should be admitted to the UK for adoption only where authorisation had been granted by the responsible authority in the UK that the adoption should proceed. Such authorisation should be given only where the adoption met standards and safeguards based on internationally agreed criteria[14]. Accordingly, it would be a criminal offence to bring a child into the UK for adoption without authorisation to proceed. Furthermore, where a child was brought into the country without authorisation and granted temporary admission by the immigration service, the relevant local authority

would have the power to seek a court order authorising the removal of the child from the prospective adopter[15].

By the time the Conservative government responded to the Review in November 1993, the terms of the new Hague Convention on Protection of Children and Co-operation in respect of Intercountry Adoption had been agreed. These were endorsed by the government, which saw the Convention as 'offering a major opportunity for improving standards and streamlining the process in intercountry adoptions'[16]. It announced that its forthcoming Adoption Bill would be used as a vehicle for ratifying the Convention. In addition, it endorsed the Review's recommendation concerning the criminal liability of people who bring children into the UK for adoption without authorisation. The Conservatives' draft Adoption Bill of 1996 did, indeed, contain provisions to this effect but, in circumstances described in Chapter 1 of this book, that Bill was never presented to Parliament. What happened next was bizarre: the 1997 Labour government, having signalled a reluctance to put forward a general reform Bill on adoption, nevertheless encouraged a Liberal Democrat MP to introduce into the House of Commons a private Member's Bill drawing on the intercountry elements of the 1996 document. The Government ensured that sufficient Parliamentary time was allocated for the consideration of this measure (although in fact its approval was never in doubt). Thus it was that the Adoption (Intercountry Aspects) Act 1999 – a minuscule piece of legislation in the context of adoption as a whole – came to be enacted with diverse inputs from all three main political parties.

The provisions of the 1999 Act fell into three main categories. The first group of provisions (sections 1–8) were designed to give effect to the Hague Convention of 1993. The Convention proceeded on the basis that signatory States would deal with intercountry adoptions in accordance with specified criteria (for example, that the authorities in the child's State of origin 'have established that the child is adoptable' and 'have determined, after possibilities for placement of the child within the State of origin have been given due consideration, that an intercountry adoption is in the child's best interests'). It also made provision for co-operation between so-called Central Authorities (in England, the Department of Health) and for mutual recognition of intercountry adoption orders. Implementation of these rules was not fully achieved by the 1999 Act: section 1 provided for the making of supplementary regulations by the UK government.

The second group of provisions in the Act (sections 9–12) concerned intercountry adoptions generally, both those arranged under the Hague Convention and those not so arranged (due to the State of origin not being a signatory to the Convention). Of these provisions, section 9 deserves mention. This made it clear that intercountry adoption fell within the scope of the statutory adoption service to be provided by all local authorities. As is noted in Chapter 4 of this book, section 2(8) of the 2002 Act is framed on similar lines. Section 9 can be viewed as a further attempt by the Government, following its 1998 circular on adoption, to promote a more positive attitude about intercountry cases within social services departments.

The third group of provisions (sections 13 and 14) concerned the highly problematic unofficial intercountry adoptions, in which authorised procedures were ignored or by-passed. Section 13 made it clear that the existing ban on making private (i.e. non-agency) arrangements for a child's adoption extended to the commissioning and production of home study reports on the suitability of prospective adopters. Cases like Re C (above) demonstrated the need to clarify the law on this point in order to prevent people using glowing but grossly deficient 'reports' – which had in effect been bought from entrepreneurial social workers – to obtain a child abroad. Section 14 of the 1999 Act was concerned with the immigration process in unofficial cases. It made it a criminal offence for a person habitually resident in Britain to bring into the UK for the purpose of adoption a child who was habitually resident outside Britain, without complying with whatever requirements were laid down by Department of Health regulations. Adoptions by relatives were excluded from the scope of the offence. Section 14(4) provided for an extended prosecution period to prevent intercountry adopters hiding a child for six months in order to avoid proceedings under the ordinary rules of criminal procedure. Proceedings for a section 14 offence could be brought within six months from the time when evidence of the offence came to the knowledge of the prosecutor, although there was an absolute cut-off point of three years. Like section 1 of the 1999 Act, section 14 could not be implemented until the government made the necessary subordinate legislation.

None of the significant provisions of the 1999 Act was brought into operation immediately, it being left to the Department of Health to decide this question. Clearly, much more work needed to be done. Section 13, clarifying the prohibition of private home study reports, was introduced in January 2000 and in December of that year the Government announced, in a short passage in its white paper on adoption, that it was planning to implement the Hague Convention provisions in January 2002. Not long after this announcement, the case of the internet twins erupted.

The Case of the Internet Twins

The case of the internet twins lasted from January 2001, when news of the placement first broke, until April 2001, when a High Court judge made care orders in respect of the children in favour of Flintshire County Council. The case was not typical of intercountry adoptions. For one thing, the children came from the USA, a far from underdeveloped country. For another, the adopters had managed to obtain an adoption order from a country whose orders could be recognised as valid under English law, which might avoid the need to secure a further order from a UK court upon their return to this country. The twins had been received by the adopters in California, following payment to an internet agency, and they were taken to Arkansas where a so-called fast-track adoption order was made. They were brought to the UK six days later, without long-term entry clearance under the Immigration Acts. As in so many unofficial intercountry cases, the adopters had procured a home study report, not from a local authority, but from a private individual. This report was described by the High Court as superficial, shallow and misleading. It had been compiled five days before section 13 of the 1999 Act (above) came into force.

It has already been noted how, amid the media frenzy generated by this case, the Prime Minister came to undertake to introduce a general adoption reform Bill during the 2000–2001 Parliamentary Session. He agreed that the case was deeply disturbing, saying that 'everyone feels that it is deplorable that children are traded in that way'[17]. He went on, however, to make a further commitment, which was to bring into force during 2001 the remaining provisions of the 1999 Act. This target date was more or less in line with the one already fixed in the Government's adoption white paper and it might well have been achievable had the Prime Minister not committed the Department of Health to the far more ambitious project of an immediate Bill on domestic adoption. This imposed a burden of very considerable proportions on the machinery of government. In the event, it managed to implement two more sections of the 1999 Act during 2001: section 9, which declared intercountry adoption to fall within the existing statutory adoption service, and section 14, which imposed criminal liability on those bringing children into the UK for adoption without proper authorisation. To make section 14 workable, the Department of Health issued the Adoption of Children from Overseas Regulations. The effect of these regulations was that prospective adopters would escape liability under section 14 only if they applied to an adoption agency for assessment and obtained the agency's approval before bringing the child into the country. They were also

required to notify the local authority within 14 days of the child's entry. A DH circular accompanying the regulations stated that local authorities should report any breach, or suspected breach, of the regulations to the police for investigation as soon as possible[18]. Ironically, this extension of the criminal law, though activated as a result of the internet twins case, would not have applied to it because the adopters in that case had travelled abroad to obtain an adoption order that would be fully recognised in the UK. Section 14 affected only those – like the adopter in *Re C* (above) – who needed an adoption order from a British court to make them legal parents. Legislation geared to the particular – and unusual – circumstances observable in the internet twins case would have to wait for the enactment of the Adoption and Children Bill.

The Effect of the 2002 Act

The general effect of the 2002 Act on intercountry adoption is as follows:

- The provisions of the 1999 Act relating to the Hague Convention have been left intact. These remain to be implemented via Department of Health regulations.
- The other provisions of the 1999 Act – including those relating to unofficial adoptions – have been repealed and re-enacted as provisions of the 2002 Act, but with some amendments.

Section 9 of the 1999 Act – bringing intercountry adoption firmly within the statutory adoption service – now appears as section 2(8) of the 2002 Act. Section 13 – prohibiting privately commissioned home study reports – has resurfaced, in a more elaborate form, in section 94 of the 2002 Act. Section 14 – prohibiting the bringing into the UK of a child for adoption without authorisation – has been superseded by section 83 of the 2002 Act. This, too, is a more sophisticated provision than its predecessor and when its terms are studied it is easy to see that it has been heavily influenced by the internet twins case. Two significant changes have been made. First, the maximum penalties following conviction have been increased (to twelve months' imprisonment and/or an unlimited fine). Second, and crucially, the criminal offence now extends to British residents who bring into the UK a child whom they have adopted abroad within the last six months. Such people – who may not be planning to obtain a further adoption order from a British court – will have to comply with whatever requirements are laid down in Department of Health regulations. These are likely to follow the pattern of the 2001 regulations made under section 14 of the 1999 Act, described earlier. Questioned in Parliament about this extension of the criminal law, the Health Minister provided the following explanation:

> The restriction applies to habitual residents in the UK who adopt abroad within a period of six months. We chose six months because we thought that it would be long enough to deter those who want just to nip abroad and adopt quickly – we felt that three months was too short – but we did not want to catch people who worked abroad for a considerable period, adopted properly and ended up committing an offence when they returned to the UK.[19]

The restriction imposed by section 83 does not apply to foreign adoptions arranged under the Hague Convention, as these will necessarily be attended by safeguards. Nor will it apply to birth parents, relatives or partners of birth parents. The 2002 Act contains the following further significant provisions on intercountry adoption:

- The Department of Health will be able to specify through regulations probationary periods for intercountry adopters (section 83(6)). The Government indicated that in cases where proper procedures were followed the prospective adopter would be able to apply for an adoption order when they had looked after the child for six months. In other cases the probationary period would be twelve months.
- DH regulations will impose particular duties on local authorities which receive

notice of intention to adopt (section 83(6)).
- DH regulations will make provision for the recognition in England and Wales of foreign adoption orders made outside the terms of the Hague Convention (section 87). This is important because not every country of origin will have ratified the Convention and yet a particular country's internal adoption procedures may be perfectly satisfactory in terms of child welfare (indeed, the UK itself has been a case in point). Where British adopters have obtained such an 'overseas adoption', they will not need to go through adoption procedures here.
- DH regulations will prescribe the range of fees that may be charged by local authorities for the provision of facilities to prospective adopters (section 11(2)). The Government acknowledged the considerable disparities already evident in local authority charges but it refused to remove the principle of local discretion.
- The provisions of the Act concerning adoption support services, described in Chapters 4 and 7 of this book, are fully applicable to intercountry adopters. This is an important matter, notwithstanding the low level of intercountry adoption experienced in the UK. Dissatisfaction with the quality and quantity of social services support in intercountry adoption cases is well documented[20] and yet such support may be badly needed. As a representative of NORCAP put it during Parliamentary scrutiny of the Bill:

> Intercountry adopters need as much support as any other adopters just in bringing up their children, and those children are likely to need at least as much if not more support, because they have more profound issues of identity and origins. Children who are adopted in the UK today are far more likely to benefit from letterbox contact or direct contact. If you are adopted through intercountry procedures the chances are you will not have that level of communication.[21]

Nobody would wish to see children who are brought into the UK for adoption suffer through lack of support that is freely available to domestic adoptees. But the sustained scepticism of intercountry placements displayed by British social workers over the years shows very little sign of diminishing. The Chairman of the House of Commons Health Committee, with a background in social work, stated in May 2002 that he had 'very grave doubts in principle about overseas adoptions'[22]. It would be unrealistic to expect massive change in this area from the implementation of the 2002 Act.

Notes

1. See further John Triseliotis, 'Intercountry adoption: Global trade or global gift?' *Adoption and Fostering,* Vol 24 No 2 (2000), page 45.
2. Circular LAC (98) 20, para 52.
3. Vincent Cable MP, *Hansard* (House of Commons), 29 October 2001, col 707.
4. Philly Morrall, Adoption UK, evidence to the House of Commons Special Standing Committee on the Adoption and Children Bill, 21 November 2001.
5. See Matthew Engel, 'My daughter's Big Brother', 'We feel so right, but it's all wrong' and 'I blame the adoption agencies', *Guardian*, 29 May 1999, 15 June 1999 and 23 January 2001, referring to an adoption process of 20 months 'mostly spent battling against a bureaucracy that was often intrusive, inefficient, uncommunicative and unfeeling'.
6. Douglas Hogg MP, *Hansard* (House of Commons), 19 December 1990, col 469.
7. Alan Travis, 'Britain will ease way for adoptions', *Guardian*, 4 January 1993.
8. Virginia Bottomley MP, *Hansard* (House of Commons), 3 November 1993, col 344.
9. Note 2 above.
10. See page 8 above.
11. The Adoption (Designation of Overseas Adoptions) Order 1973.
12. SSI letters CI (90) 17 and CI (91) 14; Home Office Leaflet RON 117.
13. [1998] 2 FCR 641.
14. *Review of Adoption Law* (DH, 1992), para 47.3.
15. Paras 56.2 and 56.4.
16. *Adoption: The Future*, Cm 2288, para 6.28.
17. *Hansard* (House of Commons), 17 January 2001, col 336.
18. Circular LAC (2001) 14 of April 2001.
19. Jacqui Smith MP, *Hansard* (House of Commons), 29 October 2001, col 719.
20. See, for example, Rutter and others, *The English and Romanian Adoption Study* described in *Adoption Now: Messages from Research* (DH, 1999); Diane Taylor, 'The lost children', *Guardian*, 31 July 2002.
21. Pam Hodgkins, evidence to the House of Commons Special Standing Committee on the Adoption and Children Bill, 21 November 2001.
22. David Hinchliffe MP, *Hansard* (House of Commons), 20 May 2002, col 29.

CHAPTER 12

Access to Information After Adoption

Introduction

Unlike the previous chapters of this book, this chapter is not concerned with the adoption process itself. It is concerned with the disclosure of information after adoption has taken place. More specifically, it is concerned with the legal right to receive information. Although it is dangerous to generalise in this area, it is probably safe to make the following introductory points:

- The issues discussed here do not usually arise in step-parent or relative adoptions. They occur most frequently in cases involving baby relinquishment, the adoption of looked after children and inter-country adoption.
- The focus is on the rights of adoptees and their birth relatives, rather than the rights of adoptive parents. As far as adoptees are concerned, the focus is on adolescents and adults rather than children.
- Disclosure of information may not be needed where a child is adopted at a late stage in childhood, because birth family and other relevant information will already be known.
- In terms of law reform, any changes in the law will be of interest not merely to people adopted in the future. People adopted in

the past, and the birth families of those people, may be desperate for information. (It should be borne in mind that adoptions in the past were attended by far less openness than is the case today.) The issue of retrospective law reform therefore arises.
- Access to information inevitably affects those who hold information. In this context, key information-holders are adoption agencies, the courts, CAFCASS and the Registrar General.
- Disclosure of information may be all that the recipient of the information desires. On the other hand, disclosure may be seen, or come to be seen, as a prelude to making contact with a relative. Making such contact may or may not involve an intermediary.

The Legal Position Before the 2002 Act

The rules relating to disclosure of adoption information prior to the 2002 Act were profoundly unsatisfactory. They were confused, contradictory and out of date. The Adoption Act 1976, the Adoption Agencies Regulations 1983 and the rules of court made under the 1976 Act made provision for disclosure of information by agencies and courts, but on a discretionary basis. None of the provisions expressly referred to adoptees or birth relatives: it was as though such people had no interest in accessing family information. The one provision that was founded upon a recognition of such an interest was section 51 of the 1976 Act. The rules contained in this provision were first introduced into the framework of English adoption law by section 26 of the Children Act 1975. Section 26 gave adopted adults whose record of birth was kept by the Registrar General the legal right to obtain from the Registrar General 'such information as is necessary to enable that person to obtain a certified copy of the record of his birth'. It was brought into force in November 1976 with retrospective effect, thereby enabling people who had been adopted previously (as far back as the 1920s, when legal adoption first became possible) to obtain family information that they had not been able to access in any other way. This last point was important. Some adoptees (the exact number was never clear) did not need to use section 26 to learn what was contained in their birth certificate because they had already received this information from their adoptive parents or from the agency that had arranged their adoption or from the court that had made their adoption order. Because section 26 had retrospective effect, some adoptees would be given information that would enable them to locate the present whereabouts of a birth mother who had relinquished them as a baby many years before in conditions of strict secrecy. In an attempt to minimise the risk of embarrassment (and worse) Parliament required a section 26 applicant who had been adopted before its enactment (12 November 1975) to attend an interview with a counsellor before being supplied with the statutory information by the Registrar General. Such counselling could be provided at the General Register Office; alternatively, it could be provided by the applicant's local authority, the local authority for the area in which the adoption order was made, or, where this was the case, the adoption society that had arranged their adoption. Section 26 applicants who were

adopted after its enactment were given a choice as to whether to receive counselling from the organisations described above. The Registrar General was obliged to inform applicants – before supplying the statutory information – that counselling services were available.

The implementation of section 26 had significant consequences. Far more people than expected exercised their legal right to receive birth records information. By 1999, over 70,000 people had made section 26 applications[1]. Inevitably, the tracing of birth relatives took place more frequently, sometimes attended by considerable publicity, and issues surrounding birth family reunion came to be openly and directly explored in films, plays and television documentaries. All these developments chimed with, and contributed to, the movement towards greater openness in the adoption process during the 1980s. The specific need of some adoptees and birth relatives to trace each other and then make contact was formally recognised in 1989 when legislation establishing the Adoption Contact Register was passed[2]. The purpose of the Register was to put adopted people and their birth parents or other relatives in touch with each other but only where this was what they *both* wanted[3]. Its use was therefore entirely voluntary.

Although the passing of section 26 and the creation of the Adoption Contact Register were significant developments, concerns about the reach of the law began to emerge. One particular cause for concern arose out of the failure of the law to confer even minimal information rights on the birth mothers and other relatives of adopted people. Section 26 acknowledged the information needs of adopted adults. Yet birth relatives could have just as strong a need to know about the current circumstances, and, indeed, the continued existence, of the child who had many years previously been relinquished or removed for adoption. Having no legal rights, these people had to pin their hopes on a liberal exercise of discretion by agencies and the courts. Agency practice, however, was inconsistent and the courts were generally unsympathetic. In 2000, the Department of Health did issue detailed guidelines to agencies with a view to promoting good practice and greater uniformity in the provision of intermediary services but the guidelines had no statutory force and in any case they served only to emphasise the width of agency discretion[4]. The Adoption and Children Bill provided an opportunity to expand the law.

The PIU Report of 2000

Access to information was, understandably, not a core concern for the Performance and Innovation Unit in its review of adoption. The emphasis was firmly on increasing the adoption rate in respect of looked after children, which meant focusing on planning, placement and the immediate needs of the child and the adopters. Long-term information needs which might never eventuate were in a different category, as were the needs of those family members who had already gone through the adoption process. The PIU's report, however, was not completely silent on this matter. It noted that local authorities generally considered birth records counselling to be low priority work and it identified a growing trend to contract out the work to the voluntary sector. It also referred to concerns about the varying approaches adopted by the courts in relation to access to court files by adoptees. It recommended that consideration be given to how to bring about consistency in this area, possibly by providing for adoption agencies to assume responsibility for disclosure[5].

The Labour Government's Initial Proposals

The adoption white paper of December 2000 signalled an intention to reform the law on access to information in at least one respect. The Government would legislate 'to set out what should be in the agency files to which an adopted person will have access, and the circumstances in which they may have access to that file and to information from their court files'[6]. Such a reform would result in the removal of some or all of the discretionary elements of the rules concerning disclosure to adoptees. This was reflected in the first draft of the Adoption and Children Bill published in March 2001. The Bill repeated the existing rules on access to birth records by adopted adults and the Adoption Contact Register. In addition, adopted adults were to be given the right to obtain information from the relevant adoption agency and information from the relevant court, as well as copies of relevant court documents. The types of information and documents covered by these entitlements would be specified by regulations. No information identifying a third party was to be given, however, without the agreement of that party.

Although the terms of this Bill broadly reflected the recommendations and proposals contained in the PIU Report and the white paper, they were seen by some commentators and organisations as inadequate. Prominent among the critics was NORCAP, which specialises in family reunion work. It took issue with a number of provisions in the Bill, including the clause restricting the disclosure of information identifying a third party. However, its fire was directed principally at an omission. NORCAP drew attention to the fact that, under the Bill, access to information would continue to operate as a one-sided service: whereas adoptees were to have express statutory rights to information, birth relatives were to have none. In the view of NORCAP, it was time to redress the balance by giving birth mothers, siblings and other relatives of adopted persons the right to what it called 'access to active service provision'. It went further than this, however, by arguing for retrospective legislation on the matter so as to give rights to those mothers who had – often unwillingly – relinquished their children as babies. Many of these cases went back a long way. 'For the mothers who parted with babies born during the Second World War,' it pointed out, 'for elderly brothers and sisters who remember a baby being born and then being gone, this is the last chance.' It argued for a clause in the Bill mirroring section 26 of the Children Act 1975 or, as a weaker alternative, the codification of the Department of Health's 2000 guidelines[7].

The demise of the first Adoption and Children Bill, brought about by the general election, and the opportunity for reflection that it gave to the Department of Health, was expected to lead to a few changes in the text of the second Bill. When that second Bill emerged in October 2001, however, its provisions on access to information were received with incredulity. Not only were the provisions far more complicated ('an enormous hotchpotch of clauses', as the Opposition spokesperson put it[8]), they would have had the effect of recasting the existing law completely, with new and controversial restrictions on disclosure. Why the Government chose to rewrite the Bill in this way remains a mystery. It gave no warning of the exercise. What is clear is that it had no great confidence in its new code because in an explanatory memorandum presented to the House of Commons, the Department of Health stated that it would welcome views on whether its provisions struck the right balance. Under these provisions, information held by an adoption agency about a particular adoption was to be divided into three categories: birth records information (which would if necessary be obtained from the Registrar General), protected information (which was information which identified a person) and other information. The disclosure of this information to adopted adults and others (e.g. birth relatives) would be governed by regulations but those regulations would have to make provision, unspecified in the Bill, for 'effective objections' to disclosure. The Government envisaged that birth parents would be asked at the time of the adoption whether they would object to the disclosure of information identifying themselves. This would mean that some adopted adults whose adoption had been a closed one would have great difficulty obtaining identifying birth records information. In other words, the principle enshrined in section 26 of the Children Act 1975, described earlier, was being abandoned. The abandonment of section 26, prob-

ably the most controversial proposal in the original draft of the second Bill, appears to have been prompted by 'a small number of cases where there could be a risk to birth parents if they were traced through the birth records'[9]. One such case had come before the courts in 1990[10]. In addition, according to the Department of Health, 'some birth relatives have experienced distress at having their identifying details passed on to the adopted person and they have complained that they were not asked for their consent'[11]. Of course, this point had been fully debated in 1975. The Government was on the defensive from day one in relation to this particular proposal and in the face of powerful criticisms made by BAAF, NORCAP and other organisations, it ultimately caved in. In fact, it rethought this part of the Bill generally, so that what finally emerged was very different from the original draft. It was not law-making at its best.

The Effect of the 2002 Act

Future adoptions: the classes of information controlled

Although the terms of the Adoption and Children Bill on disclosure were much amended by Parliament, the general level of complexity remained. The 2002 Act draws a distinction between the following types of adoption information:

- *Section 56 information.* This is information to be kept by adoption agencies in relation to particular adoptions in pursuance of Department of Health regulations.
- *Protected information.* This is section 56 information, as described above, of a particular variety. It consists of information – held of course by an agency – which (a) is about an adopted person or another person and (b) is or includes identifying information about the person in question (section 57(1)). It also consists of information which would enable an adopted person to obtain a certified copy of his birth record and

information about an entry relating to an adopted person in the Adoption Contact Register (section 57(2)). The Act recognises that birth record information may have been received by an agency from the Registrar General.

■ *Information supplied by an adoption agency to prospective adopters.* This is information supplied, in the run-up to an adoption order, under regulations made in pursuance of section 54. It is referred to in Chapter 7 of this book[12].

■ *Information about an adoption held by the court.*

■ *Information held by the Registrar General.* This is information linking entries in the registers of live-births and entries in the Adopted Children Register.

Future adoptions: the rights of adopted adults

Section 60 confers on an adopted adult the right to receive three types of information:

1. Any information which would enable the adoptee to obtain a certified copy of the record of their birth. This is the type of information first made available to adoptees by section 26 of the Children Act 1975, so their rights have been maintained. There are changes, however. Section 60 provides for the information to be given to the adoptee by 'the appropriate adoption agency' and nobody else. The agency is therefore the single gateway for this information. The appropriate adoption agency is either the agency that arranged the adoption (or, if that agency has been wound up, the one that has assumed control of its records) or, in non-agency cases, the local authority to which notice of intention to adopt was given (section 65(1)). If that agency cannot find the birth record information in its own files, it can require the Registrar General to provide it under section 79(5). Regulations will lay down a procedure for this, and a fee can be levied by the Registrar General. A further change is that there is now express provision made

for the non-disclosure of birth record information by order of the High Court following an application made by the 'appropriate agency' (section 60(3)). This can occur only in exceptional circumstances. The previous legislation contained no equivalent provision but the courts nevertheless read a limitation into it by implication[13].

2. Information supplied to the adoptive parents during the adoption process. This is the package of information about the child given by the placing agency (in three stages) to the adopters. On attaining the age of majority, the child can see for himself what was said about him in the run-up to his adoption (assuming he has not already been shown this information by his parents).

3. A copy of any 'prescribed document' relating to the adoption held by a court. The documents in question will be specified in regulations. Section 60(5), however, excludes documents to the extent that they contain 'protected information'. Such information will have to be accessed from an agency under section 61 (described below).

Future adoptions: the disclosure of other protected information to adopted persons

This covers protected information – as defined – other than the birth record information governed by section 60. It is, therefore, information held by an adoption agency that is or includes identifying information. A wide variety of people could be identified in an agency's adoption case records, of course, including siblings of the adopted child, other birth relatives and foster carers who looked after the child prior to placement for adoption. In the current climate of openness, it is to be expected that a great deal of such information will become known to the adopted child as he grows up – indeed, he may know it at the time of the adoption – but in some cases it may not be known, and it is with these cases that section 61 deals.

Section 61 prescribes a four-stage proce-dure for the release of this type of informa-tion. The first stage consists of an application made by the adoptee to the 'appropriate adoption agency'. (Section 64 enables regu-lations to be made setting out the informa-tion to be provided by the applicant.) At the second stage, the agency considers whether it is appropriate to proceed with the applica-tion. The agency therefore has a discretion, just as it did under the previous law. Accord-ing to section 61(5), in exercising this discre-tion the agency must consider the welfare of the adoptee, any matters stipulated by government regulations and all the other circumstances of the case. If the agency decides to proceed, stage three is reached: the agency must take all reasonable steps to obtain the views of any person the informa-tion is about as to the disclosure of the iden-tifying information. This particular stage could, of course, be both time-consuming and expensive depending on the circum-stances. Many years may have elapsed since the information was collected by the agency. It will be for the agency to decide when 'all reasonable steps' have been taken. The fourth and final stage consists of the agency decid-ing whether to disclose the information to the adoptee. Section 61(4) provides that the agency may disclose 'if it considers it appro-priate to do so'. Again, it has a discretion and in exercising its discretion it must consider the factors pertinent to stage two, together with any views obtained at stage three. It follows from all this that the person whose views on disclosure are sought will not have a veto. The agency can go ahead and disclose in any event.

Although section 61 gives the adoption agency a wide discretion at stages two and four (and, indeed, at stage three to a certain extent) that discretion is constrained by two factors. First, it is open to the Department of Health to make regulations relating to 'the performance by adoption agencies of their functions' (section 64(1)(a)) and these will be accompanied by guidance. It has already been announced that regulations and guidance will point towards disclosure of information

where the person whose views are sought indicates consent. Second, agency decisions will be susceptible to challenge via the inde-pendent review mechanism. As is explained in Chapter 10 of this book, that mechanism – regulated by section 12 of the Act – was orig-inally designed for the review of decisions concerning adopter assessment. The Govern-ment decided to extend its remit so as to cover the very different question of access to information. Exactly how this novelty will work remains unclear in the absence of detailed supplementary regulations but what is already clear is that in the context of disclosure of information, it will work both ways. In other words, it will be available both to adopted persons whose request for informa-tion is not being met by the appropriate agency, and also to persons whose views on disclosure have been sought and who object to the agency nevertheless going ahead and disclosing identifying information to the adoptee. It also seems clear that the indepen-dent review mechanism will not enable the reviewing panel to actually overturn the agency's decision[14].

If the subject of the protected information is a child (for example, a younger sibling of the adoptee), section 62 applies instead of section 61. This section requires the agency, where it has decided to proceed with the adoptee's application, to take all reasonable steps to obtain the views of the child's parents, and the views of the child himself if the agency considers it appropriate having regard to his age and understanding. The child's welfare must be given particular consideration; in fact, if the child has also been adopted his welfare must be the agency's paramount consideration.

Counselling arrangements are governed by section 63(2): 'Regulations may require adop-tion agencies to make arrangements to secure the provision of counselling for persons seeking information from them in prescribed circumstances in pursuance of this group of sections.' Such counselling is optional, not compulsory. The payment of fees for coun-selling will also be governed by regulations (section 11(4)).

Future adoptions: the disclosure of protected information to birth relatives

As has been seen, protected information is information kept by an adoption agency that is or includes identifying information. Identifying information being sought from an agency by an adopted child's birth relative is highly likely to consist of information identifying that child. The relative could be a birth parent, a grandparent, a sibling or someone else who (a) is not in contact – either directly or indirectly – with the adopted child and (b) is not aware of the name(s) given to the child following his adoption (because, for example, the adoptive parents used a serial number when making their application to the court). The reason for seeking the identifying information could be the proposed resumption of contact but this need not be the reason. Furthermore, the identifying information could be sought during the adopted child's childhood or it could be sought after he has attained adulthood.

The policy finally pursued by the Labour government on this difficult and sensitive issue was to construct a law that treated birth relatives in the same way as adopted persons. Consequently, sections 61 (disclosure of protected information about adults) and 62 (disclosure of protected information about children), described above, are applicable where a birth relative seeks identifying information about the adoptee from the appropriate adoption agency. This means that the four-stage procedure, and the agency's discretion, will apply. The independent review mechanism will also apply, as will the counselling provisions of the Act. In deciding whether it is appropriate to proceed with a request for information, and in deciding whether to release the information, the agency must consider the welfare of the adopted person. If the adopted person is still a child, his welfare is paramount. The effect of all this is that it will be lawful for an agency to disclose identifying information about an adopted person to a birth relative even though the adopted person and/or his adoptive parents object. (All reasonable steps will, of course, need to be taken by the agency to

contact these people.) All parties to adoptions after the implementation of the 2002 Act will need to understand this. The Minister of Health agreed with a questioner in the House of Commons that it would be extraordinary if an agency were to go against the express wishes of an adopted person on the issue of disclosure but she emphasised the undoubted fact that these sections of the Act give no absolute veto to such a person[15]. The most they get is the right to invoke the independent review mechanism. As for the financial costs of processing a relative's request for information (and it is not difficult to see how these costs could escalate if it proves difficult for the agency to trace the adopted person), section 64(5) enables regulations to be made providing for the payment of a prescribed fee.

Past adoptions: the rights of adopted adults

It was explained earlier how sections 60–62 introduce new rules for the disclosure of 'protected information' to adopted persons. None of these rules applies to people adopted under previous legislation, notably the Adoption Act 1958 and the Adoption Act 1976. For this very large group of people, the code established by the Children Act 1975, and then reproduced in the 1976 Act, continues to apply; but because the 2002 Act repeals the 1976 Act, it has had to reproduce the code once more, and it is now contained in Schedule 2 to the 2002 Act. Schedule 2 provides for the release of birth record information to adopted adults by the Registrar General. It also provides for counselling services from adoption agencies, adoption support agencies and the Registrar General. People adopted before 12 November 1975 remain bound by the obligation to attend an interview with a counsellor before being able to access birth record information in this way.

Past adoptions: the disclosure of information to birth relatives

It was noted earlier how, when the Adoption and Children Bill was first presented to Parliament, NORCAP drew attention to the weak legal position of birth mothers and other relatives who were anxious to receive information about children adopted in the past, at a time when openness in the adoption process was virtually unknown. Many, if not most, of these children had been relinquished for adoption at birth – they had not been taken into care for child protection reasons – and such relinquishment had not infrequently been brought about by family pressure. It was argued that the interests of the relatives in these cases should now be recognised and that consequently the Bill should make fresh provision for them. Such provision would, of course, be retrospective. Politicians from all parts of the political spectrum were impressed by the force of this argument and the case for reform of the law was felt to have been strengthened by the publication of research evidence from the Children's Society which had demonstrated that cases in which an adopted person is contacted by a birth relative frequently have very positive outcomes for both parties[16].

The Government's initial response on this question was negative. It placed reliance on the undoubted fact that some adopted persons definitely do not wish to be contacted by birth relatives ('we must recognise that some people hold that view, even if they are in a minority'). Then it argued that it was inappropriate to change the basis of legislation on which the people concerned had undertaken an adoption. This, however, ignored the fact that most of the adoptees in question had not 'undertaken' their adoption on any basis at all because they had been babies at the relevant time. It also ignored the fact that section 26 of the Children Act 1975, by giving adoptees new rights to birth record information, had set a precedent for retrospective legislation in this field. The Government also sought to rely on practicalities. It argued that the poor quality of past record-keeping would cause difficulties in the tracing process. Finally, it argued that giving fresh legal rights to birth relatives of past adoptees would involve adoption agencies in a potentially huge volume of additional work. The Government feared that the priorities of agencies would be skewed by such responsibilities, with the result that agencies' resources

would be diverted from what the Government regarded as the primary aim – 'to help the vulnerable and in some cases damaged children who need adoptive parents now'[17].

Whether ministers and officials within the Department of Health underwent a genuine change of heart on this issue, or whether they feared an adverse vote in the House of Lords (where strong feelings had been ventilated), is not clear. The fact is, however, that two weeks before the Adoption and Children Bill became law the Government published an amendment to the Bill that was specifically geared to past adoptions and the information needs of birth relatives. This emerged as section 98 of the Act, a provision that was said to have been warmly welcomed by adoption organisations. The terms of section 98 are remarkably vague, since they largely confer broad regulation-making powers on the Department of Health, but this was only to be expected in view of the lateness of the section's insertion into the Act. The section enables regulations to be made for the purpose of (a) assisting adults adopted before the introduction of the new information regime (described earlier) to obtain information in relation to their adoption and (b) facilitating contact between such persons and their relatives. It enables functions to be conferred on adoption support agencies, the Registrar General and adoption agencies; these can include a duty or a power to disclose information. It also makes provision for the charging of fees. The intentions of the Government at the time that it agreed to this special provision (these intentions, of course, are liable to change) were spelled out in the House of Lords. Adoption support agencies were to be given a pivotal role:

> We intend to use the regulations to establish a scheme that provides for registered adoption support agencies to operate an intermediary service for contact between adopted adults and their adult birth relatives. On receiving an application from the birth relative, the ASA would establish the identity of the adopted person, seek to trace him and, if he consents, disclose his identity to the birth relative and facilitate contact between them.[18]

Adopted adults would be able to use this procedure too, if they desired contact with a birth relative. Adoption agencies and the Registrar General would be placed under an obligation to provide information in their possession to the adoption support agency. The ASA would be prohibited from disclosing any information about the subject of an application to the applicant without the informed consent of the subject. A veto would therefore be created. Special provision would be made for cases where the subject of the application had died and other cases where the subject could not provide an informed consent. All of this would be brought into force in two stages. The first phase would cover adoptions prior to 12 November 1975. This was the cut-off date specified by the Children Act 1975 in connection with compulsory counselling for adopted adults seeking birth record information and it provided the Government with a convenient basis on which to give priority to applications made by the most elderly birth relatives. The second phase would cover all past adoptions.

One further provision of the 2002 Act needs to be noted under the present heading: section 79(4). This enables the court to order the Registrar General to disclose to a person information which links entries in the registers of live-births and the Adopted Children Register. This power applies only to past adoptions and only in 'exceptional circumstances'. The reason why it appears in the 2002 Act is that a similar provision was to be found in the previous legislation (section 50(5) of the Adoption Act 1976). The right of relatives to apply to the court – which has been known to lead to the release of identifying information – has therefore been preserved. This procedure, however, is extremely cumbersome and it is difficult to gauge its remaining significance in view of the completely new arrangements introduced by section 98.

The Adoption Contact Register

The Adoption Contact Register provides, in the words of the General Register Office (where the Register is located), 'a safe and confidential way for birth parents and other relatives to assure an adopted person that contact would be welcome'. It is not, strictly speaking, information retrieval machinery. As the above description indicates, the Register is, in effect, a notice-board on which information is *provided*. Adoption agencies are not directly involved in providing this facility.

Sections 80 and 81 of the 2002 Act have the effect of maintaining the Register, which was first set up in 1991 under the provisions of the Children Act 1989. The principal features of the 1989 legislation have been retained even though the drafting of sections 80 and 81 is different. The Register will continue to be in two parts: Part 1 for adopted adults whose record of birth is kept by the Registrar General and Part 2 for adult relatives of adoptees. Information about entries will be disclosed under government regulations. One significant change introduced by these provisions concerns the nature of the information that can be registered (and therefore passed on): although the Register was originally established to assist those who wished to make contact, it is possible under the new legislation to register a wish *not* to be contacted. The absence of such a facility was identified very early on as a gap in the 1989 Act. It should be understood, however, that, just as registering a wish to have contact does not mean that contact will actually take place, so registering a wish for 'no contact' does not guarantee that the relative in question will stay away. Not everybody connected with the adoption process is aware of the Register; those who are aware of it are not forced to use it; and those who do use it (whether positively or negatively) are not compelled to act in any particular way. If a person is given information from the Register which relates to a birth relative, they are free to use the information as they think fit. For all these reasons, the Adoption Contact Register is liable to lead to disappointed expectations as well as successful family reunions. Research undertaken in November 2000 indicated that at that point there were 18,276 adoptees and 8007 relatives on the Register. Matches between Parts 1 and 2 of the Register had been made in 490 cases in the first nine and a half years of the Register's operation[19].

The National Adoption Standards

Given the importance of information issues for both birth parents and adopted persons, it would be surprising if the National Adoption Standards made no reference to them. There are, indeed, references:

- Information from agency records will be made available to the child when they are of an age and level of understanding to comprehend it (Standard A12).
- Adoptive parents will be encouraged to keep safe any information provided by birth families via agencies and to provide this to the adopted child on request, or as they feel appropriate (Standard C5).
- Birth parents and families will be supported to provide information that the adopted child needs. This will include information about the adopted child's birth and early life, the birth family's views about adoption and contact and up-to-date information about themselves and their situation (Standard D6).
- Where adoptive parents have agreed to inform the agency of the death of the adopted child or the breakdown of the adoption, birth parents or the 'next of kin' at adoption will, if they wish, be informed by the adoption agency (Standard D8).

It can be seen that these Standards have been written with adopted *children* very much in mind. Consultation on the draft Standards led to suggestions that the needs of adopted *adults* should also be catered for and this resulted in the publication, in August 2001, of a separate draft Standards document, and draft practice guidance, on adopted adults and their birth siblings. At the end of 2002, the responses to these drafts were still being considered by the Department of Health but this was not surprising: the extraordinary twists and turns taken by Parliament when legislating on the information issue, described earlier, had created an uncertain legal context

against which any Standards would have to operate. Consequently, the shape of the definitive Standards would emerge only in 2003 or 2004.

Notes

1. Rupert Rushbrooke, 'The proportion of adoptees who have received their birth records in England and Wales', *Population Trends 104* (2001), page 26. The author concluded that 'the phenomenon of adoptees applying for their birth records is clearly mainstream adoption behaviour, and not at all the peripheral activity that had been expected in 1975'.
2. Schedule 10 to the Children Act 1989. See *The Children Act 1989 Guidance and Regulations, Volume 9* (DH, 1991).
3. Para 3.3 of the *Guidance* (note 2 above).
4. DH, *Intermediary Services for Birth Relatives: Practice Guidelines* (2000); SSI letter CI (2000) 16.
5. *Prime Minister's Review: Adoption*, paras 3.138–3.139 and para 5.40.
6. *Adoption: a new approach*, Cmnd 5017, para 6.45.
7. Memorandum submitted by NORCAP to the House of Commons Select Committee on the Adoption and Children Bill (May 2001).
8. Tim Loughton MP, House of Commons Special Standing Committee on the Adoption and Children Bill, 27 November 2001.
9. DH Memorandum to the Special Standing Committee (note 8 above), 20 November 2001.
10. *R v Registrar General, ex parte Smith* [1991] 2 All ER 88.
11. Note 9 above.
12. See page 69 above.
13. The *Smith* case (note 10 above).
14. *Adopter Preparation and Assessment and the Operation of Adoption Panels: A Fundamental Review* (DH, October 2002), para 8.27.
15. Jacqui Smith MP, Special Standing Committee (note 8 above), 10 January 2002.
16. David Howe and Julia Feast, *Adoption, Search and Reunion: The Long Term Experience of Adopted Adults* (The Children's Society, 2000).
17. Jacqui Smith MP, *Hansard* (House of Commons), 16 May 2002, col 1019.
18. Lord McIntosh, *Hansard* (House of Lords), 16 October 2002, col 946.
19. John Haskey and Roger Errington, 'Adoptees and relatives who wish to contact one another: the Adoption Contact Register', *Population Trends 104* (2001), page 18.

APPENDIX

Special Guardianship Orders

Background

Although the special guardianship order is a creation of the Adoption and Children Act, it is very different from an adoption order. Strictly speaking, the order falls outside the scope of this book but it does merit at least some attention here because it has been fashioned against the background of adoption law reform (and is therefore part of the Government's reform package) and because its significance needs to be understood by those working in the adoption field.

The origins of the SGO lie in the report of the Adoption Law Review of 1992. The Review emphasised the fact that adoption is not the only means of providing a child with a permanent home and drew attention to the availability – after October 1991 – of residence orders under the Children Act 1989. However, it went on: 'Responses to the review revealed a wide degree of concern that residence orders are not perceived as being likely to offer a sufficient sense of permanence for a child and his carers. It may therefore be beneficial to enhance the attractiveness of residence orders in certain circumstances.'[1] The Review recommended that where a court made a residence order in favour of a person other than a birth parent or step-parent, it should have a further power to appoint that person as the child's 'inter vivos guardian'. Such a guardian would have parental responsibility until the child reached adulthood. Whether inter vivos guardianship, as envisaged by the Review, would actually have conferred more real power on a carer than an ordinary residence order is debatable. This is not the point, however. It was the badge – and the public perception of the badge – that was seen as significant. It would act, in effect, as a selling point for the residence order and thereby reduce the number of inappropriate adoption applications. The Conservative government accepted the case for this new legal arrangement. In its adoption white paper of 1993 it stated that the guardianship order was intended to allow relatives or others caring for a child, including long-term foster carers, to obtain legal recognition of their role without going as far as adoption. Foster carers who obtained such an order, it said, might regard it as giving them 'foster-plus' status[2]. There matters rested until the Labour government commissioned its own adoption review from the Performance and Innovation Unit in 2000. Not surprisingly, the PIU returned to the question of alternatives to adoption but by 2000, of course, the focus had shifted to looked after children and it was in that particular context that the case for a new 'guardianship' order was resurrected. According to the PIU:

> While planned long-term fostering could offer some degree of security, and might suit some children, it still lacks real security and a proper sense of permanence in a family. Children are still subject to monthly visits by social workers

and annual medical inspections, and permission from a social worker is needed, for example, before a child can 'sleep over' at a friend's house. Residence orders were acknowledged to provide some of what was required, but are still open to legal challenge at any time, and usually ended when the child was 16. Those consulted were of the view that a new option would in particular fulfil the needs of a distinct group of older children who did not wish to be adopted.[3]

In accepting the case for a new option – now to be called 'special guardianship' – the Government singled out four groups of children who could benefit from it:

- Older children who do not wish to be legally separated from their birth families.
- Children being cared for on a permanent basis by members of their wider birth family.
- Children from certain minority ethnic communities that have religious and cultural difficulties with adoption.
- Unaccompanied asylum seekers who have strong attachments to their families abroad.

In a departure from the earlier proposals, the Government undertook that the introduction of special guardianship would be accompanied by proper access to a full range of support services, including, where appropriate, financial support[4]. This undertaking made it clear that the Government viewed special guardianship primarily as a mechanism for dealing with children in the care system.

The Effect of the 2002 Act

Special guardianship is governed by section 115 of the 2002 Act. This has the effect of inserting into Part II of the Children Act 1989 seven new sections: sections 14A–14G. These provisions prescribe the legal effect of a special guardianship order, the range of applicants, the role of the court, and the functions of the local authority before and after the making of an order. Rules, regulations and Department of Health guidance will supplement them in due course.

Applicants: section 14A

Any individual can apply for an order, except a birth parent (the exception is logical because special guardianship is aimed at people who are caring for children who are separated from their parents). Some people are entitled to apply; those not so entitled need preliminary leave from the court. Entitled applicants include holders of a residence order, people who have cared for the child for at least three years, and local authority foster carers who have cared for the child for at least one year. A local authority foster carer who has cared for the child for less than one year needs the consent of the authority as well as the leave of the court, unless they are a relative. Couples, including unmarried couples, can make joint special guardianship applications.

Notice of intention to apply: section 14A

The intending applicant must give written notice of the intention to apply to the relevant local authority at least three months before making the application. On receipt of this notice, the local authority must investigate the matter and prepare a welfare report for the court. This element of the procedure has been borrowed from the non-agency adoption provisions of the 2002 Act.

The role of the court: sections 14A and 14B

The court can make an order either upon application or in the course of any family proceedings in which a question arises with respect to the welfare of the child. In the latter situation, the court can make an order even though no formal application has been filed. Before making an order the court must consider whether, if the order were made, a contact order should also be made and any current section 8 order should be varied or discharged. Section 1(1) of the Children Act 1989 applies to special guardianship cases: the welfare of the child shall be the court's paramount consideration. The welfare checklist contained in section 1(3) of the 1989 Act also applies. This should ensure that the ascertainable wishes and feelings of the child are given proper weight. A social worker from CAFCASS will often be appointed to assist the court in its welfare role.

The effect of a special guardianship order: sections 14C and 14E

It was noted earlier how the Adoption Law Review of 1992 saw the new option for permanence as being closely linked to a residence order. The 2002 Act does not reflect this view because the special guardianship order is a free-standing order and can be made whether or not a residence order is in force. Its principal legal effect is described in section 14C(1): the special guardian has parental responsibility for the child and, crucially, 'is entitled to exercise parental responsibility to the exclusion of any other person with parental responsibility for the child (apart from another special guardian)'. This rule is similar to the one that applies to a local authority following the making of a care order (under section 33(3)(b) of the Children Act, the local authority has the power to determine the extent to which the birth parents may meet their parental responsibility) and is clearly designed to put the special guardian in firm control of the child's upbringing. This includes deciding where the child is to live. The birth mother (and possibly birth father) of the child retains parental responsibility but the ability to exercise it is constrained. The special guardian's autonomy is not total, however, and in this respect the order is different from an adoption order:

- The special guardian's legal authority is subject to any other Children Act order affecting the child. Contact orders (in favour of birth parents, for example) may accompany special guardianship in a significant proportion of cases.
- While a special guardianship order is in force, the special guardian may not cause the child to be known by a new surname and may not remove the child from the UK for more than three months without the written consent of the other holders of parental responsibility or the leave of the court. These restrictions are modelled on the ones applicable to residence orders and care orders.
- Conditions can be attached to the special guardianship order at the court's discretion.

If the child was previously looked after by the local authority, that status will cease upon special guardianship. Any care order is brought to an end automatically.

Revocation of special guardianship: section 14D

It is here that the permanence of special guardianship can be seen. Although the child's birth parents can apply to the court for the discharge of the order, they must first obtain the leave of the court. Furthermore, the court may not grant leave unless it is satisfied that there has been a significant change in circumstances since the making of the order.

Death of the child: section 14C

If the child dies, his special guardian is obliged to take reasonable steps to give notice of that fact to his mother and his father (if the father has parental responsibility).

Financial support from birth parents

Schedule 3 to the 2002 Act amends Schedule 1 to the Children Act 1989 so as to enable a special guardian to apply to the court for 'orders for financial relief' against either or both parents of the child. The maintenance liability of birth parents therefore continues, unlike the position following an adoption order.

Local authority support services: section 14F

For some children and their carers, the viability of special guardianship will hinge on the availability of ongoing support, including financial support, from the local authority. As the National Foster Care Association put it:

'Unless this is a properly funded service, it will go the way of both custodianship and residence orders, i.e. not used for those children in long-term foster care who could benefit from the stability that the order could give.'[5] The Government was pressed heavily on this issue but, as on adoption support, it refused to shift the Act's emphasis on local authority discretion. While it is true that every local authority must make arrangements for the provision within its area of special guardianship support services (which are to include financial support), the assessment of individuals' needs, and the provision of support to individuals following assessment, are in principle discretionary. Department of Health regulations and guidance may have the effect of reducing this discretion in certain types of case (for example, cases involving children who were looked after by the local authority prior to the special guardianship order) but this is not demanded by the Act.

Notes

1. *Review of Adoption Law* (DH, October 1992), para 6.4.
2. *Adoption: The Future*, Cmnd 2288, para 5.24.
3. Para 8.6.
4. *Adoption: a new approach* (2000), Cm 5017, paras 5.8–5.10.
5. Written evidence to the House of Commons Select Committee on the Adoption and Children Bill (May 2001).

Index

Adopted Children Register, 17, 19, 126, 130
Adoption and Children Act Register, *see* National Adoption Register
Adoption and Permanence Taskforce, 26, 28, 53–4
Adoption Contact Register, 123–4, 126, 130
Advance consent to adoption, 42, 46, 76, 84
Birth parents, 11, 15, 36–40, 42–9, 70, 83–5, 125, 128, 130, 134
Birth records counselling, 33, 123–4, 128
CAFCASS, 42, 74, 76, 78, 84, 108, 122, 134
Concurrent applications, 80
Confidentiality, 69
Consent to adoption, 42–6, 81–3, 101, 103–4
Contact, 16, 18, 21, 70–1, 75, 79, 85, 88–92, 128, 131, 133–4
Default power, 26
Disability, 43
European Convention on Human Rights, 39–41, 71
Extended family, 15–16, 40–1, 85–7, 133
Foster carers, 95, 99, 103–4, 126, 132
Freeing for adoption, 34, 43, 49, 54, 72–4, 77–8, 80–1, 84
Gay couples, 15
Grandparents, 19, 40, 85–6, 89, 92, 102, 128
Hague Convention, 7, 117–20
Human Rights Act 1998, *see* European Convention on Human Rights
Incest, 17
Independent review mechanism, 111–3, 127–8
Inheritance, 17
Internet twins, 8–10, 116, 118–20
Introductions, 70, 78
Lesbian couples, 15
Maintenance, 15
Matching, 59–64

National Adoption Register, 53, 62–4, 68, 112
National Adoption Standards, 26–8, 37–40, 49, 53, 57–8, 61–2, 67–9, 84, 90, 92, 95, 111–2, 131
National Care Standards Commission, 27–8, 30–2
Nationality, 17
Openness, 16, 21–2, 38, 70, 89–90, 122–3, 126, 129
Orphans, 81
Overseas adoption, 120
Panels, 3–4, 77, 110–1, 113
Parental order, 50–1
Parental responsibility, 14–15, 39, 47, 49–50, 74–5, 78–9, 81, 84, 87, 91–2, 95, 100–3, 106, 132, 134
Parents, *see* Birth parents
Partners, 102, 108, 120
Placement, 35–6, 41–2, 71–81, 95
Placement order, 3–4, 43, 45, 73–81, 84
Political correctness, 3, 5, 10, 65, 67
Probationary period, 87, 91, 101–2, 120
Prohibited degrees, 17
Race, 3, 61, 64–8, 114–5
Readoption, 14
Relatives, *see* Extended family
Removal of child from the UK, 50, 75, 79, 134
Residence order, 46–7, 49, 75–6, 78, 84, 86–7, 100–3, 106, 132–5
Special guardianship order, 76, 100, 102, 107, 132–5
Step-parents, 18–19, 27, 99, 100–2, 106, 108–9, 122
Support services, 25, 32, 37, 39, 40, 92–5, 114, 120, 133–4
Surnames, 50, 75, 79, 134
Surrogacy, 50–1
Unmarried couples, 15, 102, 106–8, 113, 133
Waterhouse Inquiry, 7–8, 10–11
Welfare considerations, 77–8, 83–4, 88, 100, 104, 133
Welfare report, 31, 84, 87, 100, 104, 133